WELFARE AND WELL-BEING

Social value in public policy

Bill Jordan

This edition published in Great Britain in 2008 by

The Policy Press
University of Bristol
Fourth Floor
Beacon House
Queen's Road
Bristol BS8 1QU
UK

Tel +44 (0)117 331 4054
Fax +44 (0)117 331 4093
e-mail tpp-info@bristol.ac.uk
www.policypress.org.uk

British Library Cataloguing in Publication Data
A catalogue record for this book is available from the British Library.

Library of Congress Cataloging-in-Publication Data
A catalog record for this book has been requested.

ISBN 978 1 84742 0 800 paperback
ISBN 978 1 84742 0 817 hardcover

Cover design by The Policy Press
Front cover: image kindly supplied by www.corbis.com
Printed and bound in Great Britain by Hobbs the Printers, Southampton

Contents

Acknowledgements

I would like to thank a number of people who gave helpful comments on various drafts of this book. In particular, I am grateful to Michael Breuer, with whom I worked on most of the material in Part One, and who made several other useful suggestions. Ian Gough read and commented on Parts One and Two very constructively. Louise Haagh and Simon Birnbaum were very helpful with aspects of Part Three. I also had some useful comments from the anonymous assessors of the proposal and a draft, which were much appreciated.

I would also like to thank Rachel Arnold for her patient and efficient typing of my handwritten text and amendments.

Introduction

It is both alarming and exhilarating when our fundamental assumptions about the world come under question. For most of the 20th century, the terms 'welfare' and 'well-being' were used more or less synonymously in discussions about human development, social justice and public policy (Adler and Posner, 2006; Baldock, 2007). Despite their often furious debates over the best outcomes of the interactions between its members, theorists of society seemed to share a rough consensus about the nature of the desirable rights and material resources for which these populations were striving.

In retrospect, it is possible to recognise that this view stemmed from a struggle between idealists and materialists in the first two decades of that century, in which the latter emerged victorious. Although many traces of idealist thought continued to influence both liberal and socialist analyses for the next half century (Offer, J., 2006), the dominant approach to issues of human flourishing was derived from economics. This was in large part due to the challenge to liberalism and democracy posed by Marxism-Leninism, which called its underlying theory 'dialectical materialism'. The economic model of Pareto (1909) and Pigou (1920) was simply the 'best response' to a version of authoritarian socialism that mobilised workers and peasants against capitalism.

So the arguments of the idealists who saw well-being as stemming from social interdependence and the common good, rather than 'mechanical laws and … necessarily determined conclusions' (Gore, 1922, p 10), gave way to a definition of welfare in terms of 'that portion of the field in which the methods of science seem likely to work at best advantage', and 'make more easy practical measures … which statesmen may build on the work of the economist', and where 'one obvious instrument available in social life is money' (Pigou, 1920, pp 10-11).

> Hence, the range of our inquiry becomes restricted to that part of social welfare that can be brought directly or indirectly into relation with the measuring-rod of money. This part of welfare may be called economic welfare. (Pigou, 1920, p11)

Another reason why this seemed an uncontentious definition was that the scope for collective action, and hence the territory of political interdependence, was expanding throughout the first half of the 20th century. This meant that more and more aspects of economic and social life were coming under government control, and in democratic countries it widened the possibilities for redistribution, and the field for debate about social justice. The economics of Keynes (1936) and Beveridge (1942, 1944) expanded the politics of welfare.

It is perhaps only now that we can fully recognise the extent to which the trend had been reversed by the end of the century, as much by a rolling revolution in economic theory as by the integration of the world economy, and the collapse of the Soviet Bloc. First, public choice theory spelt out the basic assumptions of the economic model, and – together with the protagonists of the Austrian and Chicago Schools – cast off the accretions of misleading collectivisms. These had taken the form of 'organic' theories of society and 'aggregates' in Keynesian analysis, as much as class dominance in Marxist orthodoxy. It meant that:

> [W]e are left with a purely individualistic conception of the collectivity. Collective action is viewed as the action of individuals when they choose to accomplish purposes collectively rather than individually, and the government is seen as nothing more than the set of processes, the machine, which allows such collective action to take place. (Buchanan and Tullock, 1962, p 13)

In one sense, of course, this was only restating the fundamental principle of modern liberal societies since the 17th century – that free individuals should choose both the means of satisfying their private desires, and the institutions through which they agree to be ruled collectively. But, in the hands of Buchanan himself (1965, 1968, 1978, 1994), of Olson (1965, 1982), Oates (1972, 1999), Niskanen (1975) and their many followers, it was developed into both a devastating critique of social democracy and a technology for the transformation of the public sector, first in the Anglophone countries, and then all over the world.

The individualistic basis for welfare in the economic model, along with a dynamic of self-sorting by mobile individuals, seeking self-governing collectives for the supply of various goods and services involving interdependency, appeared to have justified this transformation, and provided a basis for the new public policy agenda. This quickly extended to the social services themselves (Foldvary, 1994). Why should social housing tenants not have a 'right to buy', or parents a right to choose the best schools for their children? Government should enable these extensions of individual autonomy and independence, and allow hospitals, clinics and care homes to be self-governing, because this followed logically from the new model of welfare optimisation.

With growing confidence, economic theory laid claim to the territory of the other social sciences, insisting that it alone offered a coherent framework within which to analyse human behaviour of all kinds. Once government and public policy had fallen within the scope of its methods, all other features of the collective landscape – culture, morals, institutions, social formations of all shapes and sizes – became the targets of its methodology. For example, the Nobel laureate Gary Becker proposed an 'extended utility function', through which to explain individual 'preferences' for a whole range of psychic and social 'goods' not previously dealt with by economists. This approach:

> retains the assumption that individuals behave so as to maximize utility while extending the definition of individual preferences to include personal habits and addictions, peer pressure, parental influences on the tastes of children, advertising, love and sympathy, and other neglected behaviour. This extension of the utility-maximizing approach to include endogenous preferences is remarkably successful in unifying a wide class of behaviour, including habitual, social and political behaviour.
>
> I do not believe that any alternative approach – be it founded on 'cultural', 'biological', or 'psychological' forces – comes close to providing comparable insights and explanatory power. (Becker, 1996, p 4)

Just as actions and decisions in every context are to be analysed as rational maximisation, so relationships were now modelled as contracts. In the new 'information economics' of the 1990s, individuals' responses to each other in a variety of settings could be understood in terms of their knowledge about each other's abilities and motives, and the incentives they faced. This could be represented as a game in which the solution 'requires that at each point in time each player chooses an optimal strategy, given the situation which has been reached, and assuming that all other players will do likewise' (Macho-Stadler and Pérez-Castrillo, 2001, p 8). In this way, all the actions of members of any kind of organisation can be specified in terms of 'optimum contracts', to achieve the greatest feasible efficiency.

So the gradual extension of the economic model, to embrace the public as well as the commercial sector, and family and social as well as business life, has allowed government in turn to adopt a rationale for managing society that relies on the principles of preferences, incentives and contracts.

And yet, just as these principles seemed to have triumphed in the Anglophone countries, and to be spreading to every other type of regime worldwide, a fundamental doubt afflicted the economic model itself. First through sociological researches (Lane, 1991, 2000; Kelsey, 1995; Pusey, 2003), and then through analysis of survey evidence by economists themselves (Frey and Stutzer, 2002; Van Praag and Ferrer-i-Carbonell, 2004; Layard, 2005), it emerged that there was no reliable link between increases in average incomes and levels of self-assessed well-being. Especially in the affluent countries, economic welfare did not correspond predictably with people's overall satisfaction with their lives.

Above all, this seemed to question whether individuals were capable of choosing those goods and services that would improve their well-being. Since this was the whole basis for the economic model, the implications were potentially devastating. However we define the 'utility', which is supposed to be maximised by each actor in the economic model (whichever intended psychic or social satisfactions are included), the discovery that choices (over earning, consumption, leisure and engagement with others) are not consistently linked to positive experiences is extremely damaging. Utility-maximising individuals might make mistakes, of course, but they should not persist in these, under the assumptions of the model.

> Reduced to its barest essentials, the economic assumption
> is simply that the representative or the average individual,
> when confronted with real choice in exchange, will choose
> 'more' rather than 'less'.... Through the use of the utility-
> maximizing assumption, we shall construct logical models
> of the various choice-making processes.... In this, we must
> place certain [political] restrictions on individual utility
> functions, restrictions which are precisely analogous to
> those introduced in economic theory: that is to say we must
> assume that individuals will, on average, choose 'more' rather
> than 'less' when confronted with the opportunity for choice
> in the political process, with 'more' and 'less' being defined
> in terms of measurable economic position. (Buchanan and
> Tullock, 1962, pp 18, 28, 29)

This classic statement of the public choice approach to social institutions makes the economic model, now adapted to its requirements, doubly vulnerable to the evidence on subjective well-being (SWB). On the one hand, individuals have continued to increase their work effort, in order to consume more, even though this has made them no more satisfied, overall, with their lives. On the other hand, given the chance to design and run their own collective institutions, as they have been under the influence of the public choice approach to policy, they have failed to create an institutional framework to correct this fault, by restraining whatever perverse incentives caused them to do this.

In other words, the constituent utility-maximisers of the economic model have turned out to be several pennies short of the rational shilling, when it comes to choosing the means to satisfying their own desires, and to managing their own collective lives. Either they are caught on some kind of 'hedonic treadmill' (Brickman and Campbell, 1971), which condemns them to pedal ever faster, because they have 'adapted' to whatever pleasure they previously got from their former levels of income and consumption. Or the very institutions they designed to enable them to earn, choose and spend more have a malevolent side-effect, such as an increase in rivalry, stress and insecurity, which subtracts as much from their SWB as they gain from their increased efforts.

There is, of course, another possible explanation – that individuals in affluent societies are in the grip of some collective neurosis, which requires them to drink to oblivion, eat to obesity, fornicate to the ruin of their relationships, spend to bankruptcy, and consume to the destruction of the planet. But this kind of theory breaches all the rules of the economic model, by postulating irrational and self-destructive motives driving the average member of society and dark collective forces that have not been designed or recognised by such members.

Indeed, any such theory is 'collectivist' in the strong sense, in that it reduces individuals to the status of 'cultural dopes' – beings in the thrall of socially generated patterns that determine their behaviour. Such creatures would be no better able to make rational choices over working hours or social policy than those in the grip of Freud's death wish, or Marx's false consciousness – the denizens of theoretical constructions of society of exactly the provenances that the economic model most abhors.

Well-being and social value

So the paradox of the present situations in the affluent Anglophone countries is that the economic model is both dominant (as a basis for public policy, and within the social sciences) and fragile (in the tenability of its fundamental assumptions). While unchallenged by any alternative approach to government, and also largely shaping the agenda of social scientific enquiry, it is subject to sceptical scrutiny by some of its own luminaries, in relation to its core methodology.

So far, the doubts that stem from data about 'stalled well-being' in affluent countries have provoked two main responses. The first has been the robust assertion that evidence on SWB provides an opportunity to quantify and compare the actual satisfactions gained by individuals from their choices and interactions (Van Praag and Ferrer-i-Carbonell, 2004; Layard, 2005, 2006), and hence to strengthen the analyses on which public policy is based, albeit with more emphasis on externalities and interpersonal comparisons. The second is to pay more attention to factors influencing quality of experience, which demand a different kind of study and cultivation (Offer, A., 1996, 2006; Kahneman et al, 1999; Bruni and Porta, 2005; Huppert et al, 2005).

Neither of these directly addresses the more challenging question of whether some other basis for public policy and social analysis can replace (or complement) economics in the new century. Other sets of ideas (feminism, communitarianism, environmentalism) have attempted to do so since the waning of the socialist challenge in the 1970s. Of these, only environmentalism remains a potent force, because of climate change and resource depletion, but it has not so far been able to mobilise a popular political movement to confront the economic model directly. Some of the reasons why such challenges to the model are difficult will be considered in Chapters One and Two.

In Part One of the book, I consider how the version of welfare that is central to the economic model is crucial for its dominance. Using the example of social capital theory and research, I aim to show how a concept that promised to bring social factors and collective goods to prominence was easily absorbed into the economic model, and even served to strengthen its grip on policy analysis and planning.

In Part Two, I turn to the question of how well-being analysis might avoid a similar fate. It is here that I adopt a bolder strategy, in arguing that this cannot be achieved without a radical new approach to value, and its social origins. At this point, the difference between the economic model's version of welfare (as individual utility), and the notion of well-being as derived from social value, can be briefly sketched.

In the latest variant of the model – information-theoretic analysis – relationships between individuals in organisations are modelled in terms of the incentives they face under the conditions of their contracts. Consider this example, given at the beginning of a text on the economics of information:

> It has happened to us all at one time or another, while at a
> professional office you don't receive the service you expected.
> Sometimes there are long queues while the employees can
> be seen happily chatting away to each other, or talking
> on the phone to friends or relatives about their personal
> affairs. Often, in such a situation, someone will comment:
> 'it's obvious that their wages do not depend on how many
> clients they serve'. Behind these words is a criticism of a
> lack of incentives that is often present in certain contractual
> arrangements, such as bureaucratic labour contracts. (Macho-
> Stadler and Pérez-Castrillo, 2001, p 3)

In the sophisticated mathematical modelling that forms the rest of
that text, this is taken as an instance of one situation (moral hazard) in
which one party to a contract knows certain relevant things of which
the other party is ignorant (asymmetric information) – in this case, the
employer cannot observe the employees' behaviour after the contract
is signed. The solution proposed is that the incentives to give good
service are internalised by the employees, via the contract terms. In
other cases, prospective workers (or customers of an insurance scheme)
know something negative about themselves that their employer/insurer
does not (adverse selection), or something positive that they are keen
to communicate (signalling).

The point about all these 'relationships' is that the economic model's
solutions assume that the parties have a conflict of interest, because
each is seeking to maximise their utility at the other's expense. The
optimum contract is therefore designed to give the employee an
amount of utility that is no more than their 'reservation utility', while
ensuring that the necessary incentives exist for tasks to be performed
so as to supply the employer's maximum expected utility. This
approach is now applied on a massive scale, to relationships between
governments and firms, central banks and financial intermediaries,
and transport authorities and their contractors. It largely defines the
way in which the units in societies' organisational structure relate
to each other, as well as how the sub-units within each organisation
coordinate their activities.

But there is another way of interpreting, and hence addressing,
the dysfunctional behaviour of the staff in the imaginary office. This
focuses on the interactions between the employees, and with the public,
in terms of the *culture* that has developed within the organisation. It
assumes that how individuals behave in any social interaction will be
strongly influenced by their capacities to create a set of meanings,

interpretations and practices, through which they get things done. This in turn will be derived from claims for mutual support, recognition and the sense of belonging in their relationships. It may extend to the clients of their agency in positive ways, or it may – as in this example – be exclusive, or even abusive.

This analysis seems far more appropriate for understanding the behaviour of the characters in the cult BBC TV comedy series *The Office*. David Brent and his colleagues appear to have developed a culture in which his claims for recognition and esteem as some kind of minor show-business celebrity, and the various obsessions and neuroticisms of other staff members, have become their main preoccupations. It seems doubtful whether any contractual approach to their functioning would be effective.

Here again, a seemingly trivial example has large implications. If people seek support, recognition, esteem and solidarity through their everyday interactions, it is important to analyse how this can best be accommodated within our collective lives. In this book, I argue that the creation and distribution of *social value* is not well captured by the economic model, and indeed that the policies that derived from the model often reduce social value in the process of increasing individual utility. I reserve the term 'well-being' for the level of social value enjoyed by populations, and distinguish it from the 'welfare' that is maximised in the economic model.

The example of *The Office* illustrates one of the most difficult aspects of the analysis of interactions in terms of social value. The reason why the programme was funny (and sometimes almost embarrassing) stemmed from the fact that the culture of this group of office workers was a microcosm of the wider culture of society. In their self-indulgent concerns, their absurd posturings and their aping of celebrities, the characters laid claim to each other's valuation in terms of a culture of individualism, in which each person is supposed to realise themselves through the development of their special potentials. These bizarre identities, inappropriately acted out in the office setting, represented a parody of the type of value created and exchanged in a post-industrial, postmodern order.

Ironically, much of this culture is itself derived from the economic model, above all the idea that the individual selves that seek to maximise their utility are the main source of value, and that these have a kind of sacred quality. So the dominance of the economic model – in political discourse, in business jargon and advertising and in people's roles as consumers – shapes the culture in which social value is defined. Furthermore, in trying to be unique and original selves, the characters (and the rest of us) are often pathetic copies of cultural stereotypes. We act as 'cultural dopes' in seeking what dominant ideas and institutions define as valuable. All this will be further explored in Part Two of the book.

Finally, in Part Three I turn to the relevance of social value for public policy. The economic model has been installed as such a comprehensive guide to government interventions that it is very difficult to identify a sphere in which there is scope for an alternative approach. Whereas the post-war welfare state represented a compromise between the more collectivist concepts of the Keynes–Beveridge era and a residual idealism, represented by Tawney, Titmuss and T. H. Marshall, the present rationale for programmes and initiatives is almost exclusively one of maximising welfare according to the principles outlined in this introduction.

For the idea of well-being (as derived from social value) to gain any purchase, it is necessary to counterpose to the economic version of welfare the cultural and institutional characteristics of ways of human flourishing. The contrast between the two approaches can be illustrated with a short example.

Gneezy and Rustichini (2000) report that the management of a children's nursery in Israel was experiencing some frustration about the fact that a few parents were occasionally late picking up their offspring at the end of the day. The director therefore decided to introduce a system of cash penalties for lateness. As a result, many more instances of parents arriving late were recorded. Even when the penalty was removed a few months later, the incidence of lateness remained at the new (higher) level.

The authors explained these outcomes in terms of the economics of information. Before the penalty, the contract between the parents and the nursery was 'incomplete'; parents knew that 'something might happen' if they were late, but they did not know what. The information contained in the penalty's introduction was, in effect, a price for lateness, which several were prepared to pay occasionally, if they had other engagements at the end of their children's nursery hours. Even after its cancellation, they were better informed about likely future costs.

An alternative interpretation of these outcomes is that, before the new penalties were introduced, arrangements were regulated on a communal (moral or social) basis. Being on time to collect children was, along with inquiring about a child's progress, or exchanging greetings with a staff member, taken to be a requirement of good parenting. A culture of consideration for staff was presumably sustained among the parent group, who waited for their children together, and perhaps collected each other's children at times.

The system of penalties for lateness substituted a different kind of regulation, in line with the economic model. In effect, it redefined the relationship between staff and parents, making the latter pay for the extra staff time they required through delayed attendance. But – by putting a 'price' on lateness – it both enabled economic calculation (some parents could easily afford to be late, and might sometimes prefer to be) and weakened the other forms of face-to-face moral and social regulation, exercised through informal interactions.

The point about this example is that it illustrates the differences between welfare and well-being as I have defined them. Even though the incidence of parental lateness increased, the new system might well improve welfare. Parents could choose to be late when it would cost them more than the penalty to be punctual, so they could gain additional utility. Staff would gain through being paid for extra time spent at work. But the same change might also cause a decline in well-being. If relations between staff and parents, and within the parent group, became less respectful, considerate and supportive, because the culture of mutual concern was undermined, some parents, staff and children might feel a reduction in the quality of their experience and a deterioration in their relationships.

This example also illustrates the central problem of trying to introduce well-being (in my definition) into policy priorities. Economic welfare is easy to quantify, and to operationalise (through contractual and market mechanisms). Although the contribution of specific experiences to subjective well-being can be identified (for example, we could measure how happy parents feel while waiting for children, or how staff rate parents' considerateness), it is more difficult to specify how a culture of respect and support can be established and maintained. Whereas individual utility can be mathematically aggregated and analysed on any scale, culture demands painstaking interpersonal communication at a face-to-face level. In this example, it could not be restored by the hasty abolition of the penalty.

The economic approach argues that the choice between contractual and cultural ways of doing things is a matter of preferences. In the last resort, parents can move their children to another nursery if they prefer the style of relationships there. They can choose to give priority to community (and hence social value) over individual utility, either as a commitment to a particular way of life or as a reflection of wider cultural influences on their preferences (Becker, 1996, pp 12-23). Such actions will, in his model, still be 'rational' in the economic sense, because it is based on 'forward-looking, maximizing and consistent choices' (p 23).

But the example also illustrates how institutions influence such choices. The change in policy by the nursery immediately altered the behaviour of some parents, and soon the cultural standards adopted by all. In Part Three of the book, I shall analyse the implications of a public policy environment in which most official agencies have been required to adopt market and contractual approaches to their dealings with citizens.

The obvious question that arises from the nursery example, and in the wider policy context, is whether there is any way in which welfare and well-being can be reconciled and combined through an institutional framework that achieves efficiency by means of an economic approach, and a social-value-enhancing culture through processes of management, negotiation and deliberation. These are the big questions for Part Three of the book.

This book aims to explore whether the economic model of welfare allows any space for the kinds of social factors that might allow the addicted gerbils of the hedonic treadmill to recognise their plight and escape from it, either by modifying their own behaviour, or redesigning their cages and equipment. It also explores whether there are any alternative analyses of well-being from the cultural tradition of social theory that can account for self-defeating actions and perverse incentives without reducing their constituent actors to dopes, and taking away their democratic freedoms.

ONE

The Easterlin paradox and the dominance of the economic model

The starting point for this book is the finding that, for at least 30 years, there has been a widening gap between average Gross Domestic Product (GDP) per head and measurements of happiness in affluent countries. This divergence was first commented on by Easterlin in 1974, but it has continued to grow ever since; as income follows an upward trajectory, 'well-being' (whether counted in terms of current contentment or overall satisfaction with life) remains stubbornly flat (Easterlin, 1974, 2005).

The availability of decades of comparable individual 'happiness data' from countries all over the world (Veenhoven, 1989, 1999) is now recognised as both an opportunity and a challenge for social scientists and philosophers. It has already provoked some questioning of the basic assumptions of economics (Frey and Stutzer, 2002; Bruni and Porta, 2005; Layard, 2005). Because of the dominance of the economic model in social scientific theory and government policy, this has fed through to every other field of enquiry, from politics to social work (Jordan, 2006a, 2006b, 2007).

This is not surprising, given that all theorising about the basis for and distribution of happiness among utility-maximising and interdependent populations had come (in the 20th century) to accept the idea that interpersonal comparisons were impossible. Since each individual's preferences over sources of satisfaction were different, and the subjective outcomes of their choices could not be measured, the abstract concept of 'utility' had, mainly through its proxy (money), to stand in as such a yardstick. This in turn allowed economists, starting with Pareto (1909) and Pigou (1920), and continuing with Robbins (1932) and Samuelson (1954), to develop models in which the trade-offs between efficiency and equity in the allocation of all kinds of material resources could be analysed.

Within these, there was a fundamental distinction between those goods and services that were privately exchanged between individuals, and those that, because of the potential external costs imposed by some on others, or external gains from others' action, required collective measures for the sake of optimum outcomes (Buchanan and Tullock, 1962). It was the capacity of 'welfare economics' to handle production and exchange in markets within the same framework as taxation, transfers and the provision of public services that gave it a decisive edge as a tool of government planning, and made its analyses so influential on those of the other social sciences. As a result, the concept of 'welfare', as it has entered into debates about income maintenance, health, education and the social services, came to be founded upon a model with utility of this kind as its ultimate measure.

This book is concerned with the implications for welfare economics, government, public policy and social relations of the new evidence on happiness – or subjective well-being (SWB), as it is called in the psychological literature (Kahneman et al, 1999; Huppert et al, 2005). These studies have challenged the idea that interpersonal comparisons of utility were impossible, because they reflected *choices* rather than *satisfactions*, with data from surveys in many countries of people's self-assessed satisfaction with their lives as a whole, their incomes, health, jobs and housing.

> The empirical practice and success of these questions constitute ample evidence that individuals are able and willing to express their satisfaction on a cardinal scale. If we assume these questions to be interpreted in approximately the same way by different respondents and we find that similar respondents give similar answers, this is ample evidence that (approximate) interpersonal comparison is possible. (Van Praag and Ferrer-i-Carbonell, 2004, p 4)

This evidence has attracted enormous attention in social-scientific and government circles, but its significance is disputed. Those who are most sceptical about attempts to link it to economic analysis or public policy point out that income is only one of the factors whose increase has not provided additional happiness.

> Certainly, to claim that only one particular change – increased material living standards – makes no difference whatsoever to happiness seems a case of choosing one's evidence to fit one's argument. We would have expected the huge increase in public spending in the second half of the 20th century, or the increase in leisure time, to have had an impact on the happiness time series. They didn't. (Ormerod, 2007, p 6)

This is an oversimplification – there are significant differences in levels of SWB between populations that relate to such factors as inequalities and working hours.

But Ormerod is right to draw attention to two points. First, continuities in measured SWB levels, both of societies and of individuals, are stronger than variations. Second, theorists of well-being have been selective in their choice of evidence, and have been quick to incorporate arguments derived from the phenomenon of stalled well-being into their critiques of the current bases for government policy, without clear accounts of the wider implications of the data. So interpretations of and remedies for the Easterlin paradox have been extremely divergent.

On the one hand, as I shall show in this chapter, some 'neo-utilitarian' economists have welcomed these findings as supplying positive content for the notion of utility. In the view of Layard (2005) and others, happiness statistics (which make interpersonal comparisons possible) can generate the evidence from which to make objective judgements about welfare, which can inform a far more scientific approach to public policy, and perhaps restore trust in government. Rather than undermining economics, measuring happiness might supply a consensual basis for the allocation of distributive shares and the regulation of private interests.

On the other hand, critics of the economic model, and particularly of the utility-maximising individual at its heart, lay claim to happiness data as a possible foundation for a new approach to well-being. The gap between rising income and stagnating life satisfaction is filled by various elements of human value, put at risk by the dominance of individualism and consumerism. Both the central features of sustainable quality of life, and the principles for its distribution among populations, are called into question.

In this, they have built upon critiques of the economic model of welfare that have been developed since its rise to hegemony. They include ideas of positive freedom and capabilities (Sen, 1984, 1987a, 1987b; Nussbaum, 2000), communitarianism (MacIntyre, 1981; Sandel, 1982; Taylor, 1989), feminism and the ethic of care (Pateman, 1989; Sevenhuijsen, 2000) and environmentalism (Douthwaite, 1992; Nordhaus and Boyer, 2000). All these have challenged the economic version of how value is produced and distributed, to propose alternative accounts of the sources of well-being. Data on SWB have been grafted onto these accounts to extend these arguments.

In this chapter, I shall outline the issues at stake in these new debates, and the approach to them taken in this book. I shall argue that there are shortcomings in all the accounts of the Easterlin paradox, and all the attempts to deploy versions of well-being that adapt or challenge the welfare perspective.

In the next chapter, I shall outline the approach to the happiness data that informs this book. My analysis will argue that an alternative to the economics of welfare cannot be made coherent, except in terms of a wider theory of social value. This must both encompass the economic model, and be accountable to it, since the strength of that model lies in its capacity to explain all interactions within the same overall framework.

I shall show that the notion of social value raises many problems for societies in which economic welfare, based on individual utility maximisation in markets, is the main source of self-esteem. However, there are important clues from the happiness data of how these problems might (in the long term) be overcome, if governments are willing to risk abandoning some of the securities of quantified models in favour of the uncertainties of social and political processes.

Welfare and utility

If it is possible to measure not only individual happiness, but also its components, then the goals of public policy might be redefined. On the one hand, it could be argued that (following Bentham) we should return to the aim of enabling the greatest possible amount of happiness for the greatest number – utilitarianism. In principle, each person could be wired up to a device to measure their current contentment (a 'hedonimeter'), and governments could orient their decisions to the aggregate outcomes of these readings.

But this change has big implications for the economic model of welfare that prevails (in one form or another) in liberal democracies. This rests on the idea that there is an identifiable sphere of interdependence between members of a political community over which collective decisions are required because individuals are affected by each other's actions. Within this sphere, institutions can be agreed that set the 'rules of the game' for the economy. Because each individual can be relied on to maximise their utility in markets, and through other voluntary exchanges, collective institutions are designed to enable interactions for the pursuit of individual utility within these rules.

But 'utility' signifies a consistent set of preferences rather than any specific content (in terms of emotions or satisfactions) in the economic models developed since the early 20th century. If the goal is to promote interactions that make people happy, it may be that a different set of institutions, involving other public goods, and enabling other kinds of exchanges, should underpin collective life. For instance, instead of redistributing income and providing education and healthcare through professional services, government agencies might promote festivals, or supply leisure facilities, or award more widespread honours to citizens. After all, these were things the Ancient Romans did, with some success.

From a utilitarian standpoint, some economists have indeed argued that greater happiness, rather than the growth of GDP, should be the goal of public policy. This view has been most forcefully put by Richard Layard (2005) in his influential text on happiness. In this, he makes a set of sweeping recommendations for the reorientation of public policy, drawing on the results of well-being research (pp 247-9).

However, these proposals are made without a systematic reanalysis of the implications of a hedonic basis for political and social institutions. Existing structures purport to represent the best possible compromises, in terms of the external costs and benefits of living in the same territory, between individuals intent on maximising their utility. If the sum total of national income under these arrangements is an unreliable indication of the potential for optimising well-being, as suggested by the gap between GDP growth and happiness stagnation, then a far more thoroughgoing review of collective life is required.

In the economic model, the links between utility-based welfare and the trade-offs between efficiency and equity are so tight and embedded that marginal adjustments (more redistribution of income and work, less competition and comparison in the public sector, less mobility in civil society) such as Layard proposes cannot be logically derived from the assumptions. Something far more radical about what is to be produced, distributed and consumed, and how costs and benefits are to be accounted, is required.

So the paradox of the 'new utilitarianism' proposed by Layard and others is that the utility-based welfare with which it is associated, and which has been the target of its critics since the 18th century, has itself become the most unstable element in its analysis. If well-being is to be identified with psychological states rather than decisions and actions, and if the economic choices of 'free individuals' do not equate with its maximisation, then utilitarianism becomes detached from the economic model that has been its principal legacy.

This can be recognised in the two main theoretical attempts that have been made within the utilitarianism tradition to explain the Easterlin paradox. On the one hand, there have been those who postulated a 'hedonic treadmill'; as individuals adapt quickly to higher levels of income, they strive for more pleasure by higher earnings and consumption, but are unable to overcome the effects of this rapid adaptation (Van Praag and Frijters, 1999; Di Tella et al, 2003). But the economic model would predict that a rational utility-maximiser should identify this problem, and change his or her behaviour accordingly, for instance by preferring more leisure, or substituting other more satisfying activities for material consumption.

Alternatively, there might be other missing variables within the aggregate statistics on income and SWB that, if introduced into econometric analysis, explain the paradoxical divergence between them. Di Tella and MacCulloch (2007) show that such factors as the rate of unemployment, inflation, longer working hours, pollution, and divorce and crime rates are negatively correlated with SWB. But, as they comment:

> [A]dding the actual impact of other variables besides income leads one to expect happiness levels that are even higher, making the unexplained trend in happiness data larger, than when just changes in income are considered. In other words, introducing omitted variables only worsens the income-without-happiness paradox. (Di Tella and MacCulloch, 2007, p 25)

This points to a more fundamental problem for the 'new utilitarianism'. Perhaps the social institutions themselves, which have been designed to create the conditions for maximising utility, are at fault, because they are promoting self-defeating behaviour. If this were so, we would need to identify those public goods and decision processes that enable happiness, rather than economic welfare. This might involve a far more laborious dismantling of the structures of liberal democracy than the 'new utilitarians' seem to envisage.

Alternatively (or additionally), there might be some way of analysing utility itself to make it better at encompassing the components of well-being, rather than those of economic welfare. But utility is already supposed to be a comprehensive term, which embraces all sources of happiness. The problem is not that the economic model fails to explain behaviour that takes place outside the formal economy; as Becker (1976, 1981, 1996) and many others have shown, it is well capable of doing so. It can account for family, community and political choices in terms of the psychic costs and benefits to individuals as well as the material ones.

Furthermore, most social scientists would accept that the explanatory power of the economic model, in relating welfare gains to the decisions of millions of individuals, is far too important to sacrifice for the uncertain possibilities of a new approach grounded in psychology. The challenge therefore seems to be to explain the Easterlin paradox, and look for ways of overcoming the stagnation of SWB rates, without losing all the advantages of the economic model.

To summarise, utility can encompass psychological factors, but the decision to use Gross National Happiness, rather than Gross National Product, as an approximation for aggregate utility, might sacrifice many of the most powerfully explanatory and predictive features of the economic model, and much of its usefulness for public policy. We would need to re-examine the institutions under which private exchanges of all kinds take place, to consider whether they provide a basis for equity, in terms of happiness outcomes (fair rules and a level playing field) for such exchanges, and whether they are in any way responsible for such perversities as a 'hedonic treadmill'. And we would have to carry out a far more systematic study of the links between individual actions and their psychological consequences, to check whether people could, in general, be relied on to maximise their own (material and psychic) utility in voluntary exchanges, or if they require different incentives, or paternalistic guidance, to do so.

After all, Bentham himself, who is claimed to be the father of the 'new utilitarianism', was little concerned with liberty. He dismissed natural rights as 'nonsense of stilts', and prescribed an enormous range of officials, agencies and punishments to steer populations towards the greatest happiness.

If the pitfalls of this approach seem deterrent, there are several alternative responses to the Easterlin paradox. The obvious one is to leave the economic model intact as an analysis of material goods, but to find a more satisfactory framework for the determination of moral and political issues than welfare economics. To put this another way, we could leave questions about economic welfare to be determined within markets and voluntary exchanges, but only after revising the institutions for collective life according to criteria derived from some other evaluative standards, better related to the promotion of well-being.

Capabilities – Sen

If this task sounds more manageable than the reconstruction of the whole economic model, it is still a very challenging one. Behind all our existing institutions, and much of our philosophising about them, is a set of assumptions that are broadly 'welfarist'. This relies on information about the distribution of material resources as the basis for judging the appropriateness and fairness of rules and organisations. Without necessarily being utilitarian in the way it assesses final outcomes, 'welfarism' of this kind evaluates institutions by reference to some aspect of how such goods are distributed.

For example, in the economic model most widely adopted, the principle of equity applied is the maximisation of the incomes of the worst-off members of society. This represents a fusion between Rawls's (1971) 'difference principle' and the Pareto criterion, that no one can be made better-off without making someone worse-off. Even though Rawls's list of 'primary goods' to be equalised for the sake of justice (rights, liberties and opportunities, income and wealth, and the social basis of self-respect) embraces far more than such material distributions, its plausibility as a theory, and its influence on public policy, have largely rested on its adoption into welfare economics in that form. In this sense, the Rawlsian legacy has been welfarist, even if his theory had other moral features (Sen, 1984, pp 316-20).

Sen's own approach argued that the moral yardstick for assessing institutions should be positive freedoms – not what people have, by way of material goods, but what they can do (their 'capabilities to function').

> These freedoms are not primarily concerned with what goods or income or resources people have. Nor with how much pleasure or desire-fulfilment they get out of these activities (or from the ability to do these activities). The category of capabilities is the natural candidate for reflecting the idea of freedom to do. (Sen, 1984, p 316)

Sen argued that both Rawls's (1971) and Dworkin's (1981) principles, for justice and equality respectively, contained elements of a capabilities approach, but that both relied ultimately on versions of welfarism. He claimed that his version of equity dealt better with such phenomena as the long-suffering compliance of very poor people, and the additional needs of people with disabilities, by factoring in the positive measures required to enable them to do the things taken for granted by the mainstream population.

Does the capabilities approach deal more comfortably with issues of well-being than the welfarist one? In one way, it seems more fundamentally challenged by the findings of SWB research, both by the availability of comparative data on overall life satisfaction, and by the revelation of the principal components of such self-evaluations. If these are to be seen as having any ethical relevance, they appear to be problematic for this non-welfarist perspective.

This is because the findings do appear to show strong adaptation effects, both in terms of the rather narrow gap between the levels of SWB among wealthy citizens of any country (with many capabilities of all kinds), and poor ones (with few such); and in terms of the small differences between the average SWB of certain relatively poor countries (such as Ghana, Mexico and Vanuatu) and certain rich ones (such as the UK and the US). What seems to matter more to people than the options available for pursuing their own ends are certain widely available sources of well-being, such as close personal relationships, good neighbours and an inclusive community in which their contribution is valued (Argyle, 1999; Myers, 1999; Helliwell, 2003). Although this casts doubt on welfarism, it challenges the capability approach also.

On the other hand, long-term illness and unemployment contribute more to declines in SWB than loss of the final third of income (Helliwell, 2003), and their effects also last longer. This could be argued to reflect very much what a capabilities approach would suggest (Schokkaert, 2007). Personal, economic and political freedom are also strong influences (Frey and Stutzer, 2002). This leads Schokkaert to suggest that well-being statistics can provide answers to the problem acknowledged by Sen himself with his principle. As he observed:

> Capabilities are … directly valuable in a way that the possession of primary goods cannot be, since they evidently are means to some more human ends. Judgements of relative importance are, thus, less contingent and less remote in the case of capabilities as opposed to primary goods. Nevertheless, there are difficulties in such indexation. (Sen, 1984, p 323)

Several commentators have argued that 'overall satisfaction with life' statistics might resolve this difficulty since they indicate which functionings most influence SWB, and hence what weightings should be given to the different factors (Anand et al, 2005; Anand and van Hees, 2006). However, this overlooks the difficulty that, even if allowance is made for variations in basic pessimism or optimism between individuals, some of the most significant elements in overall life satisfaction are concerned with the personal choices (for instance, whether to get married and stay married) and beliefs (such as that in

God) of individuals. These do not represent functionings, cannot be distributed by third parties and arguably are not ethically relevant. This leads Schokkaert (2007) to argue that these factors should be given the same constant value as temperament in interpersonal comparisons that provide the basis for decisions about policies for equity.

As a defence of the capabilities approach, this is surely stretching a point. It would be more consistent with Sen's often-repeated argument that pleasure and desire fulfilment are not the important issues for evaluations of social arrangements to dismiss SWB statistics as irrelevant. These elements make up such a large part of life satisfaction that they can make a decisive difference between otherwise similar self-evaluations, or reverse the ordering between individuals, as Schokkaert's own illustrative examples show.

Close personal relationships and membership of faith communities are, after all, part of the same sets of social interdependencies in which 'functionings' such as employment, earning and civic participation are enacted. The positive freedoms that Sen's capabilities approach are supposed to enable must include all the activities that are relevant for well-being, especially those that carry such significance.

Suppose, for example, that the institutional framework under evaluation were to be concerned with people's opportunity to get satisfying work with adequate wages, but not with their opportunity to form sustainable partnerships and support their children. This would bias any assessment of the 'goodness' of these arrangements (Sen's term) towards improving the distribution and quality of work and the level of salaries, and away from the opportunities to enjoy family life. It would also relegate close personal relationships to a subordinate position among policy concerns, which might in turn lead them to be undervalued by citizens, with harmful effects on average levels of SWB. This would not matter if policy were unconcerned about overall life satisfaction; but it would be perverse if that was supposed to supply the criteria for equity among members.

Capabilities – Nussbaum

The capabilities approach challenges the priority given to individual preferences in utilitarianism, and in economic analysis generally. In doing so, it runs the risk of arguing for a version of human well-being that is disconnected from individuals' perceptions of their welfare and hence from their choices. Martha Nussbaum's work directly addresses this dilemma; she argues that it is possible to reject the 'subjective welfarism' of economics while avoiding a slip into the 'Platonism' of defining what is right and good, and what confers quality of life, without reference to people's desires and preferences (Nussbaum, 2000, pp 116-7).

Nussbaum's rejection of 'subjective welfarism' is primarily driven by the conviction that preferences (and their aggregation) cannot supply a satisfactory basis for constitutional principles or public policies. She argues that the 'basic social minimum' that defines the respect and dignity due to each person is best understood by reference to a list of *central human capabilities* and by setting political goals in terms of what people are actually able to do and be (Nussbaum, 2000, p 5). It is only as a secondary objective of her philosophical enquiry that she considers 'comparisons of life quality' (how well people are doing), as the data for normative analyses of political principles (p 6). She rejects the term 'well-being' in favour of 'quality of life' (p 14), which is intended to indicate *universal*, cross-cultural standards, derived from capabilities 'to function in a fully human way' (p 71).

To avoid 'Platonism', she insists that her approach does not pre-empt the actual choices people make, including the adoption of traditional religious or family roles and relationships, but that they should have the capabilities of pursuing other desires and activities. Using examples of women members of a cooperative movement in India, she indicates the diversity of cultures from which they draw, and how their capabilities are shaped by the institutions of India's constituent states. Her approach is intended to provide:

> the underpinnings of basic political principles that can be embodied in constitutional guarantees.... The central capabilities are not just instrumental to further pursuits: they are held to have value in themselves, in making the life that includes them fully human.... [T]hey have a special importance in making any choice of a way of life possible, and so they have a special claim to be supported for political purposes in a pluralistic society. (Nussbaum, 2000, pp 74-5)

Nussbaum's list of central capabilities comprises:

- life;
- bodily health;
- bodily integrity, senses, imagination and thought;
- emotions;
- practical reason;

- affiliation;
- other species; and
- control over one's political and material environment.

She selects practical reason and affiliation as being of special importance for living 'in a truly human manner' – being able to behave 'as a thinking being, not just a cog in a machine; and … capable of being … with and toward others in a way which involves mutual recognition and humanity' (p 82).

But Nussbaum's capabilities constitute a 'moral conception selected for political purposes only' (p 74), which is valuable from an ethical point of view (p 83).

So her approach to 'quality of life' seeks to define what each individual should be enabled to do and be – rights are conceived as 'combined capabilities' (p 98). The 'subjective welfarism' of economic analysis cannot provide this kind of basis for the value of each human being. Although she endorses most of Rawls's account of justice and political liberalism, she disagrees with his inclusion of income and wealth among his 'primary goods', because this ignores the social context in which material resources are deployed (pp 69, 89). Like Sen, she argues that Rawls did not distinguish his theory sufficiently from welfarism in this respect.

Thus, Nussbaum's purpose in distinguishing quality of life from welfare is not the same as the distinction between well-being and welfare that seems to be demanded by the Easterlin paradox. Her critique of utility-based welfare concerns its inadequacy as a basis for theories of justice, rights and other universal human values. Her analysis abstracts such principles from the rich descriptions of the lives of Indian women, which she takes as her materials. She is not directly concerned with the sources of their actual well-being, except in so far as they are facilitated by their access to 'central capabilities', or blocked by its absence or denial.

This is clear in her treatment of culture. In defending universal values as the basis for the capabilities approach, she rejects the relativism associated with cultural analyses. She emphasises that cultures are dynamic, open to change and criticism, they offer a diversity of valuable lives, but do not invalidate the search for general principles that apply across cultures (pp 41–51). Nussbaum's concern with the justification of a 'basic social minimum' focuses on diversity itself as a positive value. I shall argue that the analysis of well-being should focus on how cultures supply social value to their members.

This difference in emphasis can be illustrated by reference to the Israeli nursery example in the Introduction (pp 9-10). The financial penalty for parental lateness in collecting their children might increase the welfare of parents with busy lives, and of staff who qualify for extra payments, but harm the well-being of parents and children, in terms of a culture of care, concern, consideration and mutuality. Nussbaum's approach would not recognise this distinction, because both situations would reflect sets of individual decisions within the same structure of capabilities, enjoyed by all the parties.

Furthermore, it is hard to see what Nussbaum's analysis would contribute to the explanation of the divergence between welfare and well-being levels in affluent countries since the Second World War. Those populations have experienced large gains in capabilities, through the expansions of welfare state services (such as healthcare and higher education), and through the collective action of social movements, on behalf of women, minority ethnic groups, gay people, disabled people and so on. Yet these gains are not reflected in higher levels of SWB. This seems to make Ormerod's (2007) point – that well-being is not closely related to improvements in social rights or state spending, any more than it is to income per head. Improvements in Nussbaum's version of quality of life do not reliably yield more well-being, at least under conditions of affluence.

The gap between welfare and well-being suggests that increased earning and consumption does not enable people to achieve as much psychic satisfaction as they desire, or that institutional arrangements mislead them into behaviour that is self-defeating, and does not maximise their utility (seen as a combination of material and psychic contentment).

The latter possibility has been explored by Avner Offer (2006), in his analysis of how institutions and cultural standards for self-control and deferred gratification have decayed in the UK and the US since the 1950s. He argues that phenomena such as obesity, binge drinking, drug abuse, risky driving, debt, inadequate pension provision and marital break-up reflect the failure of 'commitment devices' to counter the availability of instant pleasures. On this account, well-being might stagnate with a decay of social processes allowing a qualitative appreciation and pacing of experience, and a proper evaluation of long-term consequences.

This goes beyond the capabilities approach, to argue that what matters is how institutions and cultures enable individuals to value their experiences, rather than simply what they have the opportunity to do. It directs attention towards the social conventions and power structures in which interactions take place, and suggests that it is these which ultimately relate behaviour to well-being. It is to this kind of analysis that the remaining challenges to welfarism are directed.

Gender and the ethic of care

If we are looking for a systematic undervaluation of experiences and people, which is institutionalised in such a way as to skew interactions away from the sources of well-being, and towards illusory forms of 'welfare', the obvious candidate is the 'sexual contract'. Feminists have long been arguing that the relegation of the emotions, informal mutuality and communal life from the sphere of civil society not only excludes women from full membership, but also impoverishes the fabric of that society, by distorting its standards and misdirecting its priorities.

In her radical analysis of the origins of these exclusions, Carole Pateman (1988) argues that they stem from a set of foundational assumptions upon which the modern world was built. She traces the present forms of women's subordination to the 'social contract' under which new versions of 'the individual' as a political and economic actor, civil society and power were constructed in the 17th and early 18th centuries. Contract as the dominant form of relationships between such individuals, seen as owning property in themselves and their material possessions, justified both the power of employers over workers and servants, and of governments over citizens. But it was built on a very different sort of contract between men and women – the sexual contract.

The most influential social contract theorists – Locke and Rousseau – located the relations between men and women in the 'state of nature', before the formation of political society and the invention of money. This relationship, of domination and subordination, in which sexual access was 'exchanged' for protection, was brought into the new order of contract in its original form. The deeply ambiguous marriage contract both recognised this pre-political arrangement, and granted the man the right to represent his wife in the public sphere, as the competent civic and economic actor. 'In modern patriarchy the difference between the sexes is presented as the quintessentially natural difference. Men's patriarchal right over women is presented as reflecting the proper order of nature' (Pateman, 1988, p 16).

The point about the new order was as much what it excluded from the contract-based sphere of political authority and economic exchange as what it enabled. Along with overthrowing the despotic, paternal 'natural' power of fathers over sons, and monarchs over peoples, it relegated the domestic sphere of sex, reproduction and family, in which women's role was defined, to a separate and inferior status, beyond the concerns of justice, rights and contractual relations.

At this crucial defining moment, in which the assumptions of the social contract were institutionalised in the legal definitions of individuals, property and legitimate power, women were defined in terms of their bodies, their (unreliable) emotions, their attractions and distractions for men, and their reproductive functions, as threats to this new order.

> Women lack neither strength nor ability in a general sense, but, according to the classic contract theorists, they are naturally deficient in a specific *political* capacity, the capacity to create and maintain political right. Women must be subject to men because they are naturally subversive of men's political order.... Women are creatures of unlimited desire, incapable of sublimating their passions in the manner of men who are to create themselves as civil individuals.... Women, their bodies and bodily passions, represent the 'nature' that must be controlled and transcended if social order is to be created and sustained.... Women's relations to the social world must always be mediated through men's reason; women's bodies must always be subject to men's reason and judgements if order is not to be threatened. (Pateman, 1988, pp 96, 100-1; emphasis in original)

On this analysis, modern society, which is built on contract 'all the way down', between individuals who – as rational maximisers of their utility, defined in terms of property-generated goods – must always relegate the 'natural' in favour of the 'right', is inherently one-sided. By excluding and dominating women, emotions and the 'nature' they represent, the contractual version of social relations deploys power to distort the potential for human well-being. Small wonder, then, that a gap develops between material prosperity and life satisfaction, since only part of the product of interactions is represented in the former.

The idea that emotions, personal relationships and informal support are seriously undervalued through our present institutional structures is intuitively highly plausible. It also fits very well with the evidence on the components of SWB (Argyle, 1999; Myers, 1999; Helliwell, 2003). But there remain many difficult questions about how this insight could be brought to bear on the measurement and analysis of the formal business of society, or inform public policy.

In a sense, the critique seems *too* radical, because it strikes at the whole basis of the modern order. If individuals, contracts, exchanges, rights and powers have all been designed to exclude intimacy, care and the bonds of empathy, what (short of a total revolution) might allow them to enter the formal systems that shape our ideas and behaviour? What is more, women have gained increasing access to the public sphere in recent years, albeit on terms defined by men, and largely by adopting masculine standards and criteria. This implies that many women now have a stake in the order of contract and property – they are at least 'honorary individuals', in Pateman's terms, and might be unwilling to put this status at risk.

Just these issues have divided the feminist movement, both in terms of theory, and over policy. Some leading writers, such as Elshtain (1981, 1998), have argued for a complete rejection of the individualist, rights-based, formal conception of the social order, in favour of communal society with women's values of 'maternalism' at its centre. Nurture and support would replace competition and acquisition as the ethical heart of this order. Alternatively, liberal feminists argue that women's rights can be established within a modified version of democracy, which is more respectful of difference (Phillips, 1993; Nash, 1998).

Nussbaum's liberal feminism, based on her capabilities approach, leads her to endorse the family as part of the 'basic structure' of society, and love and care as universal values, but to look to property rights, education and wider affiliation as offering central capabilities for women, by strengthening their bargaining rights and exit options (Nussbaum, 2000, chapter 4). Pateman sees an entitlement to a government-funded, individual basic income as the means to democratise relations within the domestic sphere, by empowering women to achieve equality (Pateman, 2004). Both therefore abstract individual social and political rights for women, as caregivers and creators of emotional well-being, from the messy ambiguity of family and kinship relations, rather than attempting to make economic value accountable to the logic of interpersonal processes of mutual recognition and respect.

In recent years, claims have converged on the arguments for recognition of the value of the informal care provided by women (mainly), as a way of balancing the allocation of time and energy in the economy (Sevenhuijsen, 2000; Williams, 2001; Meagher and Parton, 2004). The 'ethic of care' (Tronto, 1994) demands that this commitment, which follows a different logic from that of the formal economy, is allotted a value that can allow such a balance to be struck. If ways could be found to give such value to the work of informal social reproduction, this might transform people's priorities, and possibly narrow the gap between material welfare and a more holistic well-being.

Yet there is nothing new in the insight that the formal economy and polity are constructed on a foundation of informal activity in a domestic and communal sphere. The economic model readily acknowledges that such activities involve exchanges, produce utility, and represent an alternative use of resources from the formal sphere (Becker, 1976, 1981, 1996). One obvious way in which women make choices within the model is their decisions over whether to form partnerships, have children and develop careers in employment that involve paying others for childcare. The model assumes that women have utility functions that allow them to choose between various options, in which costs and benefits are attached to each of these pathways through their adult lives.

This example also illustrates the critique made by feminists of current institutions. Such dilemmas are seen as women's issues, not men's; reproduction is still part of a 'natural' sphere excluded from the formal one. The gap between material rewards in mainstream employment and the allowances available to bring up children is so large, especially in the UK and the US, that women must sacrifice much material welfare to care for children, or other family members. How might the value of care be better recognised, so as to give it greater priority?

To complicate matters, neither having children, nor time spent with children, contribute strongly to SWB among women respondents in affluent societies. Partnerships and sociability are more consistently correlated with high levels of self-assessed overall happiness (Layard, 2005, pp 62-9). So there is an additional challenge – to make informal care more satisfying (and perhaps statusful), as well as giving it an adequate economic value.

The environment and sustainability

The final major potential source for a mismatch between gains in material welfare and the stagnation of psychic well-being lies in nature itself, and the degradation of the physical environment. One possibility is that, as economic growth through technological innovation has progressed, we have become estranged from our natural world, losing touch with the true sources of satisfaction with our lives – the rhythms of the day, the seasons, the beauty of our surroundings and even spirituality. Hi-tech production and consumption, the pace of urban life, pollution and crowding may all have contributed to a lower quality of daily living. Finally, the awareness of the threat to our very survival from global warming adds another dimension to the unacknowledged costs of an overprocessed form of existence (Nordhaus and Boyer, 2000).

This critique of the economic model and its social order has much in common with the previous one. If we seek the origins of the exploitative approach to nature that characterises modern capitalism, we need look no further than the same foundational texts as those scrutinised by Pateman. For example, although the formation of political society is related to crises in the supply of natural resources by both Locke and Rousseau, the social contract rests on the assumption that economic growth can continue indefinitely because of the availability of resources from outside Europe. This is explicit in Locke (1690, section 45), where he states that, especially in America,

> There are still *great tracts of ground* to be found, which (the inhabitants thereof not having joined with the rest of mankind, in the consent of the use of their common money) *lie waste*, and are more than the people who dwell on it do, or can make use of, and so still lie in common.

Now for the first time we have a clearer idea of the natural limits on economic development. Because we recognise that tracts of wasteland are necessary for our survival, and that we are fast approaching the point where the higher productivity that Locke used to justify inequality of property and income must rely on something other than the depletion of natural resources for its continuation, we cannot assume that growth will finance a version of equity. And the quality of our lives may require us to protect diversity, beauty and nature itself more explicitly, as part of sustainability.

The environmental movement can claim to have been the first to question the viability of a model of human development based on economic growth, and to doubt whether material consumption equated with quality of life. Indeed, the first expressions of these ideas in any systematic form more or less coincided with the identification of the Easterlin paradox. The work of Nordhaus and Tobin (1972) and the Club of Rome (1972) set out the historical, scientific and economic evidence of the negative impacts and disappointing outcomes of the pursuit of growth, and argued for radically different approaches to human development and well-being.

Some environmentalists have argued that human development can be faster in the absence of economic growth. For instance, Douthwaite (1992) gives figures to claim that the largest measured improvements in standards of health, education and income equality in the UK occurred in the period between the outbreak of the First World War and the late 1940s, a period of very slow growth by the standards of the previous and subsequent eras. These statistics are largely confirmed by Sen (1999, pp 49-51). If equality of incomes and physical endowments was greatest in 1949, before the attempt to combine redistribution and public services with a productivist, growth-oriented economic strategy could take shape, this suggests that the pursuit of well-being should be detached from Keynesian welfarism as much as post-Keynesian free market capitalism.

These debates have raised interest in the possibilities for a 'non-productivist' approach to income maintenance and public services, in which the attempt to trade off equity with 'efficiency' (defined in terms of increased production and consumption) is replaced by goals concerned with quality of life. The question haunting such attempts is whether they could be achieved by modifications of the existing social contract (by bringing excluded aspects of the 17th century basis for modernity into the process of institutional settlement). For example, now that we know that economic development threatens ecological survival, the preservation of the natural environment might be given due priority by the hypothetical presence at the negotiations over institutions for justice of representatives of future generations (Dobson, 1998).

Some commentators on these debates have argued that feminist and environmental concerns might be brought together in a non-productivist design, by putting a value on both informal care and natural resources (Fitzpatrick, 2003, chapter 7). The aim would then be to modify the economic model, by including in the whole contractarian basis for political systems – both national and international – those fundamental aspects of well-being left out of the blueprints for modernity, industrialisation and liberal democracy.

The problem of global warming has made these concerns into matters of urgency for national governments, supranational bodies (such as the European Union) and international organisations. The search for treaties over the reduction of carbon emissions, and the attempt to create 'cap and trade' schemes, indicate attempts to resolve the threat within the economic model. On the one hand, governments contract with each other to take enforcement measures against rising discharges; on the other hand, they raise the costs of emissions, but allow large companies to trade in rights to discharge.

Problems like climate change point to the possibility that the pursuit of welfare within the economic model undermines well-being, but this seems to come about in two different ways, and it is not clear how these are related to each other. On the one hand, the integration of the world economy (globalisation) creates interdependencies between populations on opposite sides of the earth. Chinese and Indian industrialisation provides cheap goods, but threatens ecological disaster, for many in affluent countries. Who should pay the costs of technological fixes (like carbon capture), through which institutions, and with what ethical justification? Should it be consumers in affluent countries, or the financial intermediaries that fund rapid growth in Asia, or industrialists there, who pay for the benefits of sustainability? And are such catastrophic threats susceptible to the instruments through which other policy issues are evaluated, such as cost-benefit analysis (Posner, 2004; Sunstein, 2005)?

Welfare economics, like social contract theory, adopts the convenient fictional assumption of a single system of cooperation (interdependency) that is also a political society. Once capital and labour are located in different regions of the globe, and consumers spread throughout it, costs and benefits are contestable, and enforcement weak. If the economic model of welfare is not to become the main enemy of well-being, these intractable issues must be addressed.

On the other hand, the environmental perspective poses a strong challenge to the concepts of the rational, utility-maximising individual as the basis for well-being. Since processes of ecological damage are largely invisible, and individuals usually cannot recognise their contributions to environmental degradation (which may happen thousands of miles away), it is difficult to construct self-enforcing versions of sustainable ways of life. Although no plausible version of sustainability can exclude changes in individual lifestyles from a long-term strategy for survival, the everyday incentives for such shifts cannot be derived from the economic model itself.

While hunter-gatherers conserved the forests and the species who lived in them through their cultures over many millennia, pastoralists maintained the grasslands on which their flocks fed, and agricultural populations attended to the structure of their soil, these practices could be analysed in terms of rational maximisation of their utility within the resources available to them. There is no such set of incentives for city dwellers, who have little idea of the environmental costs of their production and consumption activities, and must rely on the signals from prices and taxes to relate their current welfare to their long-term well-being.

Both these aspects of the ecological debate direct attention towards the ways in which behaviour can be steered for the sake of well-being, by institutions that are either non-contractarian or which interpret the social contract far more widely than the version that underpinned modernity. They imply that some cultural standards that give value to environmental goods should enter the processes of mutual regulation between citizens, not as capabilities – as in Nussbaum (2000, p 80) – but as everyday practices.

Conclusions

The recent data on SWB (which provoked the debate over welfare and well-being) have confirmed longstanding doubts about the reliability of individual preferences as a basis for collective life. Within utilitarianism, theorists since Hume (1739, book 2, part 3, section 3) have acknowledged the possibility that people can be wrong about the means to their ends, or less than rational in the way they make their choices (Harsanyi, 1982). In economics itself, welfarism has been challenged by the Arrow paradox (Arrow, 1951) and by Sen's (1977) demonstration of the problems of recognising rights within a preference-based framework.

However, the concerns highlighted by the Easterlin paradox go beyond questions about fully informed decisions, social choice and normative principles. They draw attention to the interpersonal and cultural processes through which people give meaning and value to each other, and regulate each other's actions. Because these aspects of collective life are so messy and unsystematic, they have tended to be regarded as a kind of residual sludge, from which the elegant abstractions of both economic and ethical analysis must be plucked. Even social theorists have increasingly retreated into more formal accounts of such phenomena.

Perhaps the most disquieting aspect of the growing gap between welfare and well-being is that it has defied the expansion of public provision for health and education, programmes for redistribution, and action to defend the rights of minorities. So it does not reflect a crude reliance on income maximisation in government policies, and it encompasses a wide range of regimes, from the neoliberal to the social democratic, in affluent countries.

In this chapter, I have shown that, even though there are many problems in utilitarian deployments of happiness statistics, well-being does not easily equate with Sen's 'standard of living', Nussbaum's 'quality of life' or even the elements of 'nature' that were excluded from the Enlightenment versions of the social contract, and hence eventually from economic analysis. The value that constitutes well-being seems as difficult to capture in moral and political principles as it is within calculative individual maximisation.

Disturbingly, in close personal relationships, in cultures, and even in relation to the natural world, the institutions and practices through which well-being is created and sustained may not follow the pathways of justice or rationality. To say that they enrich the quality of life through their contribution to 'diversity' (as Nussbaum does), and that they are to be tolerated so long as they do not harm others, and are voluntarily undertaken by healthy, educated individuals, with other options, is scarcely an unequivocal endorsement, or a clear guide to public policy.

Yet there appears to be an immediate relevance in the issues raised by the Easterlin paradox, which may help to explain why it has been taken up by so many social commentators, as well as (selectively) by politicians. It points towards collective failures in regulation and self-regulation of social interactions of many kinds, especially in the Anglophone countries (Offer, A., 2006), which represent a reproach to liberal democracy, and even to civilisation itself. It is not just that depression, self-harm, drug and alcohol misuse and obesity have become endemic features of our societies; so have rudeness, casual violence, boorishness, lack of consideration and respect, and a general decline in civility.

Taken together with high rates in the breakdown of relationships, and concerns about the well-being of children and young people, this seems to indicate a fundamental flaw in the ways in which people create and sustain mutual value in their everyday interactions.

> It's a pathology of individual entitlement – what's crumbling is the civility that is essential to our well-being, to trust and to the conviviality of our lives. We have failed to invest the resources, both material and cultural, in the places where we interact with strangers. (Bunting, 2008, p 25)

This short passage brings together several aspects of the debate about welfare and well-being – individual maximisation, individual rights, collective regulation and the collective infrastructure. In the next chapter, I shall consider what an alternative account of social value might offer to the analysis of these issues.

TWO

Well-being and social value: 'I shall not come to your funeral'

One of the more beguiling features of the economic model, in which distributions of welfare are related to interactions between utility-maximising individuals, is the idea that such individuals can ultimately choose the social institutions that can give them the best possible outcomes. If they are free to make agreements with each other, both in terms of private exchanges and collective action, then they can also decide about the rules under which they will live together, and the boundaries between the individual and the collective (political) spheres.

The appeal of this model lies in its ability to explain how people whose desires and interests are different, and often conflicting, can enter into contracts, both to exchange private goods and to establish collective arrangements. Indeed, it is a little-recognised feature of microeconomic theory (and the individualistic assumptions and methodology on which it is founded) that actors *must* have different preferences and interests in order to explain how both markets and polities come about.

> [W]hen individual interests are assumed to be identical, the main body of economic theory vanishes. If all men were equal in interest and in endowment, natural or artificial, there would be no organised economic activity to explain. Each man would be a Crusoe. Economic theory thus explains why men cooperate through trade: they do so because they are different. (Buchanan and Tullock, 1962, p 4)

But how different are they? Although modern political economy started from the challenging assumption of a rivalrous and footloose set of beings in a state of nature that lacked any collective restraints, it quickly moved towards a set of social arrangements – the family, property and money – all of which were supposed to have come into existence before the original political contract. In the work of Locke (1690, sections 37-43), Hume (1739, pp 484-96) and Rousseau (1754, pp 159-64), these institutions were not adopted by formal contract, or by collective agreement, but through an 'invisible hand' process, by ignorant and unforesightful primitives, because they bestowed specific (universal) advantages on members (Jordan, 2004, chapter 2).

Indeed, the whole edifice of the economic model relies on a distinction between those institutions that enable private exchanges between individuals who remain entirely 'independent' of each other in all matters except the ones specified in their contract of exchange, and those that concern 'interdependence'. The latter, which create political relationships, arise from two kinds of situations.

> First, collective action may eliminate some of the *external costs* that the private actions of other individuals impose on the individual in question.... Secondly, collective action may be required to secure some additional or *external benefits* that cannot be secured through purely private behaviour. (Buchanan and Tullock, 1962, pp 43-4; emphasis in original)

These are the assumptions that have been incorporated into welfare economics; individuals are regarded as the bearers of purposes and wants that ultimately provide the justification for collective measures (Hicks, 1947, p 11). Since individuals are so diverse and the only common metric for their desires is money, those institutions and allocations that produce the highest national income are justified. As early as 1920, something like Rawls's difference principle supplied the link between efficiency and equity in the theory of optimum allocations.

> Provided that the dividend accruing to the poor is not diminished, increases in the aggregate national dividend of the community, unless they result from coercing people to work more than they wish to do, carry with them increases in economic welfare. (Pigou, 1920, p x)

So the costs and benefits of interdependence in the economic model stem from specific circumstances, and identify a sphere for group or government action. The medium of exchange – money – is useful precisely because it enables private gains from collective action as well as from private transactions to be measured within the same framework of account. This in turn allows individuals with different purposes to recognise the advantages of government regulations and policies that apply to all.

It is easy to see why those who wish to challenge this model's ascendancy are required to construct an overarching source of value that can transcend that which is measured by individual utility. This is why state socialism, fascism and theocracy (in their 20th-century forms) were all totalitarian; they insisted that what gave all members of the collective the benefits of their interactions was that they shared in an overall purpose, respectively the triumph of labour, the glory of race and the omnipotence of God. Individual value was derived from this common source, rather than the material gains they made from trade or instrumental collective action.

But it does not necessarily follow from the fact that people have different conceptions of the good life that they are best understood as accumulators of separate, private hoards of value. While economic interaction involves exchanging goods and services for money, and physically consuming resources, social interaction does not. Value is created, exchanged and enjoyed symbolically; the dynamics of these processes do not necessarily follow a logic of individual accumulation or depletion through use.

Indeed, during the period in which the utilitarian version of the economic model was gaining its ascendancy in British public policy (the first half of the 19th century), a stream of invective against its version of value flowed from the pens of authors like Coleridge and Carlyle. Such attacks drew on Tory romanticism as well as utopian socialism, and were influential on later critics of liberal capitalism, including John Ruskin and William Morris. In a furious denunciation of the political economy of John Stuart Mill, Ruskin proclaimed his alternative to the analysis of value of terms of utility.

> To be 'valuable', therefore, is to 'avail towards life'.... The real science of political economy, which was yet to be distinguished from the bastard science, ... is that which teaches nations to desire and labour for the things that lead to life: and which teaches them to scorn and destroy the things that lead to destruction. And if ... they imagine precious and beneficent things, such as air, light, and cleanliness, to be valueless – or if, finally, they imagine the conditions of their own existence, by which alone they can truly possess or use anything, such, for instance, as peace, trust, and love, to be prudently exchangeable, when the markets offer, for gold, iron, or excrescences of shells – the great and only science of Political Economy teaches them ... how the service of Death, the Lord of Waste, and of eternal emptiness, differs from the service of Wisdom.... THERE IS

> NO WEALTH BUT LIFE. Life, including all its powers of
> love, joy, and of admiration. (Ruskin, 1860, pp 209, 222)

Ruskin and his colleagues were crying out for recognition of the value
of honest work as well as aesthetic beauty – a set of standards that
judged objects and actions for their social rather than their economic
worth. These ideas did influence the politics of the next generation,
including the British idealists whose thought justified early legislation
for income redistribution and public services (see pp 196-8).

So it could be possible to construct a theory of social value that
encompasses economic exchange, and in which the utility gained by
material consumption is valued according to social criteria. This might
be a way of analysing the sources of well-being, which both explained
the Easterlin paradox and introduced a more reliable guide to quality of
life, and for public policy. As the anthropologist Mary Douglas (1973,
p 181) wrote:

> Whenever consumption goods change hands, someone is
> communicating with someone else. Commodities define
> social categories.... We define inclusive and exclusive
> categories by rules about degrees of sharing and giving of
> commodities. No amount of welfare grants calculated on
> basic needs will cancel meanings which the language of
> commodities declares. Poverty is not a lack of goods but
> exclusion from esteem and power. This will never change
> that meaning.

In this chapter, I shall introduce the idea that well-being is directly
related to access to social value, and that economic welfare must be
seen as part of a particular system for exchanging and distributing
such value. As with all such systems for symbolic interaction, negative
as well as positive transactions occur. The concepts of cost, loss, debt,
insolvency and ruin are integral to competition for esteem, success
and celebrity, in which the price for failure is exclusion, shame, stigma
and obscurity as well as material poverty. The culture of contract and
economic welfare is not a replacement for archaic systems of status,
authority, dominance and subordination; it is an instance of how these
forms of social value are embodied in the production and exchange of
material goods and services.

The economics of esteem

One way to recognise how the economic model of human interactions represents a particular version of the production and distribution of social value is to study the transformation of public institutions under the influence of the contract culture. The avowed goal of government reforms in the Anglophone countries since 1980 has been to make people like doctors, teachers, psychologists and social workers accountable in terms of a logic of costs and benefits, measured through the quantifiable outcomes delivered for each dollar of taxpayers' money. Reform programmes with titles such as Best Value stipulate targets to be achieved, and hold the managers appointed to oversee them to account to drive through the necessary organisational and professional changes that make them possible.

This transformation has been achieved as much by the symbolic humiliation of old-style professional figures as by the glitzy promotion of new models of excellence. In the business version of public service, the new professionalism is sharp, media-savvy and enterprise-friendly – a winner in the marketplace for slogans, logos and mission statements as well as soundbites. Such criteria for esteem and celebrity are intended to drive out the dusty standards by which professionals conducted their dimly-lit exchanges in the social democratic past.

There is a story, perhaps apocryphal, of the newly appointed president of one of the constituent colleges of the National University of Ireland, an economist from Harvard, being asked to address a meeting of retired professors. Rather to the surprise of the committee, he promptly accepted the invitation. Introducing him to his audience with great deference, the chair expressed much appreciation that he had given them his time at such an early moment in his tenure of the presidency. He rose to his feet and said, 'Yes, well, I give you notice I won't be attending any of your future meetings, and nor will I be coming to any of your funerals'.

This ritual humiliation of representatives of the old academic standards might be compared to the public abasement of discredited intellectuals during Mao's Cultural Revolution. The difference is that the dominant forces do not, like the Red Guards, claim honour and legitimacy in terms of the words of the leader (by adherence to a totalitarian system of social value, according to economic role), but in terms of a competition among similar figures, mobilising discourses of efficiency, effectiveness and value for money. Prestige is measured in salaries, league table places and the award of stars by inspectors.

Yet despite the obvious quantitative basis for such standards, in terms of money, measurable outcomes and accumulated points, the ultimate sources of value, even in such a system, are 'socially constructed', not in the weak sense that is constantly used in qualitative sociological research, but in the strong sense that corresponds to 'utility' in economic analysis. Success in gaining the highest salaries, or league table places, or inspectors' assessments, involves the articulation of various collective ideas, principles and images, derived from government/business discourses. These provide the medium through which such value is produced, and then validated by the arbiters of the new public sector culture.

In order to gain access to any form of social value, one has to subject oneself to the standards, requirements and constraints of the ideas and images that apply to that field, and engage with others in transactions involving 'units of culture'. These act on individuals to define the range of permissible descriptions, decisions and justifications. They enable them to make sense of social situations, to coordinate their actions with others' and to accumulate worth within that context.

In Mary Douglas's theory of social value, two kinds of social forces work on individuals, in different dimensions. *Group* membership is primarily concerned with the extent to which individuals rely on fellow members and exclude outsiders. *Grid* factors concern the rules governing interactions, in the extreme case defining social roles in such a way as to isolate individuals from transactions with each other, and segregate their roles according to external classifications.

The point about these classifications, however, is that they themselves confer value, and define actions of social worth. Following Bernstein (1964), Douglas (1970, p 57) argued that 'to the extent that roles within it are allocated on principles of sex, age, and seniority, there is a grid controlling the flow of behaviour'.

Individualism is itself a culture (Durkheim, 1898), which confers value on individuals themselves, and on certain kinds of exchange between them. In what Douglas calls 'low-group, low-grid' social relations, individuals are competitive and unconstrained by social boundaries, groups provisional and temporary, and status negotiable. However, individuals will seek social value and power over each other by cultivating 'followings' of clients and customers, as in the development of brand images and the cult of celebrity.

The old public sector culture was one in which grid relationships applied both within and between professions, while group solidarities were important sources of value in certain teams and sections. The reforms aimed to substitute a culture that relied on symbols and standards derived from commercial services.

> The way in which a service is delivered can be as important as the service itself – as retailers know only too well….
> [E]xpectations of service quality and convenience have risen – as with the growth of 24-hour banking – but public services have failed to keep up with these developments.
> (DSS, 1998, p 16)

Douglas called the value attached to various kinds of social relations 'ritual' or 'sacred' value, meaning that certain identities and transactions have intrinsic worth within the contexts of those systems of relationships. Whereas in simple societies with strong group identity the sacred value attached to the group itself, and in those with strong grid classifications it lay in those categories and their moral standards, in individualistic cultures it is found in the sanctity of the sovereign, self-realising person and the principle of free choice (see below, pp 114-6).

So the definitions of the individual and the voluntary agreements by which such free agents exchange goods and services, and rule over each other, form the basis of social value in modern commercial society. As Pateman (1988) shows, the political theory of liberty, property and government by consent creates forms of self-ownership and contract that define worth and status in terms of ability to make rational choices, in private and collective issues. This substitutes for group loyalties and grid statuses a single social relation that alone validates the sanctity of the individual. In this culture, 'one abstract principle is sacred still, that is the holiness of contract itself' (Douglas, 1978, p 192).

Choice, contract and culture

If this is right, then choice – the basis of the economic model of interactions – is as much a socially constructed process, involving the rituals of a cultural code, as are such totems of group loyalty as football chants, religious mantras or national anthems. The individuals constructed by this culture are highly differentiated in terms of their preferences for very similar symbolic commodities, and conceive of their identities in terms of such choices. Their access to social worth lies through competition for prestige, which in turn is derived from a fickle and unstable market in such items as cosmetics, clothes, cars, jewellery and gadgetry, the tastes for which are manipulated by others with interests in stimulating a perpetual dissatisfaction and craving for novelty and change.

The same cultural bias towards choice is demonstrated by economic theory itself. Since Pareto (1909), the 'utility' that is maximised by individuals in interactions of all kinds is defined in terms of 'preferences', and not the satisfactions derived from the experience of consumption. Whereas earlier economists dealt in 'pleasure', and therefore explicitly required themselves to show how decisions resulted in psychic consequences, subsequent ones have confined themselves to 'decision utility' rather than 'experience utility', assuming only that individuals can order their preferences for every bundle of goods.

> [I]f we are trying to understand the affective qualities of social interaction, the theoretical strategies of modern economics are not merely unhelpful, but actually encourage us to ask the wrong questions.... [T]he question of how far *ex ante* preferences correspond with accurate predictions of *ex post* experiences... was removed from the domain of economics by Pareto's move. (Sugden, 2005, pp 91, 95)

Far from having designed institutions that enable us to maximise our subjective well-being (SWB), we have done so in such a way as to increase our scope for choice in all forms of interaction – as a glance at any UK government policy document concerning public sector reform can confirm. But if choice is itself a ritual totem, built into our cultural code as desirable as an end in itself, then its connections with well-being are contingent. They rely on the links between a certain kind of social value, achieved by competition in which there are a few winners and many losers; and on the transfer to spheres such as family, community, public service, the arts and politics of principles and processes that are derived from commerce.

This agenda assumes that choice, contract and private accumulation map onto these other spheres of social interaction in unproblematic ways. Precisely because the informal processes of sex, parenting, kinship, friendship and communal loyalty were not included in the political and social contracts posited by the Enlightenment philosophers, there was for them some scope for other processes, dynamics and regulatory principles to govern these interactions. Indeed, Adam Smith developed an elaborate theory of how people responded to each other at the emotional level, how this could be disciplined and shaped by proper socialisation and how it contributed to sound morality. His 'Theory of Moral Sentiments' (Smith, 1759) related this primary sphere of affective interactions to a secondary one of economic behaviour, which underpinned public policy and government.

This allowed Smith to identify sources of happiness, and of consolation for sorrow, in interactions that involved 'fellow-feeling', or 'correspondence of sentiments' – what we today would call empathy. By sharing in others' joys, or in such simple pleasures as reading aloud a favourite poem or story, we create experiences that are positive for both parties. By condoling with others over losses, rejections or disappointments, we reduce their pain, without incurring an unacceptable amount for ourselves – indeed, we may actually reduce the unavoidable negative impact of their feelings on our own (Smith, 1759, pp 73-87).

In Smith's theory, therefore, the moral and political relations through which the social order was sustained (that is, the public sources of social value) were built on a foundation of everyday affective interactions. Simple as this account may have been, it is far more convincing than the ones attempted within modern economic analysis. As Sugden (2005) points out, the assumption that individuals incorporate others' utility functions into their own supplies a version of 'altruism' that yields some improbable versions of love, sociability, solidarity and contributions to collective goods. The only ways in which pleasure in others' company and success (or joint celebrations and endeavours) can be explained are by having preferences over others' consumption (Rubin, 1993; Fehr and Schmidt, 1999) or being willing to incur costs to confer benefits on them (Bernheim and Stark, 1988).

In Parts Two and Three of this book, I shall develop a theory of social value that adopts the same approach as Smith's, and attempts to analyse well-being in terms of the production and exchange of positive feelings (and minimisation of negative ones), within a framework of cultural norms and resources, which supply the institutions for such interactions. I shall argue that this provides a more plausible interpretation of the data available from well-being research, and hence a better theoretical basis for public policy that aims to improve the well-being of populations.

There is, of course, a major theoretical difficulty for any attempt to explain the Easterlin paradox within affluent modern societies. The more that the economic model supplies *both* the institutional structures for all kinds of interactions *and* the cultural resources for describing experiences (including happiness itself), the more difficult it is to distinguish between the actual social value gained within this framework and the potential social value that might be available from some other set of social relations. When people say that they 'feel a million dollars', or are going to do a spot of retail therapy, or recommend 'acceptable behaviour contracts' as an antidote to teenage gun culture, it is difficult to break out of the cultural loop in which such ideas are embedded, to examine other possible sources of well-being.

This is very much the same problem as the one that faced the early modern philosophers at the birth of the Enlightenment. They were confronted with two seemingly coherent sets of institutions and cultural resources, corresponding to the Catholic and Protestant sides in the European religious wars, consisting on the one side of absolutist justifications, resting on divine right and paternal power, together with traditional doctrine, and on the other of claims to the righteousness of individual conscience and spirituality, biblical authority and militant mobilisation. As Hirschman (1977) showed, the new theories claimed that an order, resting on the gentler vices of indolence, greed and selfishness, rather than on the violent virtues of glory and honour, would be far less costly to sustain, and might lead to a universal modest prosperity. In rather the same way, I shall argue that the costs (in terms of wasteful striving after an ideal of autonomy and choice) of the culture of competitive individualism are destructive of potential well-being.

Making competent individuals

The priority given to freedom and choice in the economic model requires all analyses of human behaviour and social institutions to be reducible to individual decisions within a framework of opportunities and costs. In reasserting the model as a basis for public policy, and rejecting the revisions of Keynes (1936) and his followers as much as those of Marx and his, writers such as Hayek (1960) and von Mises (1966) insisted that collective bodies of all kinds, including governments, were unable to make reliable decisions from the sheer volume of information that assailed them. The institutions that could best coordinate millions of different preferences and actions had evolved over time: families, markets and the common law were built out of individual choices, and supplied the means for free individuals to reach agreements and rule over themselves.

This approach, so influential on institutional reform and public policy in the Anglophone countries since 1980, assumes a kind of natural symbiosis between these three forms of interaction, all of which enable individual liberty. The family was supposed to prepare people for a life of self-responsibility and prudence, as well as enterprise; the law, while minimising coercion and refusing to impose a single rationale on society, was to provide the principles under which impartial, consistent justice between such individuals was supplied. But Hayek did not imagine that these systems, whose spontaneous and evolutionary character he constantly emphasised, were sufficient conditions for the kinds of society he favoured, unless they provided a kind of discipline for people's more disorderly desires. For example, the whole edifice might collapse if the educational system 'fails to pass on the burden of culture and trusts to the *natural instincts which are the instincts of the savage*' (Hayek, 1982, p 174; emphasis in original)

The problem, of course, is that writers of this school can give no account of such a culture, except in terms of the habits instilled by the practices of responsible liberty in families, markets and legal processes. The test of whether or not a person has been properly socialised is their ability to handle themselves competently within these frameworks – to make good choices, abide by agreements, learn from mistakes, keep the law and raise children to recognise the same principles.

If, as we have seen, the actors in the economic model are supposed to be different from each other, to be guided entirely by their own preferences and to reach agreements (in the form of contracts) simply because of the advantages they bestow on themselves, then it is difficult to find a space for the kinds of influences that might dispose them to care about, respect or show loyalty to others, still less to sacrifice their short-term interests for the sake of solidarity or long-term commitments.

Furthermore, once individuals failed to learn the lessons of self-responsibility and prudence during childhood, or were misled by some other influences (such as collectivist politics, religious fervour, drugs or alcohol), it was difficult to see how they could be re-educated into the ways of civil competence, other than by disciplinary correction through the law. Accordingly, neoliberal governments in the 1980s, notably those of Margaret Thatcher, Ronald Reagan, Bob Hawke and David Lange (the latter two in the name of Labour), used the courts to restrain and punish, not only the excesses of trades unions, social movements and local authorities, but also those sections of their populations that expressed their protest against the new regimes through disorder, deviance and crime.

As commentators such as Hudson (1993) and Garland (2001) have noted, this involved the substitution of measures for criminal justice for government interventions that had previously followed a rationale of social justice. This might have been justified as a transitional measure in the shift from the collectivism of the era of welfare states to a new order, in which markets and property were again the bases for liberty. But the need for enforcement measures, and for a widening range of corrective, educational and therapeutic interventions, has continued to increase in these countries over the following two decades.

There has indeed been a strong association over the period since the Enlightenment between the ideas of freedom, choice and contract on the one hand, and those of discipline, correction and punishment on the other (Jordan, 1996, 2003). This was clearly signalled in the foundational document of liberalism, Locke's *Second Treatise of Government* (1690, section 3): 'Political power is the right of making laws with penalties of death and all less penalties for the regulating and preserving of property'.

Since the social contract was struck for this purpose, those who violate it become outlaws within society, and the legal system becomes a way to bring various forms of sanction upon them, through physical pain, forced labour, military service or execution. Foucault (1976) charted the connections between ideas of freedom and those of incarceration and correction, within the Poor Laws and the mental hospitals as well as in prisons. In the US, the reintroduction of the death penalty and the escalation of prison populations to almost two million in 2002 (McMurtry, 2002, p 68), with several million more under some form of surveillance regime (Wacquant, 1998), and the sanctions embodied in workfare conditions around social assistance benefits (Schram, 2006), all testify to the disciplinary effort required to try to turn people into competent actors within this kind of order.

In Part Three of this book, I shall analyse just how extensive and costly these measures have been. Their intention, after all, is to create stigma and fear, and distribute it among those who might be tempted to violate the terms of the social contract, or to break their agreements under particular contracts. Among poor people in Anglophone societies, these forms of negative social value have become so widely spread that whole communities now live in a miasma of shame and blame, which leaves their members with little more to lose from alcohol or drug abuse, sexual predation or loutish behaviour.

So the paradox of a competitive social order, in which the constituent members are distinguished by their choices of material symbols of their individuality, is that it must spend increasing proportions of its resources on trying to turn people into competent participants. Because modern affluent states have gradually undermined the cultural bonds of affection, kinship, communality, solidarity and loyalty of those it previously excluded from the status of full membership of this order, and replaced them with versions of individualism and contract, they must continuously inflate and expand the range of measures required to bind people into such a society. But the permissible means of doing so must themselves be individualised and contractual – personalised advice, chosen packages of care, or contracts for behaviour modification (Jordan, 2006a).

This also helps explain the helpless ineptitude of regimes based on the economic model, when faced with situations demanding that hearts and minds be won over from some form of enduring collective commitment (whether secular or religious) to liberal materialism. In Afghanistan and Iraq, for example, the invading coalition forces made no clear plans to stabilise or rebuild these societies after their conquest, presumably because they assumed that they would welcome their liberation from the Taliban and Saddam Hussein respectively, and joyfully adopt the World Bank version of social relations. As within their own countries, the Anglophone leaders blamed small minorities of deviants, criminals and extremists for disaffection, and thought that spiriting them away to places like Guantanamo Bay would leave the majority with sufficient reasons to choose liberal democracy and capitalism – a standpoint described by the head of the British army as 'intellectually bankrupt' (Jackson, 2007).

Since the early 1990s, there has been an awareness in the social sciences of the shortcomings of the economic model, and several attempts to remedy them. Most of these have come from political theorists, who have had some influence on public policy. In the next section, I shall review the main ones of these and focus on one of them – social capital theory – to demonstrate the problems of trying to add a social element to the economic model. If well-being is to supply a genuinely transformative new perspective for policy in the fields previously concerned with welfare, it will be required to overcome these problems.

The transformation of collective life

The dominance of neoliberal political leaderships in the Anglophone countries during the 1980s led to an awareness that collective life was being transformed, under the influence of their policies, and of global economic integration. Several critiques of the economic model on which both governments and international organisations based their programmes during the highpoint of the Washington Consensus (Stiglitz, 2002) had in common the view that its assumptions distorted social relations and political processes. Each of a number of approaches – citizenship theory, communitarianism and social capital theory – sought to identify aspects of social and collective interactions that were not adequately captured by the model, and to mark out a territory over which another logic applied.

Citizenship theory purported to provide a framework for the analysis of concepts like justice, equality and liberty, while emphasising self-rule as the aspect of freedom that characterised the liberal political sphere – a system

> in which the sole power of making laws remains with the people or their accredited representatives, and in which all individual members of the body politic – rulers and citizens alike – remain equally subject to whatever laws they choose to impose on themselves. (Skinner, 1998, p 74)

These analyses aimed to counter the instrumental and perfunctory version of politics portrayed in the economic model, in which the primary aim was to minimise the costs of interdependence. So they emphasised that citizenship was active and demanding, involved obligations and responsibilities, and created civic standards (Kymlicka and Norman, 1994).

> Citizenship, therefore, is an identity that we acquire by being 'free citizens' by engagement in the institutions of self-rule of a free people…. But this condition of 'democratic legitimacy' can be made good only if the members of the association have some sort of say in the way political power is exercised over them through the laws, because it is precisely this activity of civic freedom which does in fact create or make good, the awareness of the laws as 'self-imposed' rather than as imposed 'non-democratically', 'behind our backs'. (Tully, 2000, p 214)

This assertion of the benefits of participation was contrasted with the processes of transformation of public agencies in line with the economic model, turning citizens into 'customers' and politics into 'management' (Eriksen and Weigård, 2000). Each individual citizen engaged with these services in terms of private interests (Freedland, 2001), undermining any consciousness of the public good (Somers, 2001).

But this critique offered no clear policy alternatives to the imposition of a market logic onto political processes. Above all, because it did not renounce the individualistic and contractarian basis of liberal political thought since the Enlightenment, it failed to show what alternative forms of social relations might be substituted for economic ones.

When neoliberal governments were replaced by Third Way ones in the Anglophone countries, they did indeed adopt New Contracts or New Covenants to define the rights and responsibilities of citizens (Waddan, 1997; Jordan, 1998), but these focused on the mutual obligations of individuals and the state. Indeed, they were drawn up to formalise the expectation that citizens would function as 'independent' economic actors, taking appropriate work and training, saving for retirement, supporting their families, and avoiding being a burden on their fellow citizens (or taxpayers) (DSS, 1998, p 80). They said nothing about engagement with self-rule, or involvement in civil society.

The second strand of the critique of the economic model – communitarianism – developed during the 1980s (MacIntyre, 1981; Taylor, M., 1987; Taylor, C., 1989), and came to prominence in the mid-1990s (Etzioni, 1993, 1999). Its primary target was the individualism of the economic model, and an emphasis on 'those loyalties and convictions whose moral force consists partly in the fact that living by them is inseparable from understanding ourselves as the particular persons we are' (Sandel, 1982, p 179).

This view of individuals as embedded in social structures and practices entered the policy agenda in the 1990s as a programme for devolving government functions to voluntary organisations, and engaging with deprived neighbourhoods about their 'renewal' or 'regeneration'. But here again, it was concerned mainly with holding them responsible for their problems as communities, as well as individuals. The bonds of trust, cooperation and mutuality between members who shared common resources and purposes were seen as creating special obligations to each other, which could be strengthened through partnerships involving commercial firms and government agencies (Driver and Martell, 1997; Jordan with Jordan, 2000).

While the idea of community became central to a number of government initiatives in these deprived districts over such issues as homelessness, truancy, drug dealing and crime, and provided the basis for later programmes on 'civil renewal' (Blunkett, 2003), 'community cohesion' (Blunkett, 2004) and 'respect' (Blair, 2006), this critique of the economic model suffered from shortcomings that were the obverse of those deriving from citizenship. Community represents a specific set of relationships, organisations and practices, which may be stimulated and guided to address certain issues – through the creation of 'invited spaces' (Gaventa, 2004) – but is essentially local, particular and spontaneous. In public policy, it was seen as a complement to the economic model rather than a challenge, a way of trying to involve marginal or excluded groups in mainstream issues, to engage sections of the population in conflict with each other in dialogue about their disputes or to address intractable problems in which members of a district all had some stake.

Community therefore became an important dimension in the analysis of social issues, but as a means of generating increased involvement in matters that had been seen as the province for state action, whether through criminal justice or the agencies concerned with social welfare. In this sense, community was an ad hoc response to market *and* state failures, rather than a principle that applied more generally to social relations or liberal politics.

This was why the next attempt to introduce a social or collective element into the economic model took the form, in 'social capital', of a theory about the substructure for both markets and democratic politics, which allowed both to function more efficiently. In Part One of this book, I shall analyse how social capital theorists have set about this, and what success they have had in their attempts to modify the economic model. In arguing that they have failed to bring about any significant long-term shifts in that model, I will prepare the way for considering, in Parts Two and Three, whether well-being theory can overcome the pitfalls into which social capital theorists have tumbled.

Conclusions

The idea of social value does not fit comfortably either into a notion of 'quality of life' based on universal principles of justice (Nussbaum, 2000) or into a public policy environment constructed around individual autonomy and choice. In Mary Douglas's work, such value is always defined by the culture and institutions of a particular set of social relations. It is therefore never free from the uncriticised notions of 'the sacred', which bestow legitimacy and create stability in societies. This jars with present-day orthodoxies, both in liberal political philosophy and in popular consciousness. It makes social value a controversial candidate for inclusion in government programmes. Yet current dominant ideas

> are still the principles that have emerged over the last two hundred years, along with the emergence of an economic system based on individual contract....
> Durkheim ... taught that each kind of community is a thought world, expressed in its own thought style, penetrating the minds of its members, defining their experience, and setting the poles of their moral understanding.... For

> better or worse, individuals really do share their thoughts
> and they do to some extent harmonize their preferences,
> and they have no other way to make big decisions except
> within the scope of institutions they build. (Douglas, 1987,
> pp 118, 128)

Since the birth of this version of modernity, all analyses of the social and
political order have been required to demonstrate how individuals who
are free and equal can interact in ways that are advantageous to each,
and which deal in the best possible ways with the costs and benefits
of their interdependence. The original social contract theorists left a
space for relations that were governed by different principles from those
of the economy and consensual self-rule, by allowing a large sphere
of household and communal activity. As we have seen (pp 26-8), the
exclusion of these spheres breached the principle of equality, because
it cast women and many kinds of dependants (sick and disabled people
as well as children and frail older people) as unfit to enter the public
sphere as fully rational, competent participants.

Once collectivist routes, via state socialism, fascism or theocracy, are
ruled out by assumption, the only means to emancipation for those
disempowered by these exclusions are the acquisition of rights to full
status as individuals within an order structured by contracts between
utility-maximising agents. The paradox of the social movements of the
1960s and 1970s was that they used collective action to gain such access
to full inclusion as economic agents – for women to seek promotion
and organisational power in capitalist firms, for black households to gain
positional advantage by fleeing urban ghettoes, for disabled people to
employ carers at minimum wages for unsocial hours of menial service,
for gay people to be humiliated in celebrity TV contests just like
straight ones, and so on. These shifts enabled marriage and cohabitation
contracts to become more like other service contracts, they allowed
members of different religious faiths to exploit each other without
moral scruples, and they enabled children to claim 'respect' from adults,
and then to stab or shoot them if it seemed to be denied.

In all this, theory of welfare remained locked within the economic
model, not because it shared the neoliberal assumption that unmodified
markets in most goods allowed optimum distributions, but because it
was unable to challenge the assumption that utility maximisation was
the best way of understanding individual welfare. As the scope for
collective interventions by governments narrowed, under the combined
influence of public choice theory (see Part One) and global economic
integration, social policy analysts turned to citizenship, community and

social capital as possible ways of breaking out of this trap. I shall argue that none of them allowed such escapes.

The main problem faced by all these alternative approaches is that the individuals who are free, equal and self-governing in the Anglophone political tradition are constructed (by assumption) to seek the greatest possible range of choices over their purposes, and to do so by gaining command over the most possible material resources. Any other social or political ends must find their place within this framework. Although 'utility' may include any number of different psychic or interactive rewards, these cannot, by assumption, be adopted except as choices among alternative means of maximising satisfactions.

So it is impossible to account for behaviour which follows a logic of social value that gives prestige to loyalty, solidarity or conscientiousness (strong group or grid factors) rather than individual achievements. For instance, during the Soviet regime, retirement pensions were not regarded as benefits, but as 'privileges', granted to war and work 'veterans'. When the Russian government decided to replace these with monetary payments, it faced mass protests by these holders of prestigious veterans' badges (Danilova, 2007; Rasell, 2007). The economic analysis of welfare requires a researcher to show exactly how much such privileges were worth, in terms of travel concessions, rent reductions, fuel allowances and so on, and to count how many older people were losers in this process. But it misses the symbolic value of the very concept of 'privileges', and the stigma of 'benefits', as factors in the resistance to this change.

Social value cannot be injected into the economic model as an optional extra, because (as Douglas shows) the exchange of commodities in markets is itself a symbolic system, which allocates its own kinds of esteem and shame. The Russian veterans rightly recognised that what was a badge of honour in the Soviet currency of value was a stigmatised form of income under capitalism. This is why David Cameron's (2006) efforts to introduce the notions of well-being, quality of life and commitment to relationships into the discourses of conservative politics have proved so problematic. How can there be social value in any form other than independent property ownership in the party of Margaret Thatcher?

In the next chapter I shall start to consider how social capital theory attempted to solve these problems in relation to the economic model, and where it failed to do so.

Part One
Welfare

THREE

Welfare and the economic model: 'being precisely wrong'

It was a paradox of the last quarter of the 20th century, that the economic model of politics and public policy (with its consumerist version of value) came to overthrow all possible rivals, to the point that there 'was no alternative'. Many critics pointed out that it abandoned 'being vaguely right in favour of being precisely wrong' (Sen, 1987b, p 34), and drew attention to the contradictions at the heart of its analysis of such concepts as 'quality of life', or 'standard of living'. This chapter will seek to explain how (despite these) the economic model of welfare was so widely adopted, and how this became embedded in a wider analysis of public policy.

As I showed in the previous chapter, critics of the economic approach to value from Ruskin onwards insisted that the 'sacred' and the social were intertwined as the essential elements in well-being, and therefore that the vagueness of cultural standards for the good life was always at risk from the deadly precision of calculative rationality. A politics of mutual appreciation and sharing through interpersonal communication and collective consciousness was scarcely feasible within an industrialised capitalist economy. But the dominance of the economic approach has become more total than could have been predicted. It now shapes all formal interactions and – as I shall show in this chapter – claims to explain all social phenomena, even those undertaken for the sake of love, recognition or belonging.

In a society that prized individual liberty, contractual exchange and government by consent, it was not easy to justify compulsory transfers, or amenities that were shared among members. Indeed, Locke's foundational arguments for the creation of such a society were designed to show that all citizens benefited from substantial *inequalities* of property, and from the taking into private ownership of resources, previously held and used in common (Locke, 1690, sections 37-54). This type of argument, for the scope of private assets and transactions to be maximised, subject to certain limits and provisos, became the standard one in Anglophone political economy in the 18th and 19th centuries.

It was also the form adopted in the early years of the last century in *The Economics of Welfare* by A. C. Pigou (1920). He built on the demonstration by Pareto (1909) that perfect market competition could produce an equilibrium allocation of resources such that it was impossible to make one person better-off without making another worse-off, to show how various deviations from perfect competition affected the 'National Dividend' (GDP) and distributive shares. Pigou's normative proviso, qualifying the increase in the National Dividend as the criterion for growth in economic welfare, was that 'the dividend accruing to the poor is not diminished' (Pigou, 1920, p 82).

He therefore examined a range of public policy measures designed to make distributions more equitable in the light of this qualifying criterion, and in particular the idea of a 'National Minimum Standard of Real Income' (the final chapter of his book). Stipulating that this standard 'must be conceived, not as a subjective minimum of satisfaction, but as an objective minimum of conditions' (Pigou, 1920, p 759) (such as accommodation, medical care, education, food, leisure, safety at work and so on), he concluded that:

> [E]conomic welfare is best promoted by a minimum standard raised to such a level that the direct good resulting from the transference of marginal pound transferred to the poor [in these ways, taken as a whole] just balances the indirect evil brought about by the consequent reduction of the [national] dividend. (Pigou, 1920, p 761)

But in putting forward this argument, which was to influence Beveridge 20 years later, Pigou was using a definition of his minimum standard, and indeed an approach to the evaluation of welfare, which he had rejected in the main body of his analysis. Even there he contradicted himself, having started by saying that 'the elements of welfare are states of consciousness, and perhaps, their relations' (p 10), but also that they consisted of both 'desires' and their 'satisfaction' (pp 23-4).

The foundations of welfare economics, and hence of economic judgements about better or worse states of affairs, were therefore confused and contradictory, and these difficulties were then carried over into the second half of the 20th century. It was unclear, for example, whether value lay in certain mental states (such as pleasure), which could be taken to stem from stable preferences, or whether there were other processes of evaluation at work (Sen, 1987a, pp 3-7). But none of this seemed too important at the time because, as in Pigou's account of the 'objective' national minimum standard of real income, there appeared to be an external arbiter – the state – which could make reliable decisions (based on the advice of economists) over issues of welfare that transcended individual choices.

This was because of the enormous expansion of government expenditures, understood as being required for the optimal functioning of the economy and the society. The scope for these 'public works', recognised by Adam Smith as being 'in the highest degree advantageous to a great society', even though they 'could never repay the expense to any individual' (Smith, 1776, part IV, chapter 9, section 51), was greatly extended by Keynes's (1936) theory; but much of the growth in government activity had occurred before this was published. For instance, in Britain about two thirds of the new homes built between 1924 and 1936 were constructed by local authorities (Hicks, 1947, p 27).

By 1938, about 8% of national income was going on defence, a further 8% on various boards and regulatory authorities or direct interventions in industry and 13% on income transfers, education and the embryonic social services (Hicks, 1947, p 32). So the ambiguities and confusions in the definition of welfare within the branch of economics concerned with resource allocation were largely fudged, especially in social policy. Even in 2007, it was possible for a textbook on the subject to state:

> Social welfare is ... a term which gains little from being defined very tightly. Writers use it in slightly different ways depending on the issues they wish to cover. Sometimes it refers to very material aspects of well-being such as access to economic resources. At other times it is used to mean less tangible conditions such as contentment, happiness, an absence of threat, and confidence in the future. (Baldock, 2007, p 21)

Thus, although the concept of individual welfare in welfare economics was built on shaky ground, that of social welfare was constructed on shakier still. Partly a normative idea, related to justice between members, partly an 'objective' version of minimum standards of health, education, nutrition and housing, it was, nonetheless, also still accountable to the notion of efficiency captured by the Pareto criterion. The continued expansion of welfare state expenditure after the Second World War, which was first echoed and then surpassed in most Western European countries, was therefore vulnerable to new developments in economic theory, which were not long coming.

In retrospect it seems that the relative durability of welfare states (well beyond the end of their 'golden age' in the 1960s) has lain in the fact that they balanced two entirely different notions of welfare. The first was the utility derived by individuals from choices of private goods; the second the provision, through government intervention, of income and services, which enabled certain 'capabilities' (positive freedoms and abilities to do certain things) and 'functionings' (actually doing such things), as Sen (1984, 1987a, 1987b) called them. Perhaps something specific to post-war industrialised societies – both the balance of power between firms and trades unions, and the combination of enabling and restraint achieved by their institutional systems – helped to create the mixture of autonomy and solidarity that characterised this period. But it was all highly contingent, and owed more to a special set of circumstances (including the Cold War and the fear of internal communist subversion) than to the coherence of its welfare economics. In many respects it was ripe for the attacks to come, as much from neoliberal theorists as from the integration of world markets, and the rise of transnational corporations.

The nature of collective action

With the obvious success (in terms of economic growth and democratic governance) of the European welfare states in the 1960s and 1970s, the idea that collective provision from compulsory contributions enhanced the welfare of societies' members seemed to have a solid foundation. But the weakness of the UK economy, and its susceptibility to crises, made its institutional structure a target for radical critique. New approaches to welfare economics, generated in Austria and the US as well as in the UK, were brought to bear on public policy, and came to supply a set of new analyses, first for the Anglophone countries, then for international financial organisations, and finally for the rest of the world.

In retrospect it is easy to see how the strict methodological individualism of the new approach meshed with the deepest traditions of the Anglophone political culture, and also with the frustrated aspirations of a new middle class. Theorists such as Hayek and Friedman argued that the attempt to achieve such abstract principles as equality and justice involved increasing government control over the decisions, and even the wills, of citizens, undermining the freedoms required for independence and self-responsibility:

> [T]he more dependent the position of individuals ... is seen
> to become on the actions of government, the more they

will insist that the government aim at some recognisable scheme of distributive justice, the more they must subject the position of the different individuals ... to their control. So long as the belief in 'social justice' governs political action, this process must progressively approach nearer and nearer to totalitarianism. (Hayek, 1976, p 68)

But it is doubtful whether any neoliberal programme would have had political success without a theory of collective action to complement its reliance on markets. The public choice school owed allegiance to Wicksell (1896), whose analysis showed how fully sovereign individuals, with complete control over the collective goods supplied in their community, could voluntarily consent to taxes for the funding of these goods, rather than be compelled to pay for them.

In that tradition, Tiebout (1956) had demonstrated that (under demanding assumptions about perfect information, costless mobility and absence of externalities), households could sort themselves into self-governing communities for the supply of collective amenities and services, of the quality and cost of their choosing.

The point of these analyses was to show how public goods and political institutions could (in principle) command full consent, so long as they were limited to providing for those interdependences involving external costs and benefits among citizens. In practice, this was quickly reduced to 'the "costs" approach to collective action' (Buchanan and Tullock, 1962, pp43-6).

> The individual will find it profitable to explore the possibility of organising an activity collectively when he expects that he may increase his utility. The individual's utility derived from any single human activity is maximised when his share in the 'net costs' of organising the activity is minimised.... The possible benefits that he secures from a particular method of operation are included in this calculus as cost reductions, reductions from that level which would be imposed on the individual if the activity were differently organised. (Buchanan and Tullock, 1962, pp 43, 45)

The advantage of this method was that it allowed the full range of private, voluntary cooperative and political collective action to be considered within the same framework, and to reduce all of them to a calculation of individual utility. 'Social welfare' was not to be seen as somehow derived from a separate source from the 'individual welfare' gained in markets.

> The costs of organising voluntary contractual arrangements sufficient to remove an externality or to reduce the externality to reasonable proportions may be higher than the costs of organising collective action sufficient to accomplish the same purpose. (Buchanan and Tullock, 1962, p 48)

At the same time, these theorists developed two other approaches to the analysis of collective action, which were employed against what they saw as mystifications of the role of government activity. The first concerned the identification of those collective goods that were susceptible to cost-sharing among defined memberships, because the exclusion to those unwilling or unable to pay the appropriate fees was technologically possible. These 'club goods' were therefore another means by which individuals and households could sort themselves into self-governing groups for shared amenities without government intervention (Buchanan, 1965; Cornes and Sandler, 1986). Using Buchanan and Tullock's principles of cost minimisation, this greatly extended the scope for individual choice over collectively supplied goods and services – eventually providing the rationale for a new approach to the organisation of the social services (Foldvary, 1994).

The second focused on the motives and methods of those who, through collective action, were able to organise as groups (cartels, unions, professional associations, movements) to gain advantage in the political process. By distorting markets and appropriating tax revenues, they were able to gain 'rents' at the expense of other, unorganised sections of the society (Olson, 1965, 1982; Buchanan and Tullock, 1980). This applied particularly to those groups operating within the public sector – politicians, professionals and bureaucrats – with an interest in expanding the scope for state interventions (Niskanen, 1975). The welfare state was therefore a particular target.

However, right from the start of their assault on the collectivist elements in the theory of welfare allocations, Buchanan and Tullock did make an exception in favour of a modest form of social security. This they regarded as an exception to the overall institutional configuration designed to achieve Pareto optimality and eliminate externalities. By agreement among all citizens, individuals who do not know their future fortunes may wish to insure themselves in a way which will even out their income over the life cycle, but cannot afford to do so privately in their youth. They therefore adopt the collective device of compulsory contributions to an insurance scheme.

> Such collective redistribution of real income among individuals, viewed as the working out of this sort of 'income insurance' plan may appear rational to the utility maximising individual at the stage of constitutional decision…. [T]he individual may be more willing to accept the costs of such [private] uninsurability if he knows that all members of the group are to be included in the plan. (Buchanan and Tullock, 1962, pp 193-4)

So their foundational text for public choice theory anticipated Rawls (1971) in making something like a guarantee for the poor a constitutional feature under the 'calculus of consent'. But they emphasised that the reason for adopting this at the constitutional stage (the 'social contract') was in order to limit its scope for redistribution.

> The amount of redistribution that unrestrained majority voting will generate will tend to be greater than that which the whole group of individuals could conceptually agree on as 'desirable' at the time of constitutional choice. Since conceptual unanimity is possible on this degree of income redistribution, we may, in a certain sense, call this a Pareto-optimal amount of redistribution. (Buchanan and Tullock, 1962, pp 194-5)

Buchanan and Tullock regarded such a social security scheme as a device for guaranteeing a bargain between citizens over shares of national income, as a basis for equality of opportunity, and of fair rules under which the 'economic game' is played (Buchanan and Tullock, 1962, pp 196-7). The insurance principle represented a bulwark against the imposition of excessive external costs on individuals through direct, tax-based transfers. They saw this form of collective provision as the one example of a remaining externality (in the form of a 'redistributive inefficiency') in their model, under Pareto-optimal conditions. This was a limited external cost that individuals would be willing to bear, at the point of entering into a unanimous constitutional contract with fellow citizens. But the conditions surrounding social insurance would guarantee fair contributions and forbid free riding, by enforcing available employment and self-responsibility.

This set of assumptions constructed a modified Rawlsian version of the social contract, commanding unanimous consent, because its institutions give rise to Pareto efficiency, and citizens have the option of leaving to join other polities. It therefore built equity into the terms of the public choice model (Buchanan, 1967; Mueller, 1979). It represented a formidable challenge to the comfortable ambiguities of the welfare states.

Institutions as restraints

This alternative approach was more consistent and coherent in its interpretation of welfare than the compromised version built into the public sectors of welfare states. It stated unambiguously that welfare was to be analysed in terms of the utility that accrued to individuals, and that even social security (as a residual element of the 'national minimum' concept) could be explained in terms of cost-minimisation among interdependent rational egoists, rather than some 'objective' external standards or moral principles.

At the same time, parallel developments in economic theory were busy demolishing any other extraneous 'social' elements in its analyses of institutions and cultural traditions, by reducing them to similar cost-saving calculations, leading to contracts between utility-maximising individuals. For example, Becker (1976, p 14) insisted that the most potentially valuable contribution of economic analysis was its ability to supply a 'unified framework for understanding *all* human behaviour'. This enabled apparently dissimilar types of social interaction, such as courting, family life, voluntary association and criminal conspiracy, to be explained in relation to each other, by showing how individuals allocate their resources between different kinds of exchanges, while subjecting them all to an overarching cost-benefit analysis. It allowed an overall approach to the analysis of alternative sources of welfare, previously regarded as involving quite separate values, and hence as isolated from each other.

The great strength of the economic model was therefore its robust refusal to agonise over the moral, political or social implications of institutions, or the theoretical complexities of structure and agency (Giddens, 1976). By accounting for the whole collective landscape in terms of a single calculus, and a single currency for exchange, it potentially provided policy makers with a rationale for the transformation of that landscape, which should in principle command political support across the political spectrum, from all except those with a stake in the distortions of the previous system (that is, those who had gained rents at the expense of unorganised individuals).

But the implications of this model were in some ways too radical to be attractive to real-world politicians. After all, if all collective action was to some extent an attempt to restrain competition, this must apply to firms, faith groups, families and nation states as well as cartels, trades unions and bureaucracies. By the same token, the economic approach to social interaction demonstrated the 'rationality' of behaviour such as teenage drug dealing, teachers cheating to help their students reach government attainment targets, or sportspeople trying less hard when the top prizes were already won (Levitt and Dubner, 2006). In its game-theoretical variant, it could show that benefit fraud and petty crime were the 'best responses' to state and market failure by the residents of deprived districts, whose more able former neighbours had voted with their feet to move to better-appointed areas (Jordan, 1996).

Indeed, it was difficult to explain how markets, and especially insurance markets, functioned at all, given the imperfect and asymmetric information and moral hazard that were endemic in real-life situations, and the transaction costs these entailed. In the new mathematical models generated by 'information-theoretic' approaches (Stiglitz, 1994), the theory postulated mechanisms producing suboptimal outcomes with multiple equilibria (Fine, 2001, p11).

In this 'second-best world', people could adopt many different means, both individual and collective, to overcome market imperfections. The example of the Israeli nursery, given in the Introduction, illustrates this point. According to Gneezy and Rustichini (2000), parents responded to the original 'incomplete contract' with the nursery by being (for the most part) punctual and cooperative. They thought 'something might happen' if they were not.

In other words, the economic model's rational and calculating utility-maximisers might be guided by some form of meta-organisational system, from which all might benefit in the long term, but whose advantages were not so easy to perceive, at least through the lens of individual choice. This reopened the door to a form of 'social' analysis of interactions, which could supplement rather than contradict the theorems of the economic model.

In the New Institutional Economics, there was a basic distinction between *institutions*, which constrained and shaped interactions, and *organisations*, through which individuals pursued their interests. The former provided the necessary conditions for stability; institutions were 'perfectly analogous' to the rules of the game in competitive sports, whereas organisations corresponded to the teams competing (North,

1990, p 4). Institutions provided rules and social norms, within which organisations and their members could seek competitive advantage. Although institutions could enable rent-seeking, and were a 'mixed bag' in terms of their effects on efficiency, they were necessary to promote trust and cooperation in social interactions, and to reduce reliance on third-party enforcement (North, 1990, pp 67-9).

The purpose of this distinction was clearly to differentiate between those forms of restraint on rivalry that enhance the opportunities for market and non-market voluntary exchange, by promoting advantageous social interactions and reducing reliance on third-party enforcement, and those that involve distributional and productive distortions. If this could be done in a tight theoretical way, it would allow 'good' restraints, which save transaction costs by promoting trustworthy conduct and reliable reciprocity, to be identified and developed.

However, this project seemed from the start unlikely to succeed, since the terms 'institutions' and 'organisations' may simply denote different levels of collective structure. For instance, from the perspective of a nation state, the government is an 'institution' formulating the 'rules of the game' for citizens; but from that of a supranational body, such as the European Union, it is an 'organisation', acting rivalrously in its relations with other member states to secure national advantage. In other words, at each level, a collective body is *both* an institution that restrains costly competition among its members through rules and norms, *and* an organisation that mobilises those members for competition at a higher level, conducted within the rules and norms set by higher-level institutions (Jordan, 1996, p 59).

One has only to think of national football associations for an instance of this phenomenon. They regulate clubs, but also organise their own teams for international tournaments. Similarly, universities both preside over the award of degrees and compete with each other for research funding.

North implicitly accepted that the distinction could not be sustained in any systematic way, by acknowledging that, from the point of view of efficiency, institutions were a 'mixed bag'. So, instead of analysing group interactions in terms of costs and benefits to individuals, as Buchanan (1965) and Olson (1965) had done, he advocated empirical and historical research into the consequences of alternative forms of coordination. Such comparative reviews, over time and between countries, were to be seen as concerned with marginal institutional adjustments and reforms, within the limits set by 'path dependency', rather than thought experiments leading to abstract but precise models (North, 1990, p 69).

So the idea of 'positive restraints', which reduced the costs of rivalry and mistrust, and which were at least partly generated in *social* interactions (informal or associational, rather than economic or political), had some appeal, especially for theorists of politics and public policy. It seemed that, without weakening the methodological individualism and primacy of contract in the public choice model of collective behaviour, it could add an element to the analysis, which might soften some of the harsher features of utility maximisation and cost–benefit analysis. It also appeared to offer an opportunity for political scientists and sociologists who were attracted by the elegant certainties of the economic model to offer (albeit somewhat subserviently) a contribution to that increasingly hegemonic approach to the explanation of human interactions of all kinds.

This approach was echoed in the work of theorists such as Piore and Sabel (1984) and March and Olsen (1989); institutions reduced uncertainty, and introduced stability into all interactions, by providing a kind of embodied code for decision making, within which individuals and organisations could compete. This seemed to be a variant of the work of Alexis de Tocqueville (1835-40), which emphasised the external benefits (or spillovers) from interactions, especially informal cooperation and voluntary association, for the democratic polity and the free–market economy.

In this way, the stage was set for the advent of 'social capital' as a concept to make its appearance on the social scientific scene. The idea that interactions produced some kind of lubricant-cum-balm, which in turn entered into future interactions, some in quite different spheres, had first been put forward by Loury (1977) and was developed by Coleman (1988) as the term for a resource, consisting of social structures, which enables members to accomplish mutually beneficial ends. '[S]ocial organisation constitutes social capital, facilitating the achievement of goals that would not be achieved in its absence or could be achieved only at a higher cost' (Coleman, 1990, p 304).

This went beyond the notion of institutions as restraints on costly rivalry, or mechanisms for reducing transaction costs, to seeing them as positive factors in the attainment of efficiency. Was this a way in which social relationships, and the obligations they generated, could be captured in the economic model, as a public good incorporating collective aspects within an individualistic analysis of utility maximisation?

The relevance of social capital for welfare

The concept of social capital seemed to provide a link between the everyday social, cultural and associational domains of human behaviour, which are clearly in some sense relevant for 'welfare' (however defined), and the formal abstractions of the economic model. But it seemed to do so in such a way as largely to take this out of the sphere of government and its agencies for public services, and locate it in civil society. This made it much more compatible with the transformations in the machinery of government, and in the services, which were taking place in line with the economic model.

The key to the success of social capital, which emerged as a 'master idea' (Bowles and Gintis, 2002, p F419; Bjørnskov, 2006, p 22) in the social sciences, in public policy and in the programme of the World Bank, was that it was supposed to promote *both* economic efficiency *and* well-functioning democratic governance. Hence the excitement that greeted Putnam's *Making Democracy Work* (1993), which purported to have identified the elements of this public good in certain regions of Italy, made all the more identifiable because of their absence in others. Following Coleman, he defined social capital as 'features of social organisations, such as trust, norms and networks, that can improve the efficiency of society by facilitating coordinated actions' (Putnam, 1993, p 167). It consisted of:

> resources whose supply increases rather than decreases through use and which become depleted if *not* used.... Like all public goods, social capital tends to be undervalued and undersupplied by private agents. This means that social capital, unlike other forms of capital, must often be produced as a by-product of other activities. (Putnam, 1993, pp 169-70)

Although the concept of social capital seemed to burst onto the scene with Putnam's book, its evolution can be more revealingly traced in the work of Coleman, from whom Putnam borrowed the term. As Fine (2001, chapter 5) points out, Coleman's earlier work (1966, 1973) sought to analyse how systemic behaviour could be explained in terms of individual actions, through the aggregation of specific choices and interactions. If the paradigm for individual behaviour was rational action in competitive markets, then the existence of social norms indicated a situation in which such exchanges were problematic. Where choices generated externalities or constituted public goods or bads, the internalisation of patterns of behaviour became social capital (Coleman, 1986, 1987, 1990, pp 305-60) – a kind of credit that allowed individuals to trade in non-market circumstances (Coleman, 1992).

Once we recognise these origins, it is clear that Coleman (a close colleague of Gary Becker) was committed to methodological individualism and rational choice, and aimed to show how social norms and structures filled out economists' analyses of economic rationality under conditions of market imperfection. As Fine (2001) points out, even as the concept of social capital gave prominence to non-market interactions, it did so in ways that neatly dovetailed into economic analyses, allowing methodologically individualistic accounts of extra-market phenomena. Even though Putnam made almost no reference to the economic literature, he deployed a concept that was grounded in this tradition.

The new hegemonic economists, including the public choice school, had aimed to demonstrate that markets could coordinate social relations through spontaneous ordering processes, and that most of the inefficiencies of the post-war institutional system (and especially of the welfare state) were the consequences of state failure. Social capital theory did not follow the path of those critics of the economic model who thought that welfare demanded social engineering by government, because of market failures; it accepted the basis for individual welfare in the utility maximised by each actor, but insisted that this was facilitated by processes that were not directly produced by people acting under those motives.

This notion of social capital as a 'by-product' of interactions in which participants aim to maximise individual utility might, of course, refer to an 'invisible hand' process (see pp 35-6 and 94). It could mean that the functioning of social capital works through a mechanism that is advantageous to participants in various kinds of interaction, of which they are unaware, and whose benefits they are unable to recognise. This would make the theory of social capital akin to Locke's account of the effects on productivity of the invention of money (Locke, 1690, sections 37-43), or Smith's of optimal distribution through markets (Smith, 1759, p 215). It could occur 'behind the backs' of individuals aiming at other gains to themselves, through positive 'feedback loops' among populations, quite unable to explain the advantages they gain from it (Jordan, 2004, chapter 2).

But any such claim would require social capital theorists to show exactly how this happens if it is to be integrated into the economic model. They must show what the advantages produced by social capital are, and how they come to be distributed among participants and non-participants in social exchanges, even if they do not have to demonstrate that these effects were intended, or arose directly from rational utility-maximisation by individuals.

This would demand detailed analysis of the way such a mechanism works, either at the level of the group (exchanges among members) or among a defined population in which there are a number of such groups and associations (how the by-products of group interactions enter into wider relations), or both. In fact, no such analyses have ever been attempted in the necessary detail, nor has a convincing formal demonstration been provided. Social capital theorists have relied on vague claims about the beneficial effects of interactions, and economists have used survey and macroeconomic data to test these out by statistical methods.

In order to take the step from acknowledging that 'social and cultural aspects of human behaviour ... have economic implications' (Van Staveren, 2003, p 415) to making major modifications in the dominant model of the economy and polity, any new concept must deal with the basic elements in that model. Either it must show direct effects on the functioning of markets, property rights, legal institutors, state regulation and public agencies, or show how *alternatives* (such as informal exchanges) provide superior outcomes (Durlauf and Fafchamps, 2004, p 13).

I shall argue in the following two chapters that it is quite possible to demonstrate such effects, but that these analyses do not supply important modifications in the economic model of welfare, or make social and cultural processes more central to that model. Instead, the adoption of social capital into the still-hegemonic approach to public policy of that model can be explained by the fact that it is easily accommodated, as a subsidiary feature of the main principles driving the programmes of Anglophone governments, their imitators and the World Bank.

This is because social capital comes into play only as a solution to collective action problems where there are barriers to Pareto efficiency of the kinds already well recognised in the economic model. These consist of externalities, free riding, imperfect competition, imperfect information and enforcement. Social capital's beneficial effects can be explained in terms of solutions to coordination failures, improvements in individual incentives, or upgrading the technologies of social exchanges (Durlauf and Fafchamps, 2004, p 16). But they are never the *only* way to solve such problems, and they can never represent the *best* solution.

The definition of the 'first-best world' of economic welfare – Pareto optimality – rests on private market exchange and government supply of public goods as its two fundamental mechanisms. I shall show in Chapters Four and Five that the improvements achieved by social capital are all attributable to features of a 'second-best world', in which alternatives such as informal processes may produce better outcomes. The adoption of social capital into the model is no challenge to its fundamental assumptions about the nature of welfare, or its distribution among populations, and it can therefore play only a minor role in public policy programmes.

Indeed, these distortions often do not justify government intervention, but rather require a refinement of the theory of firms, organisations and contracts, to take account of what is feasible in terms of the costs associated with asymmetric information.

> Even though asymmetric information generates allocative inefficiencies, these inefficiencies *do not call* for any public policy motivated by reasons of pure efficiency. Indeed, any benevolent policymaker in charge of correcting these inefficiencies would face the same informational constraints as the principal. The allocation obtained [in a model of a second-best outcome] is Pareto optimal in the set of incentive feasible allocations or incentive Pareto optimal. (Laffont and Martimort, 2002, p 47; emphasis in original)

Some such issues were already analysed in the economic literature on 'mechanism design', in which markets were just one institution among those overseen by governments. A development of this was the Revelation Principle, in which (given information problems such as adverse selection and moral hazard) any institution must be 'incentive-compatible'; in this way, all informed agents revealed their private knowledge to the decision-making agency (Dasgupta et al, 1979; Myerson, 1979). This supplied a framework for analysing situations of asymmetric information, and contracts appropriate for every such situation.

Conclusions

The version of welfare that was incorporated into post-Paretian economic analysis at the beginning of the 20th century fixed the dimensions of political struggle and public policy development for the rest of the century. Welfare was defined *both* in terms of individual maximisation of utility *and* in terms of the collective resolution of issues of interdependence, in such a way as to give scope for the expansion of the latter, and of some 'objective' criteria for meeting basic social needs (or minimum standards). This represented the 'best response' to the thoroughgoing collectivism of Marxist-Leninist regimes, and allowed the justification of welfare states under the aegis of Keynesian variants of that orthodoxy.

By the end of the century, a new, more all-embracing application of methodological individualism – the sovereignty of each citizen and the principle of free choice – had undermined that compromise, and with it many of the institutions of the welfare state's heyday. Most of the shortcomings of the Anglophone countries' economies in the 1970s were blamed on 'state failure' – the over-organisation of society in the name of social welfare, leading to 'stagflation' and relative decline (Olson, 1982). But the political dominance of this new model, which incorporated public choice theory, was resisted by the many who still recognised many unresolved examples of market failure. Hence, an opening was available for a concept – social capital – which seemed to offer a 'third way' (Bowles and Gintis, 2002, p F419), and this was taken up by political leaderships, who adopted both social capital theory and that title.

The attraction of social capital was that it seemed to show that purely social exchanges, and the collective units they generated, had a positive value for the economy and polity. As we have seen, the whole emphasis of public choice theory was on minimising the costs of interdependence, by reducing the scope for others to affect private behaviour in adverse ways. To this end, it aimed to maximise opportunities for individuals to switch and shift between collective units of all kinds.

If the world was made up of small political units (Inman and Rubinfeld, 1997) and specialised 'clubs' for the provision of collective goods (Cornes and Sandler, 1986), this could allow far more exit options, with national and supranational governments left to reduce externalities between these units, and supply a few residual categories of goods, such as environmental protection and poverty relief (Oates, 1972, 1999). Despite longstanding warnings about the need to balance exit with voice and loyalty in collective life (Hirschman, 1970), this threatened to make free movement for the sake of cost minimisation the first principle of public policy. Social capital offered a corrective to this view, by suggesting that interactions produced resources that improved the functioning of all types of exchanges, and hence increased individual welfare.

This went beyond New Institutional Economics, in accounting for the beneficial effects of some social contexts. Rather than simply restraining costly rivalry and enabling greater reciprocity, social capital theory suggested that interactions created collective resources, and that these were then accessible to all individuals, both among the members of the original group or association that produced them, and beyond this, among a wider population.

However, social capital entered the economic model as a residual category – a way of dealing with information imperfections where market solutions were not available. Here again, the example of the Israeli nursery (see pp 9-11) illustrates the point. On Gneezy and Rustichini's (2000) account, the parents largely observed punctuality in fetching their children before the penalty – some perhaps calling on other members to collect their offspring if they were delayed – because they thought 'something might happen' if they were late.

But after the 'incomplete contract' with the nursery was clarified, when the financial penalty fixed the 'price' of lateness, parents used this information to calculate the costs of punctuality, and could recognise when it was advantageous to be late. As we saw, this might allow them to increase their utility, and hence improve their welfare, as well as allowing staff to do the same through extra payments. In other words, if 'social capital' (the parents' norms and networks, including mutual assistance) was involved in sustaining punctuality before the introduction of the penalty, it was obsolete and dispensable once a 'market' solution to this information imperfection was introduced.

So social capital, built through interactions between the parents, had value to them only in the absence of the new opportunities for utility maximisation given by a mechanism for pricing lateness. Far from introducing a social element into the definition of welfare (in terms of individual utility) in the economic model, it merely denotes the limited circumstances in which non-market means are the second-best remedy for information asymmetries.

Even in these situations, the gains to individuals attributable to social capital can still be understood in terms of the utility that is accessible through private exchange. For example, Glaeser et al (2002), in one of the few systematic analyses that adopts 'an economic approach to social capital', stipulate that they are concerned with the decisions of individual actors, and define social capital as:

> a person's social characteristic – including social skills,
> charisma, the size of his Rolodex – which enables him
> to reap market and non-market returns from interactions

> with others. As such, individual social capital might be seen
> as the social component of human capital. (Glaeser et al,
> 2002, p F438)

Although most social capital theorists treat it (in aggregate) as an attribute of communities (populations or territories) that is accessible to individuals, the lack of a coherent analysis of how such a collective good gives value to those who use it, or a distinctive account of the nature of that value, makes the interpretation quoted above the easiest to absorb into the dominant form of analysis of interactions, and into public policy on welfare issues.

Like the rules and norms of institutional theory, the 'social value' of this collective good is simply that it enables more private value (utility) to be accumulated. In the next chapter I shall show how this can be quite easily explained within the economic model. This in turn helps to explain why the Third Way approach to welfare policies has had so little impact on the disadvantages of those it tried to assist through programmes for building social capital.

FOUR

Social capital: the missing link?

Among the many attempts to rescue the idea of welfare from the limitations and contradictions of the economic model (see Chapter One), social capital theory has been the most influential in recent years. In this chapter, I shall focus on the first of two parts of its attempt to explain the beneficial effects of certain social contexts – that 'social networks have value' to those who participate in them (Helliwell and Putnam, 2005, p 438). The second part – that they benefit non-participants also – will be examined in Chapter Five. The purpose of this analysis is partly to show why social capital theory falls short of its declared aims; but also to clarify why it is so difficult to reinterpret welfare without challenging the basis of the economic model in more fundamental ways than social capital theory can muster.

The idea that informal social interactions in groups and associations can give benefits to participants may be understood in at least three ways:

(a) that individuals find it advantageous to enter into such relationships with others, because they constitute a better way of achieving certain purposes. The benefits gained in this way can be understood in terms of the outcomes for each of the individual participants;

(b) that individuals create certain social resources through these interactions, which are of value to them across a wide range of activities and purposes. They enable advantageous exchanges to occur, which would otherwise not have been available to members;

(c) that individuals benefit directly from these interactions, because they are intrinsically satisfying, and hence valuable. Here the advantages gained by individual members are understood as stemming from participation, rather than from superior instrumental outcomes, compared with formal approaches.

Social capital theorists and researchers have made claims of all these three kinds. Putnam (2000, p 21) describes social capital as an all-purpose good to facilitate interactions, a kind of all-in-one lubricant, Teflon and salve. Its protagonists' definitions have allowed it to be a 'code word used to federate disparate but interrelated research interests and to facilitate the cross–fertilization of ideas across disciplinary boundaries' in the social sciences (Durlauf and Fafchamps, 2004, p 3). These demonstrate that it has been used to account for gains of all the three kinds listed above.

(a) Some definitions state that social capital resides in social organisation, which enables 'the achievement of goals that could not be achieved in its absence or could be achieved only at a higher cost' (Coleman, 1990, p 304). Although this refers to aggregate outcomes, these are made up of benefits to individuals, derived from interactions within groups and associations.

(b) Others define social capital in such a way as to emphasise 'the shared knowledge, understandings, norms, rules and expectations about patterns of interactions that groups of individuals bring to a recurrent activity' (Ostrom, 2000, p 176). This attributes benefits to the resources that members produce by sharing in such activities.

> [S]ocial capital may be defined operationally as *resources embedded in social networks and accessed and used by actors for actions*. Thus, the concept has two important components. 1) It represents resources embedded in social relations rather than individuals, and 2) access and use of such resources reside with actors. (Lin, 2001, pp 24–5; emphasis in original)

(c) Social capital is also linked to the research finding that people who participate in groups and associations, and meet regularly with family and friends, enjoy higher levels of subjective well-being (SWB) than those who are more isolated, passive consumers. Helliwell and Putnam (2005) use the term to describe these gains from participation, unrelated to outcomes and costs.

There are certain obvious problems in the use of the same term for all these different kinds of benefits, across such a broad range of activities. One of these occurs when social capital is defined in terms of beneficial consequences, without any attempt to identify what differentiates such 'good' interactions (or the organisations that generate them) from others that are disadvantageous for members. From a policy perspective, this makes the concept of little use, especially where gains for one group mean losses for another, so the combined effect on society may be negative (Durlauf and Fafchamps, 2004, pp 5-6).

Another difficulty stems from the huge range of possible sources for gains from these interactions. Why pick on 'rules and norms' or 'networks of reciprocity and trustworthiness' when there are so many other potentially advantageous features? In one sense, the whole of a culture, and all its institutions, facilitate exchanges by creating pathways of communication and familiar ways of getting things done; they save time and energy by establishing routines and rituals, thus 'doing our thinking for us' (Douglas, 1987). Language itself, along with all social organisations, fulfils these functions. Those definitions do not indicate anything distinctive about social capital to differentiate it from many other aspects of social relations.

However, when all these three uses of the term are taken together, there does seem to be an implicit claim that voluntary exchanges in associations contribute in a special and identifiable way, which combines the efficient achievement of purposes, the creation of collective resources, and the *satisfaction* of individual desires (as opposed to the mere expression of preferences and choices). In other words, social capital is supposed to supply, not only the 'missing link' between social context and economic behaviour (Van Staveren, 2003, p.415), but also that between utility and satisfaction, problematic since the adoption of the Paretian form of economic analysis (Van Praag and Ferrer-i-Carbonell, 2004, pp 3-5).

No wonder then that this has inspired interdisciplinary research in the social sciences, given the potential importance of such mechanisms, if they were to be discovered. In the first place, if voluntary association could be shown either to be a superior alternative to hierarchies and third party enforcement over issues of interdependence, or to be a necessary condition for their effective functioning, then this would have wide implications for the organisation of welfare benefits and services, and indeed for the analysis of social welfare generally. It could clarify the collective basis for individual welfare.

Equally significantly, if informal social interactions turned out to be the key to translating private decisions about earning and consumption into psychic satisfactions, this would unlock the problematic relationship between welfare and well-being. It could show the processes by which utility was turned into quality of experience and, more broadly, quality of life.

So the stakes concerning welfare and well-being are high in the analysis of how social capital might be produced, accessed and used in social interactions. But any such analysis is, in terms of social capital theorists' own definitions (which use economic concepts), required to set out the costs and benefits to participants, both of voluntary transactions, and of market and authority-based ones. In other words, it must deploy the economic approach to make its case.

Combining voluntary with other exchanges

This demonstration should not be too challenging, given the progress made by economists in integrating informal relations into their model of human interactions. The work of Becker and his followers aimed at showing that the economic approach could supply 'a unified framework for understanding *all* human behaviour' (Becker, 1976, p 14; emphasis added). It is the comprehensiveness of this framework that allows an analysis of utility maximisation through exchanges in markets, hierarchies and voluntary organisations.

Part of that programme consisted of showing how decisions in households combined the resources from each of them in their activities. For instance, people drawing state pensions might buy food in supermarkets to organise barbecues for friends in their gardens. But, as Becker pointed out, the productive aspects of households are more complex than this. He argued that, since more affluent families forego greater money income for increases in 'psychic income', goods and time form part of the same overall constraint, because time could be converted into goods through money income (Becker, 1976, p 94). Hence, it was meaningful to think in terms of 'the productivity of consumption time' (p 102). Accordingly,

> Households are no longer simply passive consumers of goods and services purchased in the market sector, but active producers of non-marketable commodities, such as health and prestige. These commodities are produced by combining market goods and services, the own time of household members, education, ability and other 'environmental' variables. (Becker, 1976, p 87)

More recently, in elaborating his 'extended utility functions' to include social capital, Becker has argued that social capital enters these through the choices of peers, and through the internalisation of the values of groups. This utility function includes preferences for

> advertisements ..., education, and other determinants of preferences not ordinarily considered as 'goods'.... In a more fundamental approach, utility does not depend directly on goods and consumer capital stocks, but only on household-produced 'commodities', such as health, social standing and reputation, and pleasures of the senses.... Men and women want respect, recognition, prestige, acceptance

and power from their family, friends, peers and others.
(Becker, 1996, pp 5, 12)

This insight can be extended to the analysis of all decisions concerning earning, consumption and association. Imagine a single person deciding how much time to spend during August on paid work, and whether to take a short, expensive package holiday alone in an exotic location for a break, or to spend a longer time staying with friends. The eventual decision will combine a choice over working hours (and hence income generated) with one about the relative benefits of largely passive consumption in a luxurious environment, or the more strenuous production of informal pleasures through interactions with others. The costs of the latter will be measured in terms of the time and effort required to generate enjoyable experiences; those of the former in purely monetary terms.

A more refined analysis, clarifying the associational element, becomes possible if we imagine the same individual, having decided to take a longer, cheaper holiday of informal activities, then choosing between staying with friends in another city, or spending time with a group of amateur musicians in her home town, rehearsing and performing a difficult piece. In the first choice, the expected benefits would be assessed in relation to the opportunities for shared activities, discussions, relaxing interludes and privacy, the costs in terms of possible unchosen interactions with other guests and acquaintances, as well as the efforts to produce those experiences. In the second, the expected benefits would be successful creative cooperation; the costs would be disagreements over the desired performance or the incompetence and unpleasantness of fellow performers.

The value of the goods produced by purely informal interactions such as these could not, of course, be measured in other than subjective terms, as to whether the expected benefits outweighed the expected costs. But this value is in principle comparable with that of commercially purchased goods and services (the package holiday) and could itself, under certain circumstances, be marketed. For example, in the case of the musical week, the final 'product' could be a concert to a paying audience, or even a recording, where potential buyers could compare it with a professional, commercial product.

Similarly, although the roles played by informal interactants in the production of these goods of voluntary association are never specified in terms of contractual exchange, this could in principle be done. A demanding potential guest or musical collaborator might require her hosts and potential fellow musicians to submit a prospectus, stipulating the contribution required, and the quality of outcome to be produced by their exchanges.

So voluntary association forms part of the production and consumption of goods that are carried out in everyday life by each individual, and is fully integrated with decisions about exchanges in market and official agencies. It is susceptible to the same kinds of cost-benefit analyses, and forms an element within the bundles of options that are ranked in decisions about utility. Any account of the benefits to participants in voluntary exchanges must therefore be carried out within this framework, since social capital theorists insist that their concept explains improved *efficiency* in markets and governance (Putnam, 1993).

As soon as this approach is adopted, it becomes clear that the gains attributed to social capital can be explained by conventional economic analysis. Participants benefit from positive externalities in these interactions, because some factors in their relationships allow them to economise on the costs of doing these particular things formally (through markets or state action), or to take advantage of possible benefits not available in those types of formal exchange. The stipulation of norms, values, trust or reciprocity in the definition of social capital somewhat begs the question of how these gains are achieved, but – even if this turns out to be empirically confirmed – the mechanisms at stake are familiar from the orthodox economic model.

In the example of the amateur music group, the participants put their time and skill to purposes that might otherwise be used in formal employment or the consumption of commercial products (such as package holidays). But under the basic assumptions of the economic model, the scope for gains from such informal exchange can only exist because of one of a limited number of coordination problems, already listed (p 68). Using the term social capital to denote all such informal exchanges that generate welfare gains, Durlauf and Fafchamps (2004, p 16) state:

> For social capital to increase Pareto efficiency, the decentralized equilibrium without social capital must not be Pareto efficient in the first place. Social capital can only have a beneficial effect in a second-best world.... For social capital to be beneficial, it must therefore resolve or compensate for ... sources of inefficiency.... [But] social capital will never be the only possible solution to inefficiency. There will always exist alternative mechanisms to solve coordination failure, improve individual incentives, and upgrade the

technology of social exchange – such as contracts, vertical integration, state intervention, or redefinition of property rights. Of course, there are many circumstances in which social capital is a less expensive or simpler institutional solution, but it is important to recognise that it can never be the only one.

So, in the example of the informal musical group, the niche available for this gain through amateur activity must, according to the model, exist because of imperfect information about formal alternatives, or imperfections in markets (for labour power or commercial entertainments), or undersupply of public goods (such as state subsidies for concert halls), or some such deviation from first-best (Pareto-optimal) allocations. Informal exchange could not otherwise (under the assumptions of the model) yield gains to participants.

However, the opportunity for gains through informal activities and associations may give rise to real innovations, which alter incentives or create new opportunities for beneficial exchange. Instead of remaining as a niche, the musical group might develop a new genre or style, and thus stimulate new markets, or even a whole new industry. After all, the first string quartets presumably started in these informal ways, as did the first rock groups; certainly the first punk bands, consisting of self-confessedly unskilled musicians, came together in this way. So voluntary associations of many kinds might originally have come into existence because of imperfections and problems in markets or state activities, but cumulatively shift the system of social exchange towards an improved situation in which both these mechanisms are functioning better.

Groups, clubs and change

So the benefits to participants of groups and associations cannot be explained without considering how these advantages influence the subsequent interactions between members, and between them and other individuals and groups in society. If social capital theory is to demonstrate how participants achieve gains through greater efficiency in exchange, and hence increase welfare, it should be able to show how some group and associational interactions lead to the enlargement of a particular advantageous organisation, or to other similar ones being formed, or to improved opportunities for participants to engage in beneficial market or political exchange outside the group.

But here again the formation, size and composition of such groups has already been comprehensively theorised in the economic theory of clubs (Buchanan, 1965; Cornes and Sandler, 1986) – see pp 60-1 – so social capital theory has little to add. Clubs can be made up of members with similar characteristics, in which case an efficient club must involve equality of the marginal and average cost of the collective good supplied (Starrett, 1988, p 52); or its members may be drawn from heterogeneous populations. There are much more complex issues about the advantages of segregated or 'mixed' clubs (Mueller, 1989, pp 153-4).

All this has important implications for distribution, and hence for equity in society as a whole, since many efficiency gains stem from homogeneity among members, and (especially for clubs supplying the goods that are fundamental for welfare) the exclusion of poor people, and those most at risk of poverty, is central to their dynamic (Jordan, 1996). This will be discussed in the next chapter.

However, from the standpoint of efficiency, the gains available through clubs (and through networks of clubs) are achievable only where there are barriers to the exchanges that would produce Pareto optimality. Clubs and networks improve the opportunities for advantageous exchange precisely to the extent that markets are failing to provide all the requisite conditions, and governments to supply the necessary public goods, for that optimum. 'First-best outcomes can in principle be achieved without paying attention to clubs and networks' (Durlauf and Fafchamps, 2004, p 13). If markets and contracts are functioning perfectly, all members of society will use them as their medium for private exchange, turning the whole of society into a single club, inclusive of all. This can in turn be achieved by effective administration of courts and justice.

> Because of the possibility that revenues may be collectively raised via taxation, public goods can in principle be organised by the state at lower cost in terms of public mobilisation and leadership skill.... The first-best approach is generally to develop well-functioning legal institutions and state organizations. (Durlauf and Fafchamps, 2004, p 13)

A large part of the claim to improve efficiency in social capital theory rests on the creation of trust between participants. Indeed, empirical studies suggest that trust alone among the elements in social capital is correlated with density of voluntary associations; shared norms and networks are not (Bjørnskov, 2006). But Pareto optimality can only be achieved by *generalised* trust, which allows markets and government action to function to the benefit of all. Social capital involves *personalised* trust among exclusive memberships; collective action by members then substitutes for markets and state-supplied public goods. These can provide local improvements in efficiency, but are more costly and less reliable than generalised trust. Exclusive clubs may even block members from involvement in exchange with a wider population, and hence become barriers to the achievement of greater long-term efficiency (Taylor, 2000; Fafchamps, 2002). The possibility that the trust created by groups and associations can spill over into wider society will be discussed in the next chapter.

But another possible benefit for participants is that they collectively produce goods or services that subsequently find markets, or influence the political process. In this way, even if their voluntary collective action was initially conceived as an alternative to formal exchanges in markets or official agencies, it could turn out to improve the welfare of the group's members.

Let us return to the example of the original punk bands – disaffected young musicians, rejecting the prevailing fashions in popular music, clothes and culture, and angry at the emerging political orthodoxies of their era (the later 1970s). Because they lacked access to a market for their music, and making a virtue of their lack of accomplishment or technology, they started to play together at first completely informally, then in a few pubs and alternative venues, and finally at large, commercial concerts. There they set new standards of performance behaviour, and created new markets for their genre of music.

Although this is a striking example of a swift transition from informal outsiders to commercial success and the transformation of opportunities for new private exchanges and collective activities, it is by no means unique. After all, the original group of English Romantic poets – Wordsworth, Coleridge and Southey – were impoverished young men who joined together in an unconventional lifestyle, involving long, sometimes drugs-stimulated conversations and walks in wild surroundings, first in Somerset and then in the Lake District. They were outrageous outsiders who became famed cultural figures, and spawned a whole movement in art, aesthetics and popular cultural activity, including new forms of recreation and tourism. Equally, the younger Romantics – Byron, Percy and Mary Shelley – defied conventional mores in their travels through Europe, and influenced the whole production and consumption of cultural experiences through their scandalous, chaotic and ultimately tragic lives together.

Social capital theory seems particularly unsuited to the analysis of these effects from group interactions, yet no account of the consequences of informal exchanges on efficiency, and hence on welfare, would be complete without such an analysis. Social capital is defined in terms of the shared norms and reciprocities generated by group interactions, and is supposed to operate through the greater scope for exchanges these allow. But the collective goods created in these examples did not lubricate or enhance existing patterns of interactions; they transformed them. In this sense, they were means to innovation, rather than smoother functioning, in formal institutions and transactions – part of a process of 'creative destruction', which is associated with capitalist enterprise in the theory of economic development (Schumpeter, 1911).

What these examples indicate is that social interactions cannot be seen as simply facilitating the maximisation of utility within a set of existing structures. By creating new cultural resources – ideas, images and practices – they can redefine the terms on which exchanges between individuals occur, giving value to new kinds of experiences and relationships. In the second and third parts of the book, this is exactly what will be analysed, because it indicates how cultural resources give value to material ones, so that the utility that is maximised in the economic model is itself defined by cultural processes.

This is of great importance for understanding how resources produced in social interactions give benefits to members, which are extended over time. Social capital theory seeks an explanation within the economic model, but it then fails to show how such resources are combined with human and physical capital to create new kinds of value, and new opportunities for access to it. Without such an analysis, it is impossible to account for the paradox of increased welfare (in terms of the economic model) without corresponding rises in well-being.

Incorporating social capital

The examples given in the previous section illustrate how diversely informal social interactions affect economic outcomes, and hence the welfare of participants.

From the perspective of the economists who have adopted social capital into their model, this is a way of incorporating non-market variables into an analysis of market imperfections (Woolcock, 1998), to show how these can explain (for instance) differences in rates of poverty, productivity or economic development. Economists are not concerned with the details of how this has occurred, except in case studies, for instance of development projects. They seek an integration between the new information-theoretic analysis of the second best, and one of informal contracting through non-market mechanisms, which incorporates some elements of social organisation and behaviour.

> Social capital is 'social' because it involves some non-market process which nevertheless has economic effects. The economic effects are consequently not 'internalised' into the decision calculus of each agent by the prices faced in markets. In the language of economics, they are 'externalities'. (Collier, 1998, p 1)

This allows economists to select from the literature of the other social sciences whatever elements seem to have some relevance to outcomes, either positive or negative, because what they all have in common is that they are responses to market imperfections. 'Social capital can incorporate anything and everything.... No earlier contribution to social theory is safe from re-interpretation within its expanding and accommodating framework' (Fine, 2001, pp 124-5).

As an example of this selectivity and distortion, Becker's adoption of the concept of social capital in his 'extended utility function' pays tribute to the work of Mary Douglas (1983, p 45), while largely distorting its theoretical purpose. He writes: 'the noted anthropologist Mary Douglas claims that "the real moment of choosing is ... choice of comrades and their way of life"' (Becker, 1996, p 13). However, his purpose in deploying the notion of social capital is to give a spuriously social content to the individual preferences through which he seeks to explain all interactions – for example, that 'people often choose restaurants, neighbourhoods, schools, books to read, political opinions, food, or leisure activities with an eye to pleasing peers and others in their social network' (Becker, 1996, p 12).

But this misses the whole point of Douglas's account of how social interactions of all kinds are shaped, and given meaning, by the culture in which they are embedded. In her analysis, markets are only one of a range of institutions through which social value is exchanged. Whereas for Becker the market is the primary source of the utility that is finally realised in household production and consumption, for Douglas the social relations of a society provide the cultural symbols that underlie all interactions. Becker adopts social capital to explain individuals' '"given" and stable preferences over goods' (Becker, 1996, p 17); but Douglas sees choices as always socially situated, and institutions as reflecting the categories and 'thought styles' of cultures (Douglas, 1987).

Of course, it is possible, in a purely formal way, to capture the general idea of a social institution (such as income redistribution or the sharing of food) or even an emotion (such as love or sympathy) in an equation. Becker, for example, elaborates a 'Theory of Social Interactions' in which the head of a household is motivated by benevolence to other members, or richer members of a society by benevolence towards poorer ones. In the section of his book on social capital, he gives a formal demonstration of how this 'economises' on love and sympathy in the case of the family.

> The 'family's' utility function is identical with that of one member, the head, because his concern for the welfare of other members, so to speak, integrates all the members' utility functions into one consistent 'family' function, ... because he (or she!) cares sufficiently about all other members to transfer resources voluntarily to them. Each member can have complete freedom of action; indeed, the person making the transfers would not change the consumption of any member even with dictatorial power! ...The major, and somewhat unexpected, conclusion is that if the head exists, *other members are also motivated to maximize family income and consumption, even if their welfare depends on their consumption alone.* This is the 'rotten kid' theorem.... In other words, when one member cares sufficiently about other members to be the head, all members have the same motivation as the head to maximize family opportunities.... Even a selfish child receiving transfers from his parents would *automatically* consider the effects of his actions on other siblings as well as his parents....As it were, the amount of 'love' required in a family is economized: sufficient 'love' by one member leads all other members by an 'invisible hand' to act as if they too loved everyone. (Becker, 1996, pp 179-81; emphasis in original)

It is easy to recognise that similar analyses could be offered for the benevolence of tribal heads or political party bosses, but this is scarcely enlightening in terms of the nature and outcomes of social processes. It provides no cultural context of how benevolence and its obligations might become the ruling standards for interactions, or how such norms might decay. Nor does it help explain how particular individuals might be able to appropriate the meanings associated with these cultural expectations, to gain or subvert power (Edwards and Foley, 1997, pp 670-1).

> The specific social context in which social capital is embedded not only influences its "use value", it also shapes the means by which access to specific social resources

is distributed and managed. (Edwards and Foley, 1999, p 171)

So the huge expansion of literature on social capital, instead of counterbalancing the individualism and formalism of the economic model, is instead a means by which the model expands to make ever-grander claims about its explanatory power. Social capital complements utility as an all-embracing concept in accounts of why we behave as we do, and how we gain welfare, which claims to encompass norms, institutions and rules within a highly formalised theory. It is difficult to disagree with Fine's conclusion (2001, p 199) that social capital has become 'an all-embracing residual ... absorbing and neutralising more radical and coherent alternatives' in the analysis of capitalism.

Social capital and well-being

The most recent claims by social capital theorists link it directly with well-being, arguing that – in addition to the effects already examined – informal social interactions give rise to higher levels of satisfaction with life, and do so via the operation of social capital. They therefore postulate its 'missing link' function not only between interpersonal exchanges and economic efficiency, but also between these and rewarding experiences. Social capital resolves the Easterlin paradox by showing that the gap between economic welfare and SWB exists only among those who, because they do not interact with others sufficiently frequently, and hence do not have access to social capital, instead seek satisfaction in the private consumption of goods and services, and are thus disappointed.

> People who have close friends and confidants, friendly neighbours, and supportive co-workers, are less likely to experience sadness, loneliness, low self-esteem, and problems with eating and sleeping. Indeed, a common finding from research on the correlates of life satisfactions is that SWB is best predicted by the breadth and depth of one's social connections. In fact, people themselves report that good relationships with family members, friends or romantic partners – far more than money or fame – are prerequisites for their happiness. Moreover, the 'happiness effects' of social capital in these various forms seem to be quite large, compared with the effects of material affluence. (Helliwell and Putnam, 2005, p 439)

This is in some ways the most puzzling of the claims made for social capital. On the one hand, it may simply restate the idea that marriage, kinship, friendship, neighbourliness and voluntary association all provide more efficient ways of getting things done under certain conditions, and hence that those who participate in these units achieve more of their purposes. As we have seen, this outcome can be captured in orthodox economic analysis without the intervention of social capital. But the claim sounds to be far more comprehensive than this, since it suggests a link between activism of these types and well-being, which somehow transcends utility (and hence welfare) in the economic model. Without claiming to explain causation, they postulate 'possible mechanisms linking social capital and subjective well-being', which might be discovered through further statistical or experimental research (Helliwell and Putnam, 2005, pp 455-6).

But unless such capital is defined tautologously, to mean any factor in interactions which improves SWB, it is not clear why any such concept is required. The forms of social interaction and social units that are collected together for their comparative data are very diverse (from domestic partnerships to large-scale voluntary organisations), but they all involve face-to-face exchanges between participants. Is it not entirely possible that exchanges of something like the social value discussed in Chapter Two could occur in such interactions without the mediation of any generalised collective good? The fact that, among all the units of interaction considered in Helliwell and Putnam's study, marriage has the largest positive effect on levels of SWB makes it unlikely that the link between such exchanges and well-being stems from group or wider associational participation, since marriage and activism of these kinds are weakly correlated.

The formula 'utility + social capital = SWB' adds another whole dimension to the almost magical properties of this resource. Participants in all these interactions are supposed to generate an all-purpose collective good, which improves satisfaction with experiences, and with life overall, as well as the efficient functioning of all the major institutions of the economy and polity. Yet social capital remains a hypothesis, rather than a mechanism whose operation can be systematically theorised by any of these effects.

This problem is illustrated in another context by research on 'workplace social capital' (Helliwell and Huang, 2005; Helliwell, 2006), which has found that good relations between colleagues at work lead to higher job satisfaction. But the idea that high morale and team spirit among workers may be desirable is hardly a new one. Management theory and human resources practice have dealt in these ideas for many decades, since long before the concept of social capital appeared in the social science literature. Starting with Elton Mayo (1949), they have sought ways to achieve 'spontaneous cooperation' between staff, so that they become both happier *and* more productive in their work.

These approaches, which now use methods of 'transformational leadership' (Bass, 1990; Bryman, 1992; Northouse, 1997) to 'move group members beyond their self-interests for the good of the group, organisation or society' (Bass, 1990, pp 15-16), do not require the concept of social capital to develop a theory of improved well-being and performance. But they do recognise that there are collective goods, generated by interactions within the workplace, which promote both these outcomes.

> All organisations depend on the existence of shared meanings and interpretations of reality, which facilitate coordinated action: the actions and symbols of leaderships frame and mobilise meaning. (Bennis and Nanus, 1985, p 39)

This suggests that the collective good at stake is quite concrete and recognisable – a set of ideas and images, giving rise to practices, which allow staff to identify with each other and cooperate in joint purposes. The notion of a 'workplace culture', through which staff can make sense of what the organisation is trying to do, and of their potential contribution to this, is central to this approach. This culture is initiated by managers, but reinforced through interactions between workers. The culture is designed to 'change the way, people think about what is desirable, possible and necessary' (Zalenik, 1997, p 71).

Here again, the notion that individuals exchange social value through these interactions, in the very process of making and remaking the culture (Douglas, 1978, p 189), makes the concept of social capital redundant for the explanation of these effects.

Of course, it is equally possible for workers' informal interactions to generate cultures of resistance to management strategies. There is no reason why the solidarities facilitated by discourses and practices of resistance should not give workers satisfactions of a quite different kind, particularly when trades union activity is successful in improving wages and conditions. Here again, social capital is not needed for the explanation of these phenomena. The economics of groups and collective action on the one hand (Olson, 1965), and the sociology of labour movements on the other, account for the benefits to participants, and the cultures of resistance that sustain them.

So social capital theory points towards important issues about the relationships between welfare in the economic model and well-being as positive experience and life satisfaction. But it does not supply a convincing analysis of this relationship.

Conclusions

The contribution of social capital theory to the social sciences has been as an important stimulus to interdisciplinary research, and in directing greater attention towards the benefits for participants of purely social elements in interpersonal exchange. However, as I have shown, these effects can largely be captured within the economic model of welfare, in terms of either decisions about psychic goods by utility-maximising individuals or gains in efficiency because of coordination problems in markets or government activities. The remaining aspect of its claims, concerning links between social capital and well-being, is so generalised as to be unconvincing. It provokes the question: 'How long is a missing link?' (Fine, 2001, chapter 10).

Overall, therefore, social capital emerges as something like phlogiston in premodern explanations of combustion – a hypothetical element that turns out to be unnecessary for the analysis of the phenomena in question. The research into community and civil society that it has stimulated is valuable, but the benefits of group and associational activity can either be better explained within the economic model or remain quite unexplained. The Easterlin paradox of divergence between welfare and well-being comes in the second category.

Where social capital research has proved suggestive, and opened up the field for further theoretical and empirical explorations, is in questions about how the collective goods generated by social interactions enable communities to provide neighbourhood amenities, insurance and credit where markets and states have failed. Although they are otherwise sceptical about the claims of social capital theorists, Bowles and Gintis (2002) argue that the terms can be used as a synonym for 'community governance' – cooperatives, risk-pooling, parent-teacher schools, credit unions and so on.

> Communities can sometimes do what governments and markets fail to do because their members, but not outsiders, have crucial information about other members' behaviours, capacities and needs. Members use this information, both to uphold norms ... and to make use of efficient insurance arrangements that are not plagued by the usual problems

of moral hazard and adverse selection…. This insider information is most frequently used in multilateral rather than centralised ways, taking the form of a raised eyebrow, a kind word, an admonishment, gossip or ridicule, all of which may have particular salience when conveyed by a neighbour or workmate whom one is accustomed to call one of 'us' rather than them. (Bowles and Gintis, 2002, p F423)

So, despite the fact that these uses of community, involving multilateral enforcement of group norms, are always part of a 'second-best' world, they may be important sources of beneficial exchanges, even in highly developed economies. This was recognised by Arrow (1971, p 22) in his proof of the Fundamental Theorem of Welfare Economics; the requirements for the efficient operation of the invisible hand were so demanding that 'norms of social behaviour, including ethical and moral codes', were necessary to compensate for market failures.

This version of social capital is clearly also framed within the economic model, but it does give a much more precise account of how community governance works in terms of that model. It suggests that interpersonal relationships function at a face-to-face level both to reinforce certain kinds of behaviour (reliability, self-control, mutuality) and to punish other kinds (impulsiveness, defection, opportunism). This has echoes of recent analyses of the 'commitment devices' available to individuals through various kinds of social institutions – restraints on immediate gratifications, which allow participants to take full account of the future consequences of their actions, and of their effects on others (Offer, A., 2006). These will be further discussed in Chapter Seven.

So social capital theory does point towards the need for a better account of those collective goods which enable beneficial cooperation and restrain self-defeating hedonism and opportunism in social exchanges. Although the effects of these processes can be captured in the economic model, and although they directly influence decisions over material as well as psychic resources, the processes themselves remain elusive. Can an analysis of the cultural ingredients of these goods clarify the workings of these institutions?

Finally, Bowles and Gintis also speculate that, far from diminishing in importance in affluent societies, community governance through multilateral enforcement may be gaining significance. This is because the situations in which complete contracts cannot be stipulated, or external regulation sustained, have increased along with the complexity of interactions, and the privacy of unverifiability of information among parties to transactions.

These interactions arise increasingly in modern economies, as information-intensive team production replaces assembly lines and other technologies more readily handled by contract or *fiat*, and as difficult-to-measure services usurp the pre-eminent role, as outputs and inputs, once played by measurable quantities like kilowatts of power and tons of steel. In an economy increasingly based on qualities rather than quantities, the superior governance capabilities of communities are likely to be manifested in increasing reliance on the kinds of multilateral monitoring and risk-sharing.... (Bowles and Gintis, 2002, p F433)

The notion of 'qualities rather than quantities' again hints at a way of evaluating the satisfaction of experiences (that is, well-being rather than welfare). It suggests that interactions of this kind are somehow better suited to exchanges in which something other than utility (in the economic sense) is the currency. Here again, the notion of social value of some kind becomes a candidate for the explanation of both how cultures work to pattern the actions of participants, and how they distribute the benefits of interaction among their members.

FIVE

Players, members, spectators and bystanders: benefits for non-participants

The meteoric rise of social capital as a dimension of social scientific analysis can be traced to the shortcomings of the economic orthodoxy that preceded its introduction. In the model that guided public policy under strict neoliberalism and the Washington Consensus, fiscal discipline, tax reform, trade liberalisation, competitive markets, privatisation, deregulation and well-defined property rights were supposed to supply the conditions for gains in welfare by all. But the disappointments of the 1990s (including financial crises in Russia, Latin America and South-East Asia) led to modifications of that model, in which social capital found an important place (Stiglitz, 1998). The Third Way in the Anglophone countries, and the Post-Washington Consensus in the international financial institutions (World Bank, 1997) saw social capital as highly relevant for the welfare of whole populations.

Instead of counterposing the state and the market as rival principles, the modified version of the economic model reintroduced government regulation, public services and social protection as complementary to markets. Together with the new understandings of incentives and transaction costs in the theory of the firm and contracts (Macho-Stadler and Pérez-Castrillo, 2001; Laffont and Martimort, 2002), this made space for an account of how market imperfections could give rise to more or less welfare-enhancing institutional features. Social capital theory and research was supposed to provide an account of the 'extra element that defines how individuals and societies interact, organise themselves, and share responsibilities and rewards' (World Bank, 1997, Introduction) – how what happened at the level of villages and networks could add value to the government programmes, or substitute for them. At the World Bank, in 1997, 800 economists and 3,000 other professionals were employed on research projects connected with social capital (Fine, 2001, p 146).

This approach cast social capital as a kind of collective good that was free and non-excludable once it was acquired (like language), and which did not involve the costly processes of decision making over rules and rights that were required by purposive collective action (like politics). It came into existence through interactions in civil society, including ones not directly related to the economy. How, then, did these non-market interactions, including purely social or recreational ones, contribute to the welfare of all members of a community, even those who did not themselves participate in them?

A recurrent example in social capital research is that of sports clubs, the decline of which in the US gave rise to the title of Putnam's (2000) *Bowling Alone.* Here we should contrast the notion of social capital with that of 'club goods' in Buchanan's (1965) analysis of a swimming club. Club goods are strictly reserved for members, who pay fees to enjoy facilities that are congestible (they deteriorate when crowded), but where costs of maintenance can be shared. The exclusive nature of club goods makes this model apply well to private gymnasia and fitness centres, where members pay to 'work out' occasionally, with others of like incomes and tastes.

But sports clubs proper are not merely amenities for players. They also act as social centres for a wider circle of non-playing members, such as ex-players and committee members; and they are open for non-members as spectators. Without access for a wider public, they would not be able to sustain recruitment of new players and members over time. Indeed, the whole point of many sports clubs is to win support from the local population, which in turn improves the morale and performance of players.

In these ways, the benefits produced by sports clubs cannot be adequately analysed as excludable club goods, but nor are they captured in the framework of classical public goods (such as the sea, clean air or the wilderness). There are rules surrounding access by non-members, who may have to pay to be supporters, but whose support is counted as a benefit rather than a cost, and who have a collective identity, solidarity and loyalty, focused on the team. They in turn count these factors as benefits, and they may meet elsewhere (in pubs or restaurants) with fellow supporters, as part of the interactions that stem from affiliation to the club.

But although the club has to be managed, and rules made, these decision-making activities are not central to its purposes. So sports clubs do not fit easily into the any of the main categories of collective action within the economic model. They seem to be prime candidates for the kinds of interactions giving rise to benefits for some non-members, as well as those who directly contribute and participate in their purposes.

The first claim to investigate in this chapter is that, as a 'by-product' of interactions in groups and associations, social capital has benefits even for those who do not join in these activities (Putnam, 2000, p 20; Helliwell and Putnam, 2005, p 438). I will analyse the nature of these external effects, and how gains accrue to non-participants.

The second is that a distinction can be made between different types of social capital, which accounts for the variation in their external effects. Whereas 'bridging' social capital stems from interactions between people with heterogeneous social profiles, 'bonding' social capital is produced by interactions among homogeneous populations, at a local level. Putnam (2000, pp 22-3) acknowledges that the latter may give rise to negative externalities, for instance when the groups concerned are criminals or terrorists. I shall examine the basis for this distinction.

The third concerns the role of trust in these effects. Trust is not always included within the definition of social capital (Helliwell and Putnam, 2005, p 438), but it is one of the most reliable factors in statistical correlations between frequency of interactions and positive social outcomes. The extent to which this can be explained in terms of externalities will be analysed here.

Finally, I shall explore the distributional effects of group and associational interactions, and how these relate to external effects. I shall argue that these two are often confused in the social capital literature.

Gains by bystanders

In their example of externalities generated by social capital, Helliwell and Putnam evoke the image of 'vibrant social networks' leading to lower rates of crime. 'Dense social networks in a neighbourhood – barbecues or neighbourhood associations, etc. – can deter crime, for example, even benefiting neighbours who do not go to the barbecues or belong to the associations' (Helliwell and Putnam, 2005, p 438). This goes beyond Bowles and Gintis's (2002) claims about gains for members of 'community governance' practices, because it attributes these effects to interactions in general, such as barbecues, rather than specific organisations like Neighbourhood Watch, dedicated to crime reduction. We can examine the basis for such a claim by developing the example of the sports club, given above.

Putting the most positive possible interpretation on this scenario, let us imagine that a sports team's overnight success generates a large local following, increasing both membership of the club and numbers of spectators at matches, and also interest among a wider population who simply follow its results in the local newspaper. How will this change the outcomes of interactions among the community's population as a whole?

Within the framework of orthodox economic analysis, more frequent informal interactions between members, spectators and other individuals in the community, arising from increased interest in the successful team, may improve the flow of information about local affairs, and hence the functioning of the council and other organisations, by making populations more alert to local issues (Granovetter, 1975). It may also give rise to other informal groups and associations, whose members can benefit directly from cost-sharing activities. But none of these effects is properly described as an externality from the sports team's intensified activities. All are direct consequences of interactions among members and non-members.

It may well be, of course, that these have unintended consequences, such as the reduction of crime or an increase in house prices. But this is not the same thing as an external effect, where the gains or losses to one individual can be traced to the actions of another or others. This can be shown by reference to Invisible Hand explanations of the adoption of new social institutions, such as money, markets and families (see pp 35-6 and 67-8).

These explanations, which are fundamental to the economic model of welfare, rely on unintended consequences of actions by agents who have no intention to benefit others (Smith, 1759, p 215). But the optimal distributions achieved by markets, and the advantages for children of the family as a unit of nurture and socialisation, do not stem from external effects of trading or cohabitation. The workings of markets eliminate externalities in the exchange of private goods, and the workings of families internalise many of the costs of childcare, which otherwise fall on a wider community (Jordan, 2004, chapter 2). Becker claims that the 'head' of a household integrates all members' utility functions into one consistent 'family' function, by internalising the 'external' effects of his actions on family members (Becker, 1996, pp 178-9). He calls this an example of an Invisible Hand mechanism (see p 84).

So, gains to 'bystanders' who do not participate, even though they are not intended by activists, may be a consequence of the processes of social institutions (including voluntary associations, such as sports clubs), rather than external effects.

Perhaps the improved welfare of a community with a successful sports team could result from the adoption of new social institutions throughout that community (in this case, informal conversations at the railway station, bus stops or pubs, as a way of sharing information) in spite of the interactants not being aware (or fully aware) of the benefits they get from them. This type of explanation requires the demonstration of a 'feedback loop', passing through those who adopt the institution, and giving them the advantages of which they are unaware (Merton, 1949, pp 475-90; Elster, 1985, pp 28-9; Douglas, 1987, chapter 3). In the case of Smith's (1759) account of markets, it meant that the greedy and selfish rich, and grubby traders, were led to make

> nearly the same distribution of the necessities of life which would have been had the earth been divided into equal portions among all its inhabitants; and thus without intending it, without knowing it, advance the interests of society, and afford the means to the multiplication of the species. (Smith, 1759, p 215)

It is generally forgotten that Smith's original account of the Invisible Hand was given in a chapter on the connections between aesthetic and instrumental value, entitled 'Of the Beauty which the Appearance of Utility Bestows upon all the Productions of Art, and of the Extensive Influence of this Species of Beauty' (Smith, 1759, part IV, chapter 1). Here he sought to trace the high social value placed on both luxurious amenities and complex mechanical devices to a psychological response to the appearance of 'order, art and contrivance' – a 'deception which rouses and keeps in continual motion the industry of mankind'. This prosperity led mankind

> to cultivate the ground, to build houses, to found cities and commonwealths, and to invent and to improve all the sciences and arts which ennoble and embellish human life, which have changed the whole face of the globe, have turned the rude forests of nature into agreeable and fertile plains, and made the trackless and barren ocean a new fund of subsistence and the great highroad of communication to the different nations of the earth. (Smith, 1759, p 214)

It is clear that Smith is here not seeking to explain the gains to individuals from these activities, but the adoption of social institutions which had these effects, despite the much more limited and self-regarding intentions of those who participated in them. In particular, people are moved by admiration of and desire for the symbols of affluence and distinction. When properly considered,

> Power and riches appear to be what they are – enormous and operose machines contrived to produce a few trifling conveniences to the body, ... which must be kept in order with most anxious attention, and which, in spite of all our care, are ready every moment to burst into pieces and to crush in their ruins their unfortunate possessor. They are immense fabrics, which it requires the labour of a life to raise, which threaten every moment to overwhelm the person that dwells in them, and which, while they stand, though they may save him some small inconveniences, can protect him from none of the severer inclemencies of the season ... but leave him always as much, and sometimes more, exposed than before to anxiety, to fear, and to sorrow, to diseases, to danger, and to death. (Smith, 1759, pp 213-4)

What is clear from this passage is that Smith, with characteristic irony, is showing how the desire to emulate luxurious styles of living, stemming from a psychological quirk of human nature, has the unintended and unexpected consequence of consolidating 'those institutions which tend to promote the public welfare' (Smith, 1759, p 215). This is a kind of 18th-century version of the Easterlin paradox – that people are tricked by their own perception of beauty in artificial and complex contrivance into labouring to bring about vast economic development, even though gains in wealth and power do not give them 'ease of body and peace of mind'. Those who seem excluded from prosperity get their share of material goods, and 'in what constitutes the real happiness of human life, they are in no respect inferior to those who would seem so much above them' (Smith, 1759, p 215).

Even if we reject Smith's aesthetic–psychological hypothesis, we can recognise in this account an attempt to supply a detailed analysis of the mechanism linking admiration for riches with economic growth. By explaining the psychic and social value of size, luxury and complexity, Smith aims to show how the institutions of the economic order come to be adopted, and with what unintended consequences.

Furthermore, he implies (and elsewhere shows) that there are quite other sources of value (the 'real happiness of human life') that are available to those who are left out of, or distance themselves from, these processes.

Few analyses within the current economic model attempt to stipulate the mechanisms contributing to welfare gains as specifically as Smith did. It is enough for them to discover opportunities for gainful exchange between agents. Hence, when confronted with the claims of social capital theory, economists are content to define it in terms of any factors that facilitate the existence of a cooperative equilibrium (Kandori, 1992). Routledge and von Amsberg (2003) model an economic environment in which the probability of trade between a pair of agents is the indicator of whether social capital is present. Dasgupta (2002, pp 6-7) regards social capital as social structure, but again deduces its presence from the existence of a public good which promotes 'total factor productivity'.

All these accounts use social capital as the default explanation for efficiency gains within a community. Whereas Adam Smith's Invisible Hand was an ironic, tongue-in-cheek metaphor for a mechanism he could demonstrate in detail, these economists treat social capital as a convenient Ghost in the Machine, which is supposed to be taken on trust, even if its operation cannot be specified.

Bridging and bonding

However, social capital theorists do concede that informal interactions can have negative as well as positive consequences. In his *Bowling Alone* (2000, p 22), Putnam acknowledges that groups with similar social characteristics, forming tight bonds to the exclusion of others, may limit the scope for their more potentially able members to gain from exchanges with a wider community. In this sense, even if it helps individuals in the group to get by, 'bonding social capital' does not enable them to 'get ahead' (p 23). Some networks, such as the Ku Klux Klan, can even serve 'antisocial ends'.

In their later formulation, Helliwell and Putnam argue that harmful effects from social capital are externalities, but do not link these directly to the distinction between 'bonding' and 'bridging' varieties.

> Not all the externalities of social capital are positive. Some networks have been used to finance and conduct terrorism, for example. Just as physical and human capital – aircraft or knowledge of chemistry, for instance – can be used for bad purposes, so can social capital. (Helliwell and Putnam, 2005, p 438)

This example, of course, does not describe a negative by-product, but the particular use of collective action by one group to harm another group, or random individuals in the wider population. Criminal gangs who predate upon the residents of a district are rent-seekers in economic terms (Buchanan and Tullock, 1980, pp 48-9).

A better example of a negative externality from group interactions would be loud late-night noise from the clubhouse of a sports club, causing nuisance to neighbours. But this need have nothing to do with bonding social capital, in Putnam's sense. The sports club might have very heterogeneous members, from all over a community and beyond. This would not reduce the effects on nearby residents of their roisterings. When it comes to loud interactions, those with 'weak ties' (Granovetter, 1975) make just as much noise as those with 'tight bonds of solidarity'.

More subtly, we could consider the example of a sports club that becomes notorious for racist or chauvinist chanting by its supporters at matches. This in turn affects the reputation of the district, and deters outside investment, reducing income (and hence welfare) in the population as a whole. If the chanting could be traced to a core of supporters, with similar social profiles (say young, white skinheads), this might be an example of a negative externality caused by bonding social capital (in Putnam's terms).

So it is worth considering in more detail an example of a community in which, as a result of the presence of groups and associations which are notorious outside that neighbourhood (and hence cause or add to the district's isolation from potentially gainful interactions with outsiders), does organise various kinds of exchanges between residents that are advantageous to them, within that community.

One such was the Catholic district in West Belfast researched by the sociologist Madeleine Leonard during the 'Troubles' (Leonard, 1994). Here she found:

> [A] vibrant community with strong network ties ... [where] inhabitants were involved in a host of informal economic activities, including working while claiming welfare benefits, self-help, family, kinship and friendship networks, reciprocity and volunteering. (Leonard, 2004, p 931)

All this was happening under the controlling influence of the Provisional IRA (which maintained ideological solidarity), and without the regulation of government agencies, which had little or no presence. Although some vulnerable individuals were excluded from these informal systems, this served both to reinforce loyalty to traditional identities, and to sustain gender-segregated social roles, in this community. It enabled a type of mutuality and support, which was associated with and enforced by paramilitary groups, but represented a barrier to outside involvement and investment, and to members' participation in the wider economy and civil society.

As a result of the 'peace process', energetically pursued by Tony Blair, the dominant political party in the district – Sinn Fein – agreed to collaborate in building bridges with the wider institutions of the province. As a result, efforts were made to absorb informal businesses into the formal economy. But these often forced them to close, as their costs rose, and residents could not afford their services. Alternatively, where they survived it was often by trading outside the district. Meanwhile, official and non-sectarian agencies, employing qualified professional staff who lived elsewhere, displaced local community workers (Leonard, 2004, pp 935-40).

> Bridging social capital has had limited success while the rationale for bonding social capital has had to be dismantled.... In relation to economic linkages, the West Belfast example demonstrates how bridging social capital benefited individuals rather than whole communities. (Leonard, 2004, pp 940-1)

In this case, therefore, the phenomena in question can be analysed in terms of the economics of groups. The exclusive nature of the bonds and practices of informal exchange were based on forms of cooperation that involved the expulsion and persecution of non-Catholics, and also attacks on other communities (as protection, and to maintain solidarity). The collective goods that reinforced loyalty had overall consequences for welfare in the district and the economy, by limiting the potential for gainful exchanges, rather than by externalities from these activities.

Once the community was opened up to markets and government interventions, the benefits to specific businesses and individuals could be traced to opportunities for trade or employment in those systems. In Leonard's analysis, the 'bridges' that improved the welfare of those individuals, and of the wider community outside the district, could be understood in terms of conventional microeconomic theory. Losses to businesses and individuals who were displaced were similarly explicable.

This illustrates that the economic model can accommodate the supposed external effects of both bonding and bridging social capital without recourse to the use of a concept that is supposed to introduce a social dimension to welfare analysis. Both the gains to individuals within exclusive groups, and the subsequent gains and losses to individuals through wider interactions, can be explained in terms of exchanges among rational utility maximisers.

Yet this type of explanation does not capture important dimensions of what occurred in West Belfast during the Troubles and the peace process. On the one hand, we may need another kind of analysis to understand how gender-segregated activities were sustained in this community. During the ascendancy of the IRA, women were engaged in self-provisioning such as jam-making and clothing repairs, while men did building and car maintenance (Leonard, 1999). Once the district was included in the wider economy, these activities declined, along with the traditional gender role distinctions.

It would seem that these interactions during the Troubles involved exchanges of social value that were qualitatively different from those of the wider formal economy. Similarly, the ideology generated within the community to sustain informal cooperation involved the mobilisation of a different kind of esteem, stigma and belonging than the ones at work in wider society. These issues will be examined in Chapters Six and Seven.

Trust

It is clear that trust is a valuable collective good in the economic model of welfare. A first-best world requires *generalised* trust, which stems from a knowledge of the incentives faced by others, and the socialisation and education they have received (Platteau, 1994a, 1994b). If this is in optimum supply, then the costs of delays and defections are minimised, and the opportunities for advantageous contracts maximised. Any reliance on personalised trust reduces efficiency, because it takes time and effort to establish.

However, it is not clear whether, once markets and political institutions are established, trust in them is supposed to be reinforced by the constant advantages that individuals experience in their use (that is, an Invisible Hand explanation), or whether it is supposed to reside in each individual as a kind of human capital. The literature on trust that predated the rise of social capital theory was mainly concerned with 'the making and breaking of cooperative relations' (Gambetta, 1988). It set out the findings of game theory, which showed that assuming reliable cooperation from others under Prisoner's Dilemma constraints (that is, no communication) was often irrational (Binmore and Dasgupta, 1986, p 24); even if it benefits everyone to cooperate, rational individuals may not do so. In a two-player game, the first player's non-cooperation

> may be based on the fear that the second player will not trust *him* to cooperate, and will defect as a direct result of this lack of trust. Thus the outcome converges on a sub-optimal equilibrium, *even if* both players might have been *conditionally* predisposed to cooperate. (Gambetta, 1988, p 216; emphasis in original)

Earlier theorists had focused on institutions for pre-commitment – constraints people placed on themselves, so as to restrict the extent to which others had to worry about their untrustworthiness (Elster, 1979). Social capital theory suggested that informal interactions themselves generated trust.

> [T]rust and cooperation depend on reliable information about the past behaviour and present interests of potential partners, while uncertainty reinforces dilemmas of collective action. Thus, other things being equal, the greater the communication (both direct and indirect) among participants, the greater their mutual trust and the easier they will find it to cooperate. (Putnam, 1993, p 174)

This made trust an outcome of participation and, as Putnam put it, one that spilled over from groups to networks – personal trust became social trust (Putnam, 1993, p 171). However, in his later work he modified his definition of social capital, to indicate 'norms of reciprocity and trustworthiness' (stemming from relationships between individuals), rather than trust itself (Putnam, 2000, p 19).

> Although we do not, strictly speaking, include social trust within the core definition of social capital, norms of reciprocity and trustworthiness are a nearly universal concomitant of dense social networks. (Helliwell and Putnam, 2005, p 438)

But empirical studies have not borne this out. For instance, Bjørnskov (2006), drawing on cross-country principal components analysis, found that social capital consisted of three orthogonal components, corresponding to trust, norms and associational activity. Of these, only trust correlated with quality of governance and subjective well-being (SWB). This casts doubt on whether social capital can be regarded as a single concept, involving all three elements, and whether it is generated by associational interactions.

Furthermore, survey evidence of trust in other citizens in different countries produces some surprising results. Although countries like Sweden, Denmark and the Netherlands get consistently high scores, and the former communist countries of Central and Eastern Europe consistently low ones, Northern Ireland registered a level of trust fully 10 points above Great Britain in the European Values Survey of 1990, when the Troubles were ongoing. This suggests that questions were taken to refer to members of the same local community – trust was established only after the ethnic cleansing of the previous 20 years.

In addition, others have shown that survey evidence of trust did not predict actual behaviour in trust experiments with real money, or their everyday behaviour (Glaeser et al, 2000). Finally, trust seemed to be better related to social status than to membership of groups. In Sweden, although people receiving retirement pensions and disability benefits had almost the same high levels of trust in fellow citizens as the general population, those on 'activation' programmes of welfare-to-work as conditions for their social assistance allowances had levels of little more than two thirds of mainstream citizens (Rothstein and Stolle, 2001). Trust depended on social contexts and social relations.

All this suggests that, in relation to trust as well as the other claimed elements in social capital, the concept is too vague to influence public policy in important ways (Durlauf, 2002). It has directed attention towards the social processes that underpin exchanges, but not sufficiently precisely to allow important theoretical or empirical studies to launch innovatory analyses. The economic model can afford to adopt it as a rather lazy explanation for certain phenomena (or social contexts favourable for economic and political exchanges), but its actual operation can be accommodated within the model, either as an extension of human capital, or in terms of the personalised trust that is generated among interactants in groups and associations (that is, a benefit for participants, as discussed in Chapter Four). Trust becomes no more than 'a matter of predicting the behaviour of others on the basis of imperfect information' (Dasgupta, 2000, p 395).

This failure to specify the mechanism allowing personalised to become generalised or social trust is especially limiting. It directs attention back to the 'commitment devices' by which individuals restrain their own actions, through social institutions in which they enter into agreements with others not to defect or exploit, and not to discount the benefits of such restraint for future gainful exchanges (Ainslie, 2001; Offer, A. 2006). These will be further analysed in Chapter Six.

Redistributive effects

A large part of the enthusiasm with which organisations such as the World Bank embraced the idea of social capital was that it appeared to offer a pathway for economic development by which poor people could, by their own collective action, improve their situation. If group and associational interaction created resources beneficial to whole communities, this could be advantageous for those who had previously relied on government interventions – activities that had been extensively withdrawn during the period of the Washington Consensus, when neoliberal thinking had dominated the programmes of international financial organisations. Indeed, the World Bank (1998, p 1) had defined social capital as: 'the institutions, the relationships, the attitudes and values that govern interactions among people and contribute to economic and social development'. With this optimism, non-governmental organisations were encouraged to be concerned with social capital building in poor communities (Dasgupta and Serageldin, 2000) – 'to enhance their potential by linking them to intermediary organisations, broader markets, and public institutions' (World Bank, 2001, p 10). In these ways, interactions among poor people themselves could counter market and government failures, to the advantage of poor people, especially in developing countries.

This approach has been widely criticised (for example, Fine, 2001; Van Staveren, 2003) as a convenient way of getting 'the most disadvantaged people to pull themselves up by their own bootstraps' (Harriss, 2001, p 8). An empirical evaluation of World Bank poverty programmes, with regard to projects in Mexico and the Philippines, found that only three of 10 had a pro-poor impact (Fox and Gershman, 2000).

Obviously this is because any beneficial effects from increased collective action by poor people must counter the negative consequences of similar actions by better-off people, from which they are excluded – a central feature of the economic analysis of collective goods, club goods and externalities (Cornes and Sandler, 1986). '[C]lubs and networks often have distributional consequences that may be quite inequitable. The reason is that, unlike generalised trust, clubs and networks only offer a partial or uneven coverage of society' (Durlauf and Fafchamps, 2004, p 15).

Where groups and associations select higher-income or higher-status members of the community and exclude poor people and those from stigmatised minorities, either by charging fees they cannot afford, or by their eligibility criteria, they consolidate their members' advantages, both through internalising the costs of supplying goods to members, and by externalising the costs of exclusion. When government policy encouraged parental choice in state schools in the UK, and gave parents additional opportunities to participate in the management of schools, it also gave more successful establishments many of the characteristics of economic clubs. It allowed better-off parents to sort themselves into such clubs through residential mobility or covert selection processes, and to exclude children of poor households from the benefits of those schools which achieved better examination results. The worst-off children were therefore relegated to schools with the highest concentrations of social problems, special needs and other costly disadvantages, and often also with the fewest resources (Jordan et al, 1994; Jordan, 1996).

Where clubs attract heterogeneous memberships, this may have redistributive effects in favour of greater equity. For example, to return to the successful sports club, if it draws members, spectators and followers from very different parts of the local community, this will enable informal interactions between people who would not otherwise meet, and all kinds of potentially advantageous exchanges. In so far as those with fewer resources (in terms of physical and human capital) get the chance to interact with more resourceful others, they are likely to gain most from these exchanges, which counteract the negative effects of exclusive groupings.

But it is easy to see how an otherwise similar sports club, which attracts only members from a particular income group, could consolidate or exacerbate inequitable distributions. A group of homeowners who would not otherwise get the chance to spend time together might, for instance, get together to oppose a new development in the district, on the grounds that this would reduce the value of their houses. If this development might provide employment for less-skilled workers, or lower-cost accommodation for low-income households, this would damage their interests, unless this group offered some kind of compensation.

Equally, a sports club which attracts only indigenous lower-income members might allow them the opportunity to organise a boycott of a proposed cultural event in the district, or a protest against a hostel for asylum seekers, so as to further disadvantage an even more vulnerable minority. Far from increasing equity in distribution of welfare, this would skew it still further.

The sports club example has unfortunate and poignant political resonances, because of the evidence that the young Muslim men who perpetrated the suicide bombings on the London transport system on 7 July 2007 were members of sports clubs, and used an outdoor activities facility to plan their operation. They were also well educated and trained, with good jobs or job prospects, with many informal 'bridging connections' with non-Muslim fellow citizens, through school, college, club and employment.

In this example, membership of heterogeneous associations did not ensure that they identified with British citizens on political issues; instead, they used a common interest in sports to plot retaliation for British foreign policy on behalf of their co-religionists abroad.

This illustrates the limitations of social capital analyses of the effects of informal interactions. The economic model predicts the average effects of interactions in groups with mixed and homogeneous memberships. If social capital theory were able to add anything to the economic model, or to challenge any of its analyses, it would have to be in terms of specifically *social* purposes – aspects not captured by the model of exchanges between utility-maximising individuals. It is certainly the case that this model does not convincingly capture the interactions that centre around images, ideas and practices deriving from faith, blood and ideological loyalty, enabling solidarity to the point of suicide. These require a different framework, which will be the subject of Part Two of this book.

Conclusions

It is unlikely that social capital theory would have attracted as much attention as it did if it had not claimed to explain how even 'poorly connected individuals' benefit from living in communities with many informal groups, associations and networks (Putnam, 2000, p 20). But these phenomena can either be explained within the economic model without recourse to social capital theory, or are not substantiated by empirical investigations.

This is not surprising, given that social capital theorists set out to explain the social elements in human flourishing in terms that would be compatible with the economic model of exchanges between utility-maximising individuals. In that model, choices (including those about social institutions) can only be accounted for in terms of gains in individual welfare. The cost-benefit analyses that give rise to choices of this kind are well suited to contractual relations, and trace even psychic gains to this type of exchange. The notion of social relations in which value is produced and exchanged through the medium of culture, a collective good that is created and sustained by interactions of a non-contractual kind, whose bonds and claims are not susceptible to individual decision (although they may be negotiated between members), can only be vaguely hinted at within such a theory.

Social capital analyses hope to show how social institutions can act both as a restraint on individuals (through norms and values, for instance over reciprocity), and how they can enable advantageous behaviour, from which individuals benefit. But they remain vague and ambiguous about any distinctively social elements in how this occurs. By insisting that social capital is both a private *and* a public good, Putnam (2000, p 19) characteristically tried to claim that social capital had value for a whole community, but could be reduced to resources available for individual gains (that is, economic welfare).

The kinds of questions that were addressed by the Renaissance and Enlightenment philosophers, but which are difficult to frame in terms of the economic model, are emerging from sciences such as evolutionary biology and the theory of *group* evolution. For example, as Bowles et al (2003, pp 135-6) enquire:

> Is the remarkable level of cooperation among unrelated humans a result of the distinctive capacities of humans to construct institutional environments which limit competition and reduce phenotypic variation within groups, allowing individually costly but group-beneficial behaviours to co-evolve with these supporting environments through a process of interdemic group selection?

Using simulations of a standard fitness accounting framework, they investigated this question, testing the hypothesis of Boehm (1982, 1993) that the suppression of within-group competition might be a strong influence on evolutionary dynamics, as it was for eusocial insects and other species (Smith and Szathmary, 1995; Frank, 1995). What they found was that intergroup conflicts among humans explain the success of altruistic and inclusive forms of interaction with non-kin members of an individual's group and group-level institutional structures such as food-sharing that have emerged and diffused repeatedly in a wide variety of ecologies during the course of human history.

This form of analysis sees groups as the bearers of institutions, through cultural transmission, just as individuals are the bearers of genes (Boyd and Richerson, 2002). The model is therefore an example of a gene-culture evolutionary process (Boyd and Richerson, 1985), where group selection is very important because of the advanced level of human cognitive and linguistic abilities. Food-sharing and prohibition of non-conjugal sex are mutual best responses if all expect similar behaviour from others, and these institutions turn out to be evolutionarily successful under conditions of resource scarcity and intergroup conflict.

This analysis contains some elements of an Invisible Hand explanation (the genetic processes), and some of a distinctively social one (the cultural processes). It explains what would be impossible to account for in terms of the economic model – 'the evolutionary success of individually costly but group-beneficial behaviours in the relevant environments during the first 90,000 years of anatomically modern human existence' (Bowles et al, 2003, p 135). A model based on individual utility maximisation and intergroup competition would predict that several public goods would be supplied, but not the protection of the most vulnerable; there would be a 'race to the bottom', in terms of assistance to those least able to fend for themselves (Brueckner, 2000), without the intervention of a superior authority.

We may be reluctant, especially in the Anglophone countries, to adopt explanations that rely on strong group forces, seeming to reduce the autonomy and moral sovereignty of individuals, and reducing them to 'cultural dopes'. However, in Part Two of this book I shall argue that this alone opens up the possibility of a convincing explanation of the Easterlin paradox. It is only if social value, derived from culture, is an important source of well-being that we can understand the divergence between economic welfare and quality of life.

Part Two
Well-being

SIX

Social value and well-being: paying tribute

The Easterlin paradox suggests that – especially in the Anglophone countries – societies are trapped within an economic model that fails to improve their members' quality of life. Individuals who are free to choose private exchanges, and to create their own collective institutions, seem condemned to strive for greater economic welfare, which does not satisfy their desires. They appear to be addicted to ever-higher income and consumption, driven by the compulsion to maximise a form of utility that does not correspond to well-being – and the gap between economic welfare and satisfaction with life is growing (see Chapter One).

In Chapter One, I reviewed the main challenges to economic welfare and its derivatives as the best proxies for well-being, and in Part One I considered social capital as the most recent attempt at an account of the 'missing link' between welfare and life satisfaction. I argued that the weakness of this concept was that it defined no distinctive social source of well-being that could account for quality of experience in terms other than those of the economic model. Not only can that model explain all the phenomena claimed to be effects of social capital; conversely, social capital theory cannot resolve the Easterlin paradox, because it is couched in terms of gains in utility.

In this chapter, I shall start to develop an alternative account of social value, in which the type of economic value that is produced and exchanged in the dominant model is but a particular version. Writing of 'the sociology of primitive exchange' in premodern societies, Sahlins (1974, p 186) argues: 'A material transaction is usually a momentary episode in a continuous social relation. The social relation asserts governance: the flow of goods is constrained by, is part of, a status etiquette'.

The economic model of welfare, of course, claims to have transcended such processes. In the founding texts of modernity, free individuals extricated themselves from the bonds of ritual obeisance (the giving of tributes, the performance of rites and the donation of peace offerings) in favour of the pursuit of their differing desires, under institutions of their own choosing. But I shall argue that these can themselves be analysed as conventions for the creation and exchange of social values, and that the Easterlin paradox can be resolved only if we recognise that this is what they are, and where they fail to meet these purposes satisfactorily.

The economic model has been spectacularly successful in abstracting from all the elements in human interactions a set of principles which yield broadly accurate predictions of outcomes, given certain institutional conditions. But these abstractions deliberately exclude from consideration all those dimensions of the use of material resources that bear on social relations. More than this, the institutional structures created to enable the efficient functioning of these principles come to obscure, or to substitute for, those social dimensions.

So the terminology of the economic model – of customers, credit, assets, contracts, investments and so on – comes to have its own symbolic social significance, linking commodities to the creation and maintenance of social relations. These ideas define the meaning of transactions between people in ways that determine their social status, the esteem they can command, and their inclusion in or exclusion from circuits of social value. Whereas the hunter-gatherer tribes of yore quite transparently used goods as parts of a system of communication, manifestly serving to sustain social relations, under the aegis of the economic model we bestow upon commodities a ritual significance that is all the more powerful because it is presented as 'objective', 'scientific', 'efficient' and 'realistic'.

Think of a middle-class couple in an affluent country contemplating retirement. By then they are likely to have accumulated several property rights – to own a house, and perhaps a holiday home abroad; to have occupational and state pensions, insurances, investments and savings. Their retirement plan will seek to deploy these resources in such a way as to ensure that, in leaving their professional roles, with their access to various kinds of prestige, social contacts and wider associations, they still retain some connections with these sources of social regard – or that direct substitutes for these are gained, for instance in roles as volunteers or in voluntary organisations.

At the same time, they will try to maintain or improve their links with their children and grandchildren, and with a far-flung network of kin and friends, and ensure that their accommodation and transport enable these connections. But this must be done in ways that sustain the value of their assets, and yield an income sufficient to meet their needs for social care and domestic assistance, should these arise. Alternatively, if they plan to move right away from their former social circles, they will seek to create a new situation in which they can mobilise the same resources to replace the former ones with comparable relationships.

It is perhaps only at key moments in the life cycle of affluent households – moving to new accommodation, when all the children leave home, and retirement – that these processes are made conscious and negotiated (often revealing conflicts of interest or priority between household members). What is distinctive about such moments is that they explicitly concern the use of material resources to sustain social relations of prestige, power, loyalty, reciprocity, affection, dependence or whatever. Economic categories like ownership and consumption are then understood in terms of the ability to bring about symbolic exchanges in which social value is created and exchanged. As Douglas (1976, pp 23– 25) commented:

> Modern industrial man needs goods for the same reason as the tribesman. They need goods in order to commit other people to their projects. [A]ny individual … needs goods to involve others as fellow-consumers in his consumption rituals. The fact that in the course of these rituals food gets consumed, flags waved and clothes worn is incidental.…
> [T]he ultimate object of consumption activity is to enter a social universe whose processes consist of matching goods to classes of social occasion.

Where complex affluent societies differ from simple subsistence ones is that the social categories that are marked by consumption activities, and the types of value that are mobilised by individual and collective projects, are far more various, graded, subtle and exclusive. Because the range of goods available in hunter–gatherer tribes is very limited, so too are the social distinctions and the kinds of esteem that they can represent.

Because such tribes are quite small in comparison with industrialised societies, and their collective resources usually confined to a communal hut, the scope for collective action, power and domination is also very limited. One only has to think of a celebrity wedding (as depicted in photographs in a celebrity magazine) to recognise that the guest list, the gifts given, the clothes worn and the splendour of the setting all convey layers of meaning about the social value of the participants, and tell those *not* invited exactly how much they fall short of the requirements for attaining this value.

However, this is not the end of such processes of display and recognition. Photographs of these occasions (and of celebrity birthday parties and so on) are then pored over by yet other magazines and websites, which analyse the success or failure of various celebrities in pulling off a convincing version of the esteem-attracting performance to which they aspire. By detailed analysis of clothes, jewellery, facial expressions, conversational exchanges and bodily contacts, they are able to assess who has amassed the most social value through such gatherings, and devise an up-to-the-minute pecking order of celebrity, complete with ascending and descending scales, indicating whose star is rising, and who is doomed to a humiliating exit from the next guest list.

The point here, of course, is that, unlike tribal societies, where status and esteem are relatively stable, in affluent societies (especially in the Anglophone ones) they are a constant flux, with fierce competition for the highest social value, and the constant threat of humiliation and loss of esteem. While the taking of drugs, for instance, is part of a collective ritual in tribal societies, and has a symbolically transformative significance, in affluent societies its meaning is ritualised in individual ways, as an indication of self-identity, whether practised by junkies or wealthy celebrity partygoers.

It is not that economic behaviour is interpreted as lacking social significance in our present culture, but that these meanings are all given by reference to the individual, as author of their chosen lifestyle. What is bought, worn, eaten, displayed or owned is taken to be inert and objective (the product of impersonal economic forces) until it is transformed by the act of choice, and incorporated into a personal biography.

> If there is one value that seems beyond approach, in our current confused ethical climate, it is that of the self and the terms that cluster around it – autonomy, identity, individuality, liberty, choice, fulfilment. It is in terms of our autonomous selves that we understand our passions and desires, shape our life-styles, choose our partners, marriage, even parenthood. It is in the name of who we really are that we consume commodities, act out our tastes, fashion our bodies, display our distinctiveness.... This ethic of the free, autonomous self seems to trace out something quite fundamental in the ways in which modern men and women have come to understand, experience, and evaluate themselves, their actions, and their lives. (Rose, 1996, p 1)

One paradox of the economic model is that it insists *both* that society is governed by impersonal, objective forces (supply, demand, productivity, profit) and mechanisms (Invisible Hand, moral hazard, adverse selection) *and* that the utility that is maximised by individuals is deeply personal, and what gives them unique identities. As Rose points out, this cultural interpretation has now been adopted as a means of regulating society.

So, the workings of government itself have been transformed so as to harness citizens' 'projects of self' as means of rule.

> Contemporary regulatory practices – from those which have sought to revitalize the civil and public services by remodelling them as private or pseudoprivate agencies with budgets and targets to those which have tried to reduce long-term unemployment by turning the unemployed individual into an active job seeker – have been transformed to embody the presupposition that humans are, could be, or should be enterprising individuals, striving for fulfilment, excellence and achievement. (Rose, 1996, p 154)

So the idea of *shared* social value – that goods and people derive their worth from a set of *collective* meanings, standards and practices – is made invisible (or incomprehensible) in at least three ways. First, material reality is taken to be constructed through economic laws that transcend human agency, and have no social context (Fine, 2001, chapter 2). Second, value resides in individuals and their projects in defiance of social traditions, customs and rules, which are perceived as stifling the expression of true personhood. And third, government itself denies the value of the collective, and instead seeks to improve aggregate welfare outcomes by nurturing self-responsibility and choice among rational, utility-maximising subjects.

In this chapter, and in this second part of the book, I shall analyse the implications of this transformation of the collective life of Anglophone societies. First, I shall show that the 'objective' categories of economic analysis are in fact socially constructed; they vary between societies through factors other than the mechanical laws that are taken to govern them. Second, I shall consider the nature of the collective culture of individualism as a source of social value – its strengths and weaknesses.

My overall argument will seek to demonstrate that – as a way of understanding and distributing social value – individualism (in this broad sense) makes people vulnerable to a set of harms (types of stigma, exclusion, isolation, and consequent feelings of helplessness, self-blame, the sense of failure and despair) that can become endemic in society.

This is not surprising, given the ruling economic model's emphasis on competition between self-responsible individuals for self-realisation.

It is a culture that, for all its benefits in terms of overall welfare, 'also divides, imposes burdens, and thrives upon the anxieties and disappointments generated by its own promises' (Rose, 1996, p 3).

Consumption

From what has just been argued, it follows that the utility maximised in the economic model, and manifested through consumption decisions, is socially constructed in a strong sense. It is not just that preferences and tastes, ultimately what is seen as desirable, are determined by cultural factors (Becker, 1996). It is that consumption serves social purposes, both communicating claims to esteem and influence, and enabling the shared activities through which relationships are conducted. This is the case whether societies are highly communal, with few private possessions or distinctions between individual members, or highly individualistic, with much emphasis on self-reliance, achievement, competition and private property.

The theory of consumption in the economic model constructs it as the goal of activities and exchanges, and the expression of the outcomes of choices. This makes the behaviour of hunter-gatherers, who seem content with very low levels of consumption, a puzzle to observers from affluent economies. They have an 'undeveloped sense of property' and a 'lack of interest in developing their technological equipment' (Warner, 1964, pp 136-7).

> They do not know how to take care of their belongings. No one dreams of putting them in order, folding them, drying or cleaning them, hanging them up, or putting them in a neat pile…. Actually, no one clings to his few goods and chattels which, as it is, are often and easily lost, but just as easily replaced. A European is likely to shake his head at the boundless indifference of these people who drag brand-new objects, precious clothing, fresh provisions, and valuable items through thick mud, or abandon them to their swift destruction by children and dogs. (Gusinde, 1961, p 86)

In one way, this makes the Yahgan Indians sound very like present-day teenagers in affluent societies, but for very different reasons. If the latter are careless of their possessions, it is partly because they expect their parents to pay for new ones, and partly because they know they will soon go out of fashion, and that they will need new, up-to-the-minute ones to retain the regard of their circle of acquaintances.

Hunter-gatherers, by contrast, put no value on material goods, especially large and heavy ones, because they can live well enough on what they can kill and find, so long as they remain mobile. Possessions can be replaced in new territories, and simply slow them down (Sahlins, 1974, chapter 1).

So the admiration for large and complex constructions, and the desire to emulate their owners, which Adam Smith took to be a universal feature of human psychology (see pp 94-6) turns out to be a specific construct of developed economies. 'It is not that hunters and gatherers have curbed their materialistic "impulses"; they simply never made an institution of them' (Sahlins, 1974, p 14).

Even in other societies, with weaker group ties, and more competition between individuals, the balance between household and collective consumption is very different from that in modern affluent economies. In societies where more durable items were bought and sold, food was shared in various ways. It could be given away 'to kin, friends and strangers passing the village as an act of courtesy' (Powdermaker, 1933, p 195), but not sold. 'Food has too much social value – ultimately because it has too much use value – to have exchange value. For a wide range of social relations, balanced and direct food-for-goods transactions (conversions) would rend the solidary bonds' (Sahlins, 1974, p 218).

The collective consumption of food at feasts, given by a Polynesian chief, is both an act of redistribution and a ritual consolidating his authority. It therefore affirms a set of social relations, and creates a common interest in the midst of conflicting ones. In this sense, it communicates a social hierarchy.

> Such a feast gathers together chiefs and their clansfolk who at other times are rivals ready to criticise and slander each other, but who assemble here in an outward show of amity…. In addition, such purposive activity subserves certain wider social ends, which are common in the sense that every person or nearly every person knowingly or unknowingly promotes them. For instance, attendance at the *ana* and participation in the economic contributions does in fact help support the Tikopia system of authority. (Firth, 1950, pp 230-31)

In affluent societies, the priority given to personal and household consumption makes the maintenance of social relations more insecure, because image and style are integral to the processes of social exchange. In this order, subsistence represents a cost that must be met before social interaction can be attempted. To be poor is to fear that, through a cumulative decline in income, subsistence will require more and more resources, until nothing is left for social relations.

> [I]n the field of consumption alone, without regard to other aspects of the economy such as the labour market, there is a selective bias working in favour of some and against others. This is a serious problem concerning relative poverty which is lost to sight. The subjective experience which looks like plain jealousy is partly due to fear of being unable to meet social commitments and partly due to the consumer who finds the cost structure working against him. Whether the downward spiral leads to destitution or anywhere near it is a difficult matter to demonstrate. But the existence of descending and ascending movements in the ability to command goods and services is worrying enough when the normal consumption project is recognised to be ... the creation of a network of interpersonal obligations. (Douglas, 1976, p 23)

The symbolic significance of consumption has again become the focus of much social theory with the postmodern turn. Postmodern social theory recognises the social construction of consumption value, but interprets this in terms of subjective meanings and their communication to others. Instead of challenging the economic model's neglect of the social contexts of commodity uses, it focuses on how individuals express themselves through what they purchase, display and consume – 'the consumerist system of signs' (Baudrillard, 1983).

> Each commodity is imbued with a 'personal' meaning, a glow cast back upon those who purchase it, illuminating the kind of person they are, or want to come to be. Design, marketing, and image construction play a vital role in the transfiguring of goods into desires and vice versa, through the webs of meaning within which each commodity is located, the phantasies of efficacy and the dreams of pleasure that guide both product innovation and consumer demand. (Rose, 1996, p 162)

Saving, credit and debt

The obverse of the cultural features of consumption behaviour analysed in the previous section is the cultural influence on savings and debt

Social theory has paid attention to this because of its connection with economic development. Both Weber (1905) and Tawney (1926) linked Protestantism with the rise of capitalism in Western Europe, through the ethic of saving and investment that it fostered, and which distinguished some of its teachings from those of Catholicism (or the Eastern Church). Hence, ot is not necessary to dwell on the absence of thrift from the cultures of many less developed tribes to recognise that the social value of savings (and the stigma of debt) varies between groups in societies, as well as between whole nations.

Despite the already extensive sociology of saving and debt, modern economists have tried to frame general laws governing the proportion of income that is withheld from consumption. For instance, Keynes stated as one of his first principles that there was a psychological propensity to spend a lower proportion of one's earnings as these increased. 'We take it as a fundamental psychological rule of any modern community that when income rises it will not increase its consumption by an equal absolute amount, so that a greater amount must be saved' (Keynes, 1936, p 3).

This axiom was soon being challenged by sociologists, who insisted that both consumption and savings decisions were embedded in social institutions (Duesenberry, 1949). People do not have independent utility functions, which govern their responses to price changes of specific commodities; they form part of a culture that ranks goods, and bestows esteem on members partly through which goods they have and how they deploy them in social interactions. Better-off people can achieve social expectations and still have enough for saving, so long as their cultural reference group is restricted to those whose earnings compare unfavourably to their own. Duesenberry found that black people in New York and Columbus saved more than white people at the same income levels, because at that time the black and white communities in those cities were largely separate. At any level, because black people as a whole community were poorer, an individual with a given income was better-off than their white counterparts on the same income, in cultural terms. But, as Douglas (1973, p 180) put it:

> Individual savings are not necessarily less visible or less subject to public pressures than consumption. For once commodities have been conceived as the expression of sub-cultures it is clear that the culture is just as likely to impose a careful allocation of consumption behaviour between the present and the future as to require emulative display. Communal pressures to provide for the future can be strong.

This has become more evident in recent years. There are now dramatic differences in the savings ratios of affluent countries, with Germany and Japan showing very high levels in savings, while Australia, Ireland, the UK and the US have very low ones. Among the newly industrialising countries, the Asian states have high savings ratios, particularly China. Through the mediations of international financial organisations, the savings of Chinese and Japanese households now fund large parts of the indebtedness of American ones, just as those of German households fund the borrowing of UK and Irish citizens. Through globalisation, high consumption levels in the Anglophone affluent societies are therefore substantially financed by high savings levels in those other countries (Jordan, 2006a, chapter 3).

Conversely, of course, this reveals very different cultural rules concerning debt in the various countries. The economic model adopted in the Anglophone countries as the basis for the transformation of their economies and public policies in the 1980s relied on changing people's perceptions of the role of government, and that of private financial organisations. During the 25 years after the Second World War, it became acceptable for a government to borrow money from its population and from abroad, and to provide benefits and services for all citizens. With the stagflation of the 1970s, this orthodoxy was discredited, and neoliberal governments set out to reorientate their populations towards borrowing from banks and other financial intermediaries to fund their personal projects for consumption and self-development. The UK government was, to its embarrassment, forced to nationalise the Northern Rock Bank, when its risky loans to customers could no longer be sustained by borrowing from other banks.

In the new economic model, the ideal of the autonomous, choosing, self-reliant and self-realising individual replaced that of the social citizen (Jordan, 2004). Part of this change consisted in the rejection of traditional gender roles, and the adoption of more egalitarian, negotiated forms of partnership (Giddens, 1991, 1992). With women more involved in the labour market, individual identity was reframed in terms of combinations of work and personal skills, deployed in the realisation of emotional and psychological self-development. This new definition of the social value to be accumulated through life projects and interactions was consolidated in Third Way discourses of personhood (Cruikshank, 1994).

> Contemporary individuals are invited to live as if making a *project* of themselves; they are to *work* on their emotional world, their domestic and conjugal arrangements, their

relationships with employment and their techniques of sexual pleasure to develop a 'style' of living that will maximise the worth of their existence to themselves. (Rose, 1996, p 157; emphasis in original)

The point here is that these redefinitions of individuality and its economic basis were linked with institutional shifts that enabled the transformation of collective life, making it possible for people to pursue their projects of self-development even in their decisions about education, health and social welfare (Jordan et al, 1994; Jordan 2004). Along with regular responsibility for self and family came more opportunity to seek positional advantage through mobility between options, for schooling, health and social care, thus claiming and communicating social value through achieved status and salary.

Corresponding with this institutional transformation, and enabling these identities and choices, were new forms of credit, which differentiated strongly between status groupings in society. With homeownership as the major marker of mainstream status, housing finance became the focus for the competitive struggle for secure inclusion and positional advantage, with a growing diversity of mortgage and insurance 'products', to cater for a range of 'risks'. The concept of 'sub-prime' (or self-certified) mortgages is but the latest and most notorious example of marginal access to a status that has come to be the defining one in these societies.

So the stigma of debt has been replaced by the positive value of credit, with a characteristic type of borrowing for each level of a credit hierarchy. In the Anglophone countries, personal borrowing is at far higher rates than in the other affluent states, with Australia recording the highest rates in the world (Pusey, 2003). In the European Union, UK citizens hold about 75-80% of total credit card debt, with Ireland next highest in terms of proportion per head of population. This might be compared with the Scandinavian countries, where government transfers through social insurance finance a far higher proportion of consumer spending, with France and Germany where there are lower proportions of owner-occupiers (and hence of mortgages) and with the Southern European countries, where government debt is higher.

For lower earners, the system of tax credits, which was an innovation of the 1980s in the US (Newman, 2002), have provided supplements from the public purse for those unable to reach subsistence outcomes; the fact that these are supplied through the Treasury (Revenue and Customs) in the UK denotes their higher status than the benefits that go to those outside the labour market. The rhetoric of work and

121

responsibility, of avoiding being a burden on fellow citizens, sustains the social value accumulated by those who attempt to be 'independent' (DSS, 1998, p 80).

> Liberal democracy, if understood as an art of government and a technology of rule, has long been bound up with the invention of techniques to *constitute* the citizens of a democratic polity with the 'personal' capacities and aspirations necessary to bear the political weight that rest on them.... Governing in a liberal-democratic way means governing *through* the freedom and aspirations of subjects rather than in spite of them ... in order to bring their own ways of conducting and evaluating themselves into alignment with political objectives. (Rose, 1996, p 155; emphasis in original)

The new approach, pioneered under neoliberalism and extended by Third Way regimes, is to encourage citizens to see the banks as both the providers and the limit-setters for their aspirations. The obvious problem for this culture of borrowing, which legitimates various types of mortgage and credit, is that it is based on a hypothetic shift, somewhere in the life cycle, from debt to saving. For the generation who bought houses in the 1970s and early 1980s, this has been largely accomplished, because the value of these assets has risen faster than general price inflation. Even so, there are large numbers of individuals and households in all age groups with serious deficits in their savings and pension provision (*Guardian*, 2006). Finally, the generation who are now joining the UK labour force are facing the situation that excessive proportions of their earnings are required for them to gain access to the housing market, and hence the mainstream.

Looking at the system as a whole, the transformation achieved in the Anglophone countries has enabled the governments to step down from central responsibility for the redistribution of income, requiring individuals and households to manage their borrowing and saving through the life cycle to finance their projects of self-development. The banks, insurance companies and financial intermediaries have become the main arbiters of this system, with governments as regulators and overseers. The financial intermediaries, in turn, through advertising and marketing their products, create the cultural resources by which individuals and households understand and manage their indebtedness, and the hierarchy of status within which this occurs.

Within the rhetoric of freedom and choice that sustains this approach to government, risk is managed through a well-regulated contractual relationship between all the parties (individuals and organisations). It is only when something like the 'credit crunch' of 2007-08, triggered by the 'sub-prime' mortgage crisis in the US, causes the fundamental assumptions of the model to be questioned that the culture of credit and debt becomes a matter of debate and concern.

Work effort and work roles

In the economic model, each individual chooses hours of work and labour market position according to cost–benefit analysis of the required effort and return, given their consumption preferences. Since each is individually responsible for managing a life cycle in which projects for personal development are funded by career earnings, under conditions of shifting demands for skills and experience, this is conceived as involving a series of decisions about education, training and mobility, in which the self-responsible person should demonstrate competence. The fruits of good management (human capital acquisition, organisational power, pension rights and so on) can be claimed as individual achievements, and are reflected in lifestyles.

However, there has always been enormous variation in the work effort sustained by different societies, which requires explanation in collective rather than individual terms. In her famous comparison between the Lele and Bushong peoples of Central Africa, Mary Douglas showed how the former produced only for subsistence, redistributing their output among members as gifts and feasts, while the latter produced for markets, and accumulated wealth (Douglas, 1962). Despite having languages with similar roots, and sharing styles of clothing, crafts and houses, as well as a common physical environment, the Lele used both technology and human labour power less efficiently; yet they did less work than the Bushong, because their social institutions, beliefs and practices encouraged large families with strong reciprocity among members, but gave little status to material wealth. By contrast:

> For the Bushong, work is the means to wealth and wealth the means to status. They strongly emphasise the value of individual effort and achievement, and they are also prepared to collaborate in numbers over a sustained period when this is necessary to raise output.... The Bushong talk constantly, and dream about wealth, while proverbs about it being

the stepping stone to higher status are often on their lips.
(Douglas, 1962, p 161)

As a result, a Bushong man was actively involved in productive work about twice as long as a Lele one over a lifetime. But such variations in total work effort within a society are still evident in affluent modern economies. Whereas the effect of the institutional transformations of Anglophone countries since the 1970s has been to increase labour market participation by adults, and this has been achieved in the main through increases in women's activity, French and German institutional adaptations to globalisation have been towards limiting access to labour markets.

In the French case, this has taken the form of statutory lowering of the numbers of working hours; in Germany, it has involved delaying the entry of young people into formal employment, and organising the early exit of older workers, as well as continuing to exclude many married women (Esping-Anderson, 1990, 1996, 1999).

In the Scandinavian countries, by contrast, women had since the Second World War participated in high proportions in paid work, which was predominantly part time and in the public sector. These variations stemmed from a whole set of economic strategies, state institutions and domestic practices, woven together in the collective lives of the societies.

The scope for these variations was derived from the extra-contractual nature of household and subsistence work, from the early days of commercial societies. Since much that was done to reproduce social relations was outside the formal economy, it represented both a potential 'reserve army' of workers for paid labour and a set of activities that could be formalised as services, either by government provision (as in education and healthcare) or by commercial firms. In the Scandinavian case, the expansion of the public sector absorbed women workers directly from the household and subsistence economies in rural areas in the middle years of the 20th century.

Economic theory has periodically redefined the nature of this kind of work, and its impact on welfare. Adam Smith (1776) considered that the type of value it produced, even when it was performed under contract, was different from that of commodities. This was because the latter embodied the value of the labour going into them, and could be exchanged for other commodities, whereas services 'perish in the very instant of their performance' (1776, pp 330-1). For this reason, the production of commodities contributed to the wealth of nations, whereas services constituted costs against national income. Not only were flunkeys, chambermaids and other servants to be regarded as 'unproductive'; so too were 'some of the most respectable orders of society'.

> The sovereign, for example, with all the officers both of justice and war who serve under him, the whole army and navy, are unproductive labourers.... In the same class must be ranked ... churchmen, lawyers, physicians, men of letters of all kinds; players, buffoons, musicians, opera-singers, opera dancers, etc. (Smith, 1776, p 331)

Furthermore, Smith regarded the relationships between economic agents in the various branches of activity as qualitatively different. Whereas artisans and traders retained their 'independence' because their resources embodied physical labour value, 'unproductive' service workers were part of the 'systems of authority' by which a social hierarchy was maintained. So Smith seems to have seen services as dealing in the type of value through which power and status differentials were consolidated, giving society its stability and structure, but needing to be linked (for instance through the ownership of land) to the productive economy of industry and trade.

By the 19th century, the professions, science and the arts had come to be seen to confer 'independence' on their practitioners, but the roles of paid household members remained ambiguous. Although servants were seen as part of the formal workforce, the authority of their employer over them, and the expectation of deference and respect, was non-contractual and traditional. In many European countries, rural workers were indentured, and had no freedom of movement between farms; the local authorities helped employers to enforce the conditions of bonded labour.

It was not until between the two World Wars that proportions of the workforce in private domestic service began to decline, and self-provisioning through women's unpaid work in households began to increase. The political project of welfare states was to turn some of these tasks into universal public services. For example, social care was to be an issue for local government agencies, which were to give these amenities in a 'democratic spirit' (Cole, 1945, p 29), whose social significance was to be equality of status as citizens, even though inequality of income and property continued (Marshall, 1950). Accordingly, in the UK, whereas private domestic service had constituted 10% of the workforce in 1911 (Feinstein, 1976, table 60), by 1948 national and local government represented 8% of all employment (table 59).

These shifts in the social significance of what had been household work signalled the attempt to establish a territory of social welfare in which new scope for gains in household incomes and political interdependence could be created, so that interactions between members of different occupations and work statuses could involve exchanges of some kind of political fellowship and solidarity. Subsequent history shows that this project was far more successful in the Scandinavian countries, with their more egalitarian traditions, than in the UK, with its deeply individualistic, competitive culture (MacFarlane, 1978).

Meanwhile, another whole dimension of work roles, and the standards and value they sustained, was also being subjected to transformative forces. Skills and crafts, their acquisition and organisation within the economy, had historically supplied the basis for 'grid-based' social distinctions, practices and membership systems, and provided the categories through which the collective life of cities was structured. These cultures and institutions had evolved in the advanced industrialised economies from the medieval guilds, and had become the organising principles behind these societies' democratic politics.

Richard Sennett (2008) has analysed the nature and social relations of skills, crafts and quality in the production of material goods. He considers these as aspects of cultures in which techniques for doing things well become central to particular ways of life (Sennett, 2008, p 8). His account spans the traditional crafts of work with wood, stone and metal, the human service practices of medicine and social care, and the electronic expertise of computer programming. He argues that the institutions and cultures required to support and sustain high-quality practice are complex, and not reducible to either hierarchical command or individual reward under competition (pp 28-30).

His approach allows him to trace common features in the achievement of quality in practice in very diverse contexts and also to show how these can be undermined by ill-considered innovations. Machinery is not in itself a threat to craftsmanship, but it may disturb the balance between intellectual and manual expertise, either within individuals' practice, or in the organisation of work. Soviet bureaucratic control destroyed much everyday skill, but sustained cutting-edge scientific and military work. Japanese corporations generated a culture of 'collective craftsmanship', in which managers and workers could encourage and criticise each other in direct exchanges on the shop floor (pp 29-31). Computer-assisted design inhibits 'the tactile, the relational and the incomplete' (p 44) – practical aspects of designing objects and buildings for human use – because 'people may let the machines do this learning, the person serving as a passive witness to and consumer of expanding competence, not participating in it' (p 44).

The point here is that neither skill nor technology can be adequately conceptualised outside the social relations in which they are combined. The attempt to 'rationalise' or 'modernise' work practices, or to improve performance through new contractual arrangements, is always in danger of being counterproductive if it ignores these factors. Sennett quotes the reforms of the UK National Health Service (NHS) as examples of a 'long debate about the nature and value of craftsmanship in a mechanical, quantitative society', citing the reduction in informal interactions between nurses and elderly patients, and the increase in fabricated diagnoses by doctors, as unintended consequences of 'Fordist reforms' (pp 48-9).

> In the higher stages of a skill, there is a constant interplay between tacit knowledge and self-conscious awareness.... Craft quality emerges from this higher stage, in judgements made on tacit habits and suppositions. When an institution like the NHS, in churning reform, doesn't allow the tacit anchor to develop, then the motor of judgement stalls. People have no experience to judge, just a set of abstract propositions about good-quality work. (Sennett, 2008, p 50)

Global economic restructuring has brought about a reorganisation of work roles in the affluent Anglophone countries – processes resisted and delayed in France, Germany and Japan. As male manual jobs have disappeared, the 'new economy' of financial and business service work, often involving electronic technology, has expanded; but this work is fragmented, constantly shifting, and under pressure of competition from South and East Asia (Sennett, 1998, 2006; Pusey, 2003). Workplace cultures are more individualistic and instrumental; 'competition has disabled and disheartened workers, and the craftsman's ethic of doing good work for its own sake is unrewarded or invisible' (Sennett, 2008, p 37).

Conclusions

It would, of course, be misleading to argue that the economic model can offer no explanations for the variations in patterns of consumption, savings, credit, work effort and work roles identified in this chapter.

On the contrary, it would claim to be able to explain all these, in ways that are consistent with its assumptions about individual utility maximisation and cost-benefit calculations. Such analyses would be undertaken in terms of social institutions and path dependency, accounting for the adoption of apparently sub-optimal solutions to individual and collective action problems in terms of imperfect information under conditions of uncertainty.

The point here is that the economic model makes these claims by subsuming the whole world of social relations within its economic categories. Whereas I have argued that the social value associated with power, status, esteem, respect, membership and belonging stems from social relations, often communicated through the exchange and sharing of commodities, the economic model reverses this analysis, insisting that social elements in all interactions are explicable in terms of utility maximisation. In the last resort, there is no way of settling this dispute; the economic model is an elegant abstraction with the power to offer persuasive accounts in societies organised around markets and private property. But – as I shall argue in the rest of this book – the Easterlin paradox is a good example of a phenomenon that it is unable to explain in its own terms.

Faced with the gap between economic welfare and subjective well-being (SWB), the economic model is driven into circular arguments and tautologous definitions. It is forced to draw on concepts such as social capital that, although they are claimed to provide missing links between the economic and the social, actually turn out to be versions of the Ghost in the Machine. If well-being can be shown to be related to esteem, regard and empathy, it demands a social explanation, because these stem from and reside in relationships, not individuals or their material possessions.

This is why the adoption of social capital in economic explanations of social interactions by economists has become a kind of marker of the shortcomings of the economic model. For instance, in Gary Becker's (1996) extended utility function, affecting both welfare and decisions, social capital implies influences outside the choice or control of the individual (see pp 83-4). 'The effects of the social milieu, an individual's stock of social capital depends not primarily on his own choices, but on the choices of peers in the relevant network of interactions' (Becker, 1996, p 12).

On this account, social capital is an interpersonal externality, because choices that are made by others, with limited effects on their own welfare, strongly influence each individual in this context. This allows the extended utility function to explain a large range of decisions in terms of the social impact of forces outside the individual, who in turn takes on many of the characteristics of the 'cultural dope'. The extended utility function is stable 'because it includes measures of past experience and social forces' (Becker, 1996, p 5). This in turn allows the economic approach to explain issues in sociology, history and other fields that postulate almost arbitrary variations in preferences and values, and hence to account for otherwise puzzling phenomena 'in the modern world, and probably in the distant past as well' (Becker, 1996, p 6).

But as we have seen, faced with paradoxical examples of everyday behaviour, the economic model often offers unconvincing analyses. For example, in the case of the Israeli children's nursery (described in the Introduction), parents were supposed to have observed conventions of punctuality before the financial penalty was introduced because they lacked complete information about the consequences of lateness (Gneezy and Rustichini, 2000). Once they knew the 'price' of lateness, more were late. A more plausible account would suggest that the creation and exchange of social value through cooperation between parents and staff minimised lateness under a regime regulated through a culture of mutual consideration. The adoption of a contractual approach, signalled by the financial penalty, made lateness more socially acceptable, and undermined the value of cooperative relations.

If we take the example of decisions about their retirement by the couple given at the start of this chapter, the economic model would account for these in terms of the effects of choices by work colleagues, kin, family and neighbours on this household's options. Their extended utility function must take all of these into consideration. The social model would consider in detail how the couple's long-term attempt to sustain their well-being through the accumulation of social value, and the maintenance of their relationships, uses economic assets to communicate symbolically both meanings and emotions concerning significant others. The management of job and housing careers, pensions and insurances, savings and credits, would be understood as parts of strategies pursued within social institutions that reflect a culture of competitive individualism, in which family, kinship and friendships are sustained within market and property relations.

In the rest of this book, I shall argue that the latter type of analysis is a far more fruitful way to address the Easterlin paradox, but that economic and social explanations must be mutually accountable, because of the demands of individual freedom and welfare that the economic model so impressively serves. Social theory must also refute the accusation that its agents are not individuals, let alone rational individuals, but 'cultural dopes'. Any theory that is to convince and impress an Anglophone liberal readership must make space for individual economic welfare as well as social well-being.

SEVEN

How social value works

Despite the dominance of the economic model, there has been increasing interest in the idea of social value among economists themselves (Offer, 1996), and much of this has been related to the concept of well-being (Bruni and Porta, 2005). Feeding off psychological analyses of the components of subjective well-being (SWB) (Argyle, 1999; Myers, 1999), economists have investigated the interpersonal factors that correlate with high levels of self-reported happiness; a few have also addressed the mechanisms through which well-being is generated in informal interactions, even returning to Adam Smith's (1759) accounts of 'correspondence of sentiments' in this process (Sugden, 2005).

The quantitative analyses that have been undertaken to chart these links have revealed striking contributions to SWB from marriage and employment satisfaction, which rank with good health as the largest single elements in overall happiness with life, from three to four times more significant than the final third of income (Helliwell, 2003). Conversely, the breakup of partnerships, the death of a partner, the loss of employment and the onset of long-term illness are much more damaging and enduringly negative for SWB than loss of that proportion of income. It seems reasonable to assume that a large fraction of what is lost through unemployment and illness or disability is the value gained from informal interactions at work and in the community, since these in turn contribute strongly to SWB (Layard, 2005, p 16).

These studies either do not go beyond the statistical evidence to investigate the mechanisms at stake in such interactions, or attribute gains in SWB to social capital (Helliwell and Putnam, 2005, p 439; Helliwell, 2006), in terms that were criticised in Chapter Five. This chapter will examine some of the analyses of the dynamics of social value that have appeared in the economic literature, and go on to show what is missing from them, and what can be derived from social and anthropological theory to fill these gaps.

The main deficiency in the economic analyses carried out so far is that, since they start from methodologically individualistic assumptions about interaction, they are restricted to accounts of *exchanges* in social relationships. What is seen as to be explained in 'the economy of regard' (Offer, A., 2006, chapter 5) is how interactions involve the giving and receiving of some kind of social recognition. Important as this is, I shall argue that it is not the primary purpose of such interactions. It has long been argued by social theorists that interactions, even in affluent, individualistic societies, involve elements of *ritual* (Goffman, 1967a, 1967b). These are not simply exchanges of social value (ultimately 'sacred' value); they actually create this value. In this sense they are *productive* activities, in which the parties cooperate to bring this value into being, before distributing it among them.

This is far more obvious in the ritual activities of hunter–gatherers than it is in modern, affluent societies. One of the more cryptic utterances of a group of islanders from Vanna in the South Pacific, who were brought to England for a visit and filmed for a television programme called *Meet the Natives* (Channel 4 TV, 2007), concerned their visit to a large disco in Manchester. While obviously enjoying the experience, they commented afterwards that 'your English custom-dance is not very *productive*'.

Of course, this might be taken to refer to 'primitive superstition' – the attempt to use ritual of various kinds to appease angry deities, to win wars with neighbouring tribes, to bring luck in hunting and so on. But anthropological evidence shows that ritual served other, very practical purposes. Dances and other rites mobilised the group for conflict and hunting in the sense that they strengthened bonds between members, thus enhancing the potency of the group, and reducing the vulnerability of individuals – this is still clearly the purpose of the *haka* performed by the New Zealand rugby team, and the various other warlike dances that precede matches by Fijian, Samoan and Tongan teams. Other rites served the purposes of peace-making, by including non-members in ritual giving and sharing.

Ritual group activity is also productive in the way that it seeks to instil values and qualities in members. A remote people of the upper Amazon, shown in the television programme *Tribe* (BBC2 TV, 2007), carry out ritual whippings of children by members dressed as animals, in order to give them courage and endurance. Within this tribe, children are never chastised as punishment for bad behaviour. Rites of passage in all societies similarly prescribe demanding, frightening or bizarre experiences as a way of testing the initiates, instilling the qualities needed for the next stage of life, and producing an appropriate new being for this stage by a process of rebirth.

These rituals have survived in the military services, in certain schools and colleges, and in some sports, in the individualistic, affluent societies. They represent markers of strongly group-oriented niches within such cultures. But they may well survive also in families and neighbourhoods in disguised or hidden forms. My grandfather's elder brothers persuaded the younger boys in the family to hold wasps and bees in their hands, in order to learn to bear pain and conquer fear. Two of them went on to play rugby for Ireland.

Whether in pairs or groups, the production and exchange of social value involves processes that are not well captured by the economic model. Commodities are used for symbolic as well as practical purposes, and take on qualities that defy description in material or scientific terms. This is all very obvious in the context of religion, politics, the arts and even the rituals of sexual relationships; but it can also be dimly perceived in discourses about financial markets – the symbolism of bulls, bears and dead-cat bounces.

I shall argue that this is because the Enlightenment project for modernity sought to exclude the symbolic value of interactions from the public sphere of economy, polity and international relations, as subversive of order and harmony. As the heir to this tradition, the economic model subsumes the production and distribution of the potentially volatile goods of interpersonal relations under the predictable metric of cost-benefit analysis by utility-maximising individuals.

The relevance of all this for explaining the Easterlin paradox is twofold. On the one hand, the creation and distribution of social value may help to explain why certain activities and exchanges are more enduringly satisfying than others, when they are reflectively evaluated, and why certain losses or missing elements in experiences are more enduringly damaging. If there is a social element in interactions that derives from the nature of relationships themselves (a 'ritual' or 'sacred' quality of some kind), and if the economic model fails to capture this element, then people living in societies whose dynamic is fuelled by the economic model may discount or be unaware of this dimension of the benefits and costs of their behaviours.

Why, for instance, is a ring given by one person we love of such enormous value to us, whereas the same ring, or a much more expensive one, would be of far less value if given by someone we do not love? Why is the respect of other people whose abilities we most admire, so much more valued than the lavish praise of those whose talents we do not rate? Why does it matter so much to belong to a fellowship of others with whom we identify, in bonds of strong loyalty and membership, but affect us little which of many superficially prestigious associations we can join?

In terms of the economic model, all these sources of value are simply preferences concerning positional goods. Only one person can be first in the desires of a lover, only a few can be honoured by the ablest intellectuals or musicians, and membership of closely bonded groups is necessarily limited to those who share certain affinities of blood, soil or faith. But in reducing these benefits, and the quality of their experience to preferences and utility, on a par with the flashiest car or the best seat in the theatre, the economic model may be missing some very important factors in the nature and consequences of the value they bestow. This is the issue that will be explored in this chapter.

Second, the feature of the Easterlin paradox that is most puzzling in terms of the economic model is why people do not learn from the discovery that their overall desires for a higher quality of life are only being satisfied to a limited extent by the pursuit of higher incomes and more extravagant material consumption, and why they do not recognise that they could gain more from closer emotional relationships, less but more satisfying work, and greater involvement in community life. The obvious explanation is that they are trapped in a kind of race for higher material gains and key positional advantages, from which as individuals they cannot escape, because it is related to institutional features of their social environment. Here again, the economic model can capture this feature in terms of a coordination problem, information imperfections and so on. But – given the dominance of the economic model – the suspicion is that these problems stem from the model itself, and require its radical modification to be rectified. This will be addressed in Chapter Eight.

Social sources of well-being

Up to now, much of the economic literature on well-being has focused on showing which features of individuals' lives are most influential on their assessments of their SWB. For those economists whose aim is to restore a modified version of utilitarianism at the heart of economic analysis, this is to demonstrate that specific and overall satisfactions can be reliably measured (that is, that cardinal versions of utility can be specified), and hence that interpersonal comparisons (and thus policy choices) are possible (Van Praag and Ferrer-i-Carbonell, 2004; Layard, 2005, 2006). For those who wish to claim that individual utility contains a social element, such as social capital, it provides a basis for their argument that interactions influence outcomes in terms of well-being and efficiency (Helliwell, 2006).

The first of these approaches investigates whether survey evidence of satisfactions in various domains yields consistent evidence, and whether these satisfactions are commensurable, and can yield an aggregate indication of satisfaction with life as a whole, with trade-offs between different domains (Van Praag and Ferrer-i-Carbonell, 2004, chapter 4).

This has led to the claim that we 'may deal with satisfactions as with other economic variables and that we may use them in econometric analysis in almost the same way as "objective" variables' (Van Praag and Ferrer-i-Carbonell, 2004, p 10). The implication of this is that it is ultimately possible to calculate monetary compensations for such losses in well-being as occur through illnesses and disabilities – for instance the cash equivalent of the 'quality adjusted life years' (QALYs) used in health economics (Van Praag and Ferrer-i-Carbonell, 2004, chapter 9). Ultimately, the methodology can be applied to political systems, climate, taxation policy, inequality and so on.

This approach acknowledges a large debt to psychological research and theory, for instance, to Kahneman et al (1997), and it calls for closer collaboration between economists and other social scientists. However, it defines the tasks for this collaboration in terms of the economic model.

> [T]he direct observation of utility functions opens a whole new area of research. In neoclassical theory the basic assumption is that individuals are in equilibrium. That is, they are in the situation that is optimal for them. However, if one is able to observe utility functions directly, then we can check whether the neoclassical marginalist assumption holds. If not, we can evaluate how far the individual is away from the situation of equilibrium, what is the utility loss associated with the disequilibrium, and what is the most efficient way to reduce the gap. (Van Praag and Ferrer-i-Carbonell, 2004, p 321)

Layard, too, recommends collaboration between social scientists (2005, p 145; 2006, p C32), but he moves straight from the statistical evidence on 'stalled well-being' in the affluent countries to a three-part explanation of the Easterlin paradox.

> First, a person's happiness is negatively affected by the incomes of others (a negative externality). Second, a person's happiness adapts quite rapidly to higher levels of income (a phenomenon of addiction). And third, our tastes are not given – the happiness we get from what we have is largely culturally determined. (Layard, 2006, p C24)

Layard notes that cross-national variance in rates of SWB can be explained largely in terms of divorce rates, unemployment levels, generalised trust, membership of associations, religious belief and quality of government, but his response to the Easterlin challenge deals with none of these directly. How, for instance, are we more negatively affected by the rise in others' incomes than by the success of their marriages or robustness of their religious faith? How do we become addicted to money and consumption in ways that reduce their utility, but not to relationships with others to similar effect? The explanation does nothing to clarify the positive and enduring aspects of social relations, or how they withstand the negative impact of rivalry, adaptation and consumer culture. (Layard's policy recommendations and strategies will be discussed in Chapter Nine.)

The second approach addresses these questions, but in very general and abstract ways, which fail to identify the processes at work. As we have seen in Chapters Four and Five, social capital theory, the correlation between frequent interactions in various types of social unit – such as family, kin, friendship networks and associations – and higher levels of SWB directs attention towards the satisfactions of these relationships (and the negative consequences of their absence or failure) without explaining what differentiates them from other types of experience, or why they seem to be undervalued by rational utility maximisers.

This is particularly evident when researchers report that *frequency* of such contacts raises SWB by a full point on a 10-point scale, and summarise the findings in the phrase 'The More We Get Together the Happier We'll Be' (Helliwell, 2006, p C38).

It is not necessary to be a psychologist or an anthropologist to recognise this as being almost as vacuous as any of the maxims that moved Voltaire's unfortunate *Candide*. Relationships, whether of exclusive passion or political mobilisation, are hazardous, because they demand forms of personal commitment that go beyond the rational allocation of resources, and they risk forms of failure that damage identity and social standing, as well as mere satisfaction of preferences.

In what follows in this chapter, I shall analyse the sources of well-being in social relations in terms of *intimacy*, *respect* and *belonging* (Jordan, 2006b). While the mechanisms at stake in all three have similar elements, intimacy is concerned with close physical and emotional relationships, and involves the generation and sharing of intense feelings (including love and hate). Respect comprises the recognition and regard that are produced and distributed in public life, including economic activity, the associational and the political sphere, and involves the civil interactions of the street, the workplace and the official agency. Belonging refers to the stronger feelings and bonds that are generated in teams, groups, communities and membership organisations, and which contribute directly to identity and security. In this sense, belonging is more closely related to intimacy, as a warm and emotional form of social value, than to respect, as a cooler, more formal type of social exchange.

These categories indicate forms of value, each of which involves complex codes for interactions, varying widely between societies and over time. The meanings and standards that apply to love and friendship (Bauman, 2003), to civility among citizens (Sennett, 2003) and to collective identity and membership (Taylor, 1989), shape the way that value is generated and distributed in social relations, and differentiated between spheres of activity.

One obvious difference between the social value derived from these sources and the material value of the physical economy is that negative value ('costs') are not simply the absence of, or loss of, positive value ('benefits'). To be hated by someone is not the same as to experience indifference from them; to be rejected from a closely bonded membership group is not simply to forfeit the benefits of belonging. Even respect, while it can in a sense be accumulated and lost incrementally, a bit like wealth, it turns into its opposite – humiliation – if one acts in a way that is totally inappropriate to one's status and reputation. To feel humiliated is not like being robbed of one's possessions (with or without insurance); it feels more like being irrevocably, permanently robbed of one's identity as a valued member of society (a kind of social exile).

To illustrate these features of social value, one may take the example of the intimacy associated with a love affair. Couples who fall passionately in love with each other do not 'exchange regard', even in the politest circles; the fascination for today's readers of the novels of Jane Austen is that she is able to convey the explosive chemistry of falling in love through the semi-formal conversations between her characters, often in public places. Love of this kind is not stored up, waiting for desire to trigger an occasion for its expenditure. It is a potential in people of which they are often only partially aware, and which requires some special and hard-to-specify qualities of another person to release. The consequent interaction of feelings and communications gives rise to certain almost tangible new entities (as recognisable in their effects as electricity or radio waves), and which are the products of these aspects of the relationship.

In this sense, communications between lovers have about them something of the qualities of poems or novels, whether these take the form of spoken words, letters or embraces; and like poems and novels they are open to several interpretations. Because each word or action is seen as such a potent source of value to the other, each misplaced glance or ill-chosen expression is also potentially destructive of value. The power of novels in particular to move us seems to lie in their ability to capture the type of ecstasy and agony that are characteristic of a passionate relationship. It would, of course, be possible to analyse the central love affairs of *Wuthering Heights*, *Madame Bovary* or *Anna Karenina* in terms of the gains and losses in utility available to their protagonists, but any literary critic who attempted to do this would be constructing some kind of parody of cost-benefit analysis, not a study of passion. Even those novels that rely for their dynamic on calculation and social climbing through sexual relations, such as *Fanny Hill* or *Vanity Fair*, succeed in gaining literary attention because their central characters are not quite able to pull off these forms of ruthless ambition and materialism.

Much the same kinds of volatility and hazardousness apply to the other sources of social value. Because a sense of belonging has historically been derived from common bonds of blood, soil and faith, and has provided the basis for military mobilisations against other groups, nations or empires, it has always been a highly combustible element in human societies. To use such bonds as a basis for political authority has historically involved disastrous conflict; but they have also supplied the fuel for resistance movements of heroic courage. Even in the economic model, ambivalent acknowledgement of the bonds of locality, faith and ethnicity as the principles for organisation (in schools and welfare agencies, for example) is part of a new orthodoxy that relates to the prominence of social capital theory.

Even the cooler value of respect can generate passion and conflict in some of its manifestations. One only has to substitute the term 'honour' to recognise how, in the premodern period, the code that demanded complex gradations of homage among monarchs, warlords and bishops led to the mass slaughter of wars, and the private combat of duelling. Equally, if we substitute 'celebrity', we can see in today's media how individuals are prepared to risk humiliation for a brief period in the limelight, and how either success or failure in competition for celebrity can cause the implosion of lives and careers. Finally, the links between respect and a murderous code of honour have been restored in some neighbourhoods and ethnic communities, where perceived 'disrespect', however slight, can lead to retaliation by knife or gun.

So there is nothing cosy or secure about the social value that can be traced to intimacy, respect and belonging. Indeed, the modernity that emerged with the Enlightenment (see pp 44, 133) was based on the deliberate attempt to substitute the production and exchange of economic value for these traditional systems of social value.

As A. O. Hirschman showed in his study *The Passions and the Interests: Arguments for Capitalism before its Triumph* (1977), philosophers like Locke, Montesquieu, Hume and Adam Smith sought to show that the milder and more peaceful vices – greed and covetousness – could supply a more reliable basis for the social order than the combustible passions of honour, pride and patriotism.

Indeed, they used Invisible Hand explanations of the kind examined on pp 67-8, 94-5 to explain how the social institutions of family living, female chastity and private property came into existence (Jordan, 2004, chapter 2), and how orderly government by consent under a political and social contract relied on such institutions to restrain the warlike passions. The economic model itself can be seen as the logical extension of the principles of individual sovereignty and interpersonal contract into the spheres of social relations and political authority. Economic value is installed as the source of all activity, and social value seen as a subset of this concept.

So, if we are to attempt to address the Easterlin paradox in terms of the factors identified by research on well-being, it is absurd to reduce the value of personal, associational and community relationships to the metrics and mechanisms of the material economy. That form of analysis can trace its origin to a political project for turning the excesses of power, mobilised in the cause of the patriotic, monarchical, religious and sexual passions. If today's sources of well-being are somehow derived from these same passions, and the interactions they inspire, we need to distinguish such processes from those concerning the production and exchange of commodities into which the economic model subsumes them. In the next chapter I shall examine how today's social institutions attempt to bring informal interactions under the regulation of a logic of economic exchange, and how this contributes to the Easterlin phenomenon.

The ritual nature of social value

Surprisingly little sociological research has focused on the nature of social value, its production and exchange. The work of anthropologists, and of the pioneering sociologists such as Garfinkel (1967) and Goffman (1967a, 1967b), has been carried forward mainly by 'qualitative research methods' (Silverman, 2005) – the approach to the analysis of research interviews which recognises that they are mutual constructions, or exercises in ritual collaboration (Jordan et al, 1994, chapter 1).

Goffman, whose researches had been mainly carried out on a small Scottish island and in mental hospitals, approached the topic of social value from the analysis of the 'glances, gestures, positionings, and verbal statements that people continuously feed into the [interpersonal] situation, whether intended or not' (Goffman, 1967a, p 1). Writing about interactions in affluent societies – but often in their less accessible niches – he analysed these in terms of the claiming, giving and saving of 'face'.

> The term *face* may be defined as the positive social value a person effectively claims for himself by the line others assume he has taken during a particular contact ... as when a person makes a good showing for his profession or religion by making a good showing for himself. (Goffman, 1967a, p 5; emphasis in original)

This might make interactions sound like competitions for social value among rivals, and of course they may be just this. But in many situations, indeed the vast majority, people help each other to make and sustain 'face'. What Goffman calls 'face-work' is not an individual activity but a collaborative endeavour, through which people create and share out social value in their interactions.

> The combined effect of the rule of self-respect and the rule of considerateness is that the person tends to conduct himself in an encounter so as to maintain both his own face and the face of the other participants.... This kind of mutual acceptance seems to be a basic structural feature of interaction, especially the interaction of face-to-face talk.... The mutual acceptance of lines has an important conservative effect upon encounters. Once a person initially presents a line, he and others tend to build their later responses on it, and in a sense he becomes stuck with it. (Goffman, 1967a, pp 11-12)

This cooperation in face-making or face-saving is not, of course, sustained in random ways. 'The line maintained by and for a person in contact with others tends to be of a legitimate institutionalised kind' (Goffman, 1967a, p 7). Goffman contends that this is 'conventionalised' and 'morally proper' within particular cultures and subcultures. It consists of a 'repertoire' of 'habitual and standardised' practices with a 'logically coherent framework' (Goffman, 1967a, p 13). This is what makes the value constructed by individuals part of the culture of a community, sustained within its institutions.

It also implies that this value comes from some source outside the individual, even if it eventually attaches to an individual person. When someone acts inappropriately, and loses face, they are required to re-establish themselves within the 'judgements of social worth' that are made under these codes. This he describes as re-establishing a satisfactory ritual state for them.

> I use the term *ritual* because I am dealing with acts through whose symbolic component the actor shows how worthy he is of respect or how worthy he feels others are of it.... One's face, then, is a sacred thing, and the expressive order required to sustain it is therefore a ritual one. (Goffman, 1967a, p 19; emphasis in original)

In relation to this ritual element in interaction, Goffman quotes the anthropologist Radcliffe-Brown:

> There exists a ritual relation whenever a society imposes on its members a certain attitude towards an object, which attitude involves some measure of respect expressed in a traditional mode of behaviour with reference to that object. (Radcliffe-Brown, 1952, p 123)

However, Goffman makes it clear that he is writing about modern Anglophone societies, and the 'objects' in question are people's selves – the sacred entities that derive ritual value from a society in which members' individuality is itself taken as the most holy totem, and the focus of moral rules. Concerning informal interactions, in which smaller salutations, compliments and apologies are 'status rituals', or 'interpersonal rituals', he writes that these contain a ritual element 'because this activity, however informal and secular, represents a way in which the individual must guard and design the symbolic implications of his acts while in the immediate presence of an object that has a special value for him' (that is, himself, and the other person) (Goffman, 1967b, p 57).

This use of the term 'ritual' may be confusing, because the notion of 'ritualised' activities has come in modern affluent societies to mean something like 'conventional', 'routinised' or even 'meaningless'. But the sense in which it is employed here implies almost the opposite – deeply meaningful, and symbolic of something beyond material worth. This notion of ritual activity is now confined, in our sort of society, to certain ceremonials, such as funerals, weddings and memorials for fallen service personnel or to the practices of certain sports elites and faith groups. As Mary Douglas (1970, pp 8-11) pointed out, ritual in this sense means that practitioners see nothing but meaning in these symbolic actions, and attach the greatest significance to their performance in the correct order.

But not all premodern tribes have rites involving symbolic goods or magical formulae. Peoples with loosely structured social groups and fluctuating physical and social boundaries have few such rituals; their religions concern states of mind, including trances and bodily dissociation (Turnbull, 1962, 1965). Accordingly, the Pygmies of the Congo rain forest find the solemn rituals of their Bantu neighbours ridiculous, and are reduced to giggling at the most sacred moments in their ceremonies (Douglas, 1970, p 15).

We would therefore expect that, in so far as ritual elements persist in the cultures of modern affluent societies, we might have difficulty in recognising many of them. We are confronted with (the absence of) sacred social value only when others fail to pay respect in the ways that we regard as due to us, or to the symbols we venerate. It was not fully acknowledged that Princes Diana was quite literally an icon before her death; and the indignation of a public, thrown into the deepest mourning, at the Queen's initial refusal to share in the rituals of this grief, indicated exactly the status of the occasion. The 'spontaneous' display of acres of flowers, notes and soft toys conveyed the sacred value of Diana for her public, whereas the Queen's adherence to the formalities of royal precedence seemed 'ritualised'.

Indeed, it is a mark of modern affluent societies that respect is demanded for the 'spontaneous' performance of individuality, and that the rules of interaction prescribe quite complex codes for when and how people can be ridiculed for such expressions of their 'inner' or 'true' selves, and when these should be acknowledged as deeply serious and meaningful. On certain kinds of occasions, poems and songs (however bad) must be listened to with reverence, because of the sincerity of the emotions that inform them. Even dancing must sometimes be recognised as the outward manifestation of an individual's true feelings. The islanders of Vanna were right to recognise the Manchester disco as a 'custom-dance' with some affinities to their own, even though they politely doubted its productivity.

So the ritual or sacred social value that is characteristic of interactions is deeply influential on behaviour and decisions, but in ways of which we, in affluent modern societies, are largely unaware. Instead, we experience it only through the joys and humiliations of our encounters with others, whether in business meetings or on binge-drinking nights. Because in our culture social value is seen as accruing to individuals, and largely through merit, it seems to be the product of a rational order of income and consumption within which such interactions occur, and of the projects of self-development that, under the individualistic requirements of our societies, we are realising.

The contribution of social theory

If social relations involve a whole dimension of the value of interactions that is inadequately analysed in the economic model, why has social theory and research been so reticent in its critique of that model, often adopting it for its own analyses? The answer seems to be that this critique has largely been directed at those features of modernity – the belief in science, progressive politics and human improvement through reason – that underpinned the social institutions of the post-war state, but much less at the economic model itself.

In the 1980s, the new orthodoxy in social theory took its cue from Lyotard's (1984) attack on the 'Grand Narratives' of the Enlightenment, whose claims to universality were challenged in the name of plurality, diversity and decentralisation. The 'postmodern turn' evoked contributions from many leading theorists, such as Habermas (1981), Foucault (1984), Bauman (1987) and Harvey (1989), about the potentially abusive impact of these privileged norms, whose discourses were mobilised to justify oppressive power. But few of these texts directly addressed the economic legacy of the Enlightenment philosophers' theories (liberty, contract, property, the Invisible Hand), or developed the insights of anthropologists into the social bases of economic life (Douglas, 1970).

This did not imply that postmodern social theory was unconcerned with symbolic value in social relations. On the contrary, in the hands of theorists such as Baudrillard (1983) it was primarily involved in the analysis of commodities as signs of social status. But this analysis focused on consumption as an expression of symbolic claims, rather than a deeper examination of the implications of the economic model.

So this critique of the Enlightenment foundations of modernity often fails to identify the dominant 'metanarrative' of that structure – that rules and institutions are to be justified according to their utility for individuals, with property in themselves and their material possessions. While sociologists like Giddens (1991, 1992) and Beck (1992) have theorised the new social relations of intimacy and risk, they have done so in terms of individuals ('selves') who realise themselves and develop their potential in markets, and through the accumulation of property. Far from challenging this order in the name of social value, they argue for a 'new politics' that transcends the economic categories of class and power (Beck, 1994; Giddens, 1994).

Indeed, these theorists have claimed that the new individualism of the 'late-modern age' (or the 'risk society') somehow transcends culture and convention, by adopting 'institutions which undercut traditional habits and customs' (Giddens, 1991, p 1). These link 'the most personal aspects of our experience' to new forms of open, negotiated and democratic relations (for instance, of intimacy in partnerships and families), which enable reflexivity and choice.

> The reflexive project of the self, which consists in the sustaining of coherent, yet continuously revised, biographical narratives, takes place in the context of multiple choice as filtered through abstract systems.... The more traditional life loses its hold ... the more individuals are forced to negotiate lifestyle choices among a diversity of options... [B]ecause of the 'openness' of social life today, the pluralization of contexts and diversity of 'authorities', lifestyle choice is increasingly important in the constitution of self–identity and daily activity. (Giddens, 1991, p 5)

This approach deals with the social value of intimacy as the medium through which 'sacred selves' of individualism realise their development, but it fails to connect such processes with the institutional contexts in which they occur. Indeed, it implies that the crucial transformation that has taken place since the 1970s is the escape from 'tradition' and 'convention' in social mores rather than the consolidation of individualism as the dominant cultural force in Anglophone societies. It fails to notice that these forms of individualism and intimacy also consolidate markets, property and capitalism as the economic institutions that are best adopted to these cultural forms, and the economic model as the most comprehensive way to analyse them.

Individualism as self–realisation through market choice and the negotiation of intimacy leads to a politics in which diversity and opportunity redefine equality and justice. For example:

> Equality must contribute to diversity not stand in its way....
> The cultivation of human potential should as far as possible
> replace 'after the event' redistribution....Active risk taking

is recognised as inherent in entrepreneurial activity, but the same applies to the labour force.... [S]uch risk taking is often beneficial both to the individual and to wider society. (Giddens, 1998, pp 100-8, 116)

As theorists such as Cruikshank (1994, 1996) and Rose (1996, 1999) have noted, Third Way governments have promoted 'self-responsibility' and 'self-improvement' as the replacements for the redistributive and sharing principles of welfare states. The individuals who cultivate these forms of intimacy through negotiation are encouraged to provide for themselves and each other through private pensions, insurances and investments, rather than to participate in collective, state-sponsored systems. These approaches to government harness the sacred value of individuals to themselves and the chosen others with whom they share their resources, to construct institutions that promote these forms of individualised value.

Social theory and research has only recently begun to balance such accounts with analyses of the erosion of such sources of social value as work satisfaction, quality and security, solidarity and friendship (Sennett, 1998, 2003, 2008; Pusey, 2003), or to trace this to the decay of public sector systems.

As part of the institutional transformation that has taken place in line with the economic model, the collective landscape has been reconfigured to consist of clusters of people with similar social and economic profiles (in terms of income, age, taste, and often also ethnicity), who have sorted themselves in homogeneous residential districts, associations, schools and clinics (Dorling and Thomas, 2003). Faced with these consequences, in terms of polarisation and inequality, social theorists have reverted to analyses in terms of social capital, which – as we have seen – do little to challenge the economic model.

The very term social *capital* denotes the spreading of an economic understanding of social relations beyond the sphere of material production and exchange. As Fine (2001, chapter 2) points out, it would be hard to imagine this term being adopted in anything other than a capitalist society, in which all resources of value, in terms of gains of utility, are seen as forms of capital.

Social theory has supplied a range of concepts in which social value can be analysed in far more powerful explanatory ways than the ones developed since the 'postmodern turn'. But these require a bolder approach to the economic model itself than many of the leading social theorists of recent years have been willing to adopt.

Conclusions

The celebrated economist, Vilfredo Pareto, opened his famous *Manuel d'économie politique* (1909) with the example of a 'well-bred man' who takes off his hat and makes polite gestures on entering a drawing room, 'because it is customary', but then goes to his office to buy a large consignment of grain, in order to make a profit. He called the first type of behaviour 'non-logical', and the second 'logical', because it involved reasoning from evidence. On my account, the first set of actions dealt in ritual social value, the second in economic value (utility).

In this chapter, I have argued that the generation and sharing of social value follows principles that are not adequately analysed in the economic model. Although they may be accounted for in terms of gains in utility, this is profoundly uninformative, since the model in which utility is installed as the metric of all value was designed by its originators as a *replacement* for social value (perceived as the product of passions, rites and rivalries, deriving from sex, kinship, blood, rank, faith and territory). The quest for utility, by individuals who accumulated property and contractual rights, not traditional status, honour or patriarchal authority, was supposed to allow liberty and consensual government. It was intended to reframe murderous hatreds over sexual access, racial supremacy, religious dogma, paternal authority and dynastic succession in terms of marriage contracts, legal claims, pay settlements, parliamentary votes and boundary treaties.

In other words, the daring philosophical innovations of the Enlightenment intentionally subsumed social value into economic value as the basis for a public order of prosperity, civility and welfare, rejecting any attempt to give priority to the volatile goods of earlier collective systems. This transformation was remarkably successful in increasing the welfare of populations during the following 200 years, although it faltered in the face of totalitarian regimes in the mid-20th century. It is arguably still successful in the newly industrialising countries, such as Brazil, China and India, where gains in economic welfare are on average accompanied by comparable increases in levels of subjective well-being (Frey and Stutzer, 2002; Layard, 2006).

The economic model is strictly neutral about the interactions that give rise to gains in utility, at least to those that fall within the law. It does not attempt to explain, for instance, why sex within a loving relationship might be more significant than sex with a stranger; why playing in an orchestra or a sports team might yield more fulfilment than accompanying a recording, or hitting a ball against a wall; or why a walk down a familiar street in which we are warmly acknowledged by others might be more emotionally satisfying than an exotic journey among indifferent strangers. It merely points out, quite accurately, that none of these generalisations is universally true – some individuals find sex with strangers more exciting, some prefer to exercise in private and some choose to travel anonymously; and many prefer these options at one time or another. According to the economic model, the world should be designed to accommodate this diversity of tastes, and markets, property, free movement and consensual collective units are best able to fulfil this requirement.

Yet the question raised by the Easterlin paradox is whether this success story is the whole story. Increasingly, it is clear that the very excesses that were associated with premodern codes of social value have not been completely tamed or eliminated from the margins of affluent societies. Young people engage in bloody feuds over status symbols and territory, especially in the UK and the US. Ethnic rioting and the destruction of property became the currency of political action in France in 2006. Terrorism in the name of religion has been defined as the greatest threat to security in the West, ironically in part because of the military attempts to install the economic model as the basis for the regimes in Iraq and Afghanistan.

But even more threatening to the claims of the model are the manifestations of irrationality and self-destructive choices among the populations of affluent states. In defiance of the assumptions of the model, very large groups of people eat to excess, damaging their own health and the prosperity of their societies. Binge drinking and regular alcohol consumption cause greater physical harm to a smaller proportion of the population; drug addiction is an ever more intensive and concentrated health hazard. Despite the claims made for reflexive and egalitarian relationships, separation and divorce cause measurable harm to the well-being of children and adults. Almost half of middle-aged UK citizens have not saved enough for a comfortable retirement.

Conversely, the rise of China and India as economic superpowers challenges individualistic assumptions, because these societies have combined rapid growth and expanding consumer markets with the preservation of many traditional family and cultural patterns. These phenomena demand an analysis of how systems of social value (crafts, communes and faiths) can continue to influence quality of life amid rising affluence. This issue is less one of how such practices can be consistent with liberal justice (Nussbaum, 2000) than how they are accommodated within market relations, and remain so little modified.

These social phenomena are not evenly distributed within or between societies. The variation in the propensities to criminality, addiction, obesity and divorce both in and among communities gave rise to the renewed interest in social factors, and the widespread adoption of social capital theory. But if such activities such as sex, eating, drinking, drug-taking and partying are responsive to a logic of social value, and if this is different from, and often in tension with, the logic of utility maximisation, then it demands a more comprehensive theoretical exposition, outside that model.

Above all, we need to be able to analyse how certain forms of activity and interaction transform ordinary human and material resources into ritually valuable goods, and how these in turn contribute to well-being. According to the economic model, the value derived from sex with a particular partner, or recognition from specific colleagues, or playing in a named musical ensemble, is a matter of taste, albeit taste that is influenced by social capital, in the sense defined by Becker (1996) (see pp 76-7). But the participants themselves would perceive these experiences differently, and attribute their value to qualitative aspects of their interactions, similar to the ones claimed by dancing or feasting tribespeople, or those who throw stones at Satan in Mecca.

These transformations of ordinary resources into ritually valuable ones (as in the transformation of bread and wine into the body and blood of Christ in Christian rites) do not occur spontaneously. They are produced through cultures and institutions that give these symbols and experiences meaning. This will be the subject of the next chapter.

EIGHT

Institutions and culture

In order to explain the Easterlin paradox in terms of social value, it is necessary to show how the interactions promoted by the economic model increase welfare but not well-being. This implies that people in affluent countries act in ways that overlook opportunities to improve their quality of life. Given that the economic model itself provides cultural resources and institutions for producing a certain kind of social value, how is this possible?

In the example given in the Introduction (pp 9-11) of the Israeli nursery (Gneezy and Rustichini, 2000), I argued that the installation of a financial penalty for parental lateness shifted interactions between the various parties from a social and moral mode of regulation to a calculative one. Instead of observing punctuality as a matter of consideration and respect for children and staff (giving rise to the creation and exchange of social value in interactions), parents could choose to pay the 'price' of lateness, if they had more advantageous ways to use some extra time. This allowed welfare (that is, some individuals' utility) to be increased, but could lead to a reduction in well-being (social value) among others.

The example is telling because it offers a microcosm of many of the reforms of the public services, and of the social infrastructure more generally, introduced by neoliberal regimes, especially in the Anglophone countries. But it poses questions about the nature of the coordinating conventions through which people sustain the order of families, schools, associations, faiths, communities and polities. If social and moral 'rules' coordinating times for collecting children could be so quickly subverted by this apparently minor change, and could not be recreated by its hasty abandonment, in what sense are these coordinating conventions 'institutions', and what role does culture have in sustaining them?

In the economic model, institutions become established because individuals find them advantageous; organisations and rules are chosen because they are 'efficient' in terms of minimising each person's external costs (Buchanan and Tullock, 1962, pp 43-6, 63-8). As we have seen, the Enlightenment accounts of the adoption of families (Hume, 1739, pp 483-95; Rousseau, 1754, pp 187-96), money (Locke, 1690, sections 37-43) and property (Hume, 1739, pp 571-3) explained them in terms of chance technological innovations with unforeseen positive consequences, undertaken by ignorant primitives. At the other end of the scale of rational foresight, present-day contract theory sees institutions as designed by principles (including governments) to provide good incentives for economic agents' performances (Laffont and Martimort, 2002, p 1; Stiglitz and Greenwald, 2003, pp 3-4; Bolton and Dewatripont, 2005, chapter 11). But both types of analysis use individual gains in utility as the consolidating factor.

From an anthropological perspective Mary Douglas argued that stable conventions require cultural legitimation, in the form of an analogy with nature, or some aspect of the culture's cosmology (Douglas, 1987, pp 46-7). In the case of the Israeli nursery, parents' widely observed rule of punctuality before the change might have been justified by reference to the nature of children's needs, and parents' duties towards them – the vulnerabilities of infancy, and the protective role of adults in the natural world. This might explain the persistence of punctuality among most parents, even after a larger minority of their colleagues defaulted on the standard, preferring to pay the financial penalty.

To understand how a contractual approach to institutions undermines the cultures through which social value is produced is largely beyond the economic model. For instance, Becker (1996, p 131) understands culture purely as tradition that stabilises 'obedience to institutions' – a habit of conformity. He admits that this explanation 'may seem to be an *ad hoc* trick invented to solve intractable commitment and collective choice problems'.

In the Enlightenment accounts, a more convincing analysis was possible, because the most important institutions of the social order were precontractual. Rousseau, for instance, insisted that the institutions that sustained equality in families and associations before the social contract were subverted by the new order of property, egoism and subjection.

> In a word, there arose rivalry and competition on the one hand, and conflicting interests on the other, together with a secret desire on both of profiting at the expense of others. All these evils were the first effects of property, and the inseparable attendants of growing inequality. (Rousseau, 1754, p 203)

Adam Smith's (1759) *Theory of Moral Sentiments* (see pp 42-3) was an attempt to supply a psychological explanation for the kinds of intimacy, empathy, respect and mutuality that underpin civil society, but are not susceptible to accounts in terms of rational self-interest. He postulated two main impulses: 'sympathy' or 'correspondence of sentiments', which led people to share each others' joys, and console each other for sorrows; and 'benevolence', which was naturally recognised as virtuous and good.

> It is the benevolent passions only which can exert themselves without any regard or attention to propriety, and yet retain something about them which is engaging. There is something pleasing even in mere instinctive good will which goes on to do good offices without once reflecting whether by this conduct it is the proper object either of blame or approbation. (Smith, 1759, p 36)

These tendencies were made parts of our psychological endowment by the 'wisdom of the Deity' (p 35). So, like others in his school of thought, Smith saw the (moral) value of interpersonal behaviour as different from material value as a source of well-being, as stemming from different innate drives, and as expressed in different social relations. Political institutions and other organised features of society should sustain good character and guard against vice (p 218).

In this chapter I shall examine the roles of contract and culture in the construction, maintenance and subversion of institutions, and the consequences of these processes for welfare and well-being.

Negotiating culture

The besetting problem for cultural analysis has been how to explain the social order without reducing individuals to automatons or dopes. The Enlightenment philosophers encountered a different version of the same dilemma when they relied on 'nature' or 'instinct' to account for certain features of cooperation in premodern societies, which persisted in commercial ones. They explained these in terms of 'conventions' (Hume) or 'institutions' (Smith), whereby, without any such intention, people adopted common ways of understanding each other that facilitated harmonious and predictable relations.

This approach was developed by Durkheim (1893, 1912) in his account of 'collective representations' or 'thought styles' – sets of ideas and classifications being taken as 'given' and unquestionable, with 'a special sort of moral necessity, which is to intellectual life what moral obligation is to the will' (Durkheim, 1912, p 30). He argued that in tribal societies, individuals internalise their social order and grant it sacred qualities, whereas in modern societies it is the individual who is regarded as sacred. In both, cognition – the social construction of the concepts through which we understand our lives – is the fundamental collective good through which social bonds are sustained.

Mary Douglas (1987) claimed that there was no inconsistency between maintaining that culture of this kind (rather than coercive power, selective incentives or sanctions) was the main factor in the explanation of the social order, and arguing that this same order was 'built continuously by a process of rational bargaining and negotiation' (Douglas, 1987, p 29). Within the categories given by a culture, concepts are constantly being interpreted and stretched to accommodate specific actions and interests, both in tribal and in modern societies.

> The individual cost-benefit analysis applies inexorably and enlighteningly to the smallest micro-exchanges, with them as well as us. [Anthropological evidence] destroys the case for extra-rational principles producing a community at some unspecified point of diminishing scale. It is when making threats and offers that individuals often invoke the power of fetishes, ghosts and witches to make good their claims. The resulting cosmology is not a separate set of social controls. In Durkheim's work the whole system of knowledge is seen to be a collective good that the community is jointly constructing. (Douglas, 1987, p 29)

So Douglas restated the puzzle addressed by Hume and Smith – how rational actors with individual expectations and aspirations create collective goods for agreed use among members. Religious symbols and beliefs are not an explanation here, but what has to be explained. Both science and religion are created by negotiations among individual thinkers, jointly producing a cultural resource that enables communicative cooperation.

Douglas argued that this process can be explained in terms of a 'functionalist formula' (Merton, 1949, pp 475-90; Elster, 1985, pp 28-9), since this production of a collective good is not planned, intended, noticed or consciously valued – in this sense it is more like the operation of the Invisible Hand in the Enlightenment tradition. The thought style survives because individuals see benefits of cooperation that are consistent with acceptable autonomy (that is, there is scope for negotiation). These features of cultural resources might be expected to be common to all societies and organisational spheres, even though the content of their cultures would vary enormously.

This view is consistent with the economic model of institutions in most respects. Institutions are there seen as ways of making routine decisions on behalf of individuals, thus saving transaction costs – as in large firms saving on the costs of accessing information (Williamson, 1975). They solve problems of bounded rationality as a limitation on individual rational choice (Simon, 1955), encapsulating past experience in their rules, as guides to future action (Schotter, 1981, p 139). Hence, they coordinate the actions of members, starting as rules of thumb and institutionalising reliable predictions.

However, such social arrangements can never give rise to binding forces for cooperation if they are perceived as merely 'conventional' or 'contrived', or the consequences of human manipulation. They must be derived from some feature of the 'natural', 'supernatural' or 'socially sacred' order, culturally recognised as a principle of legitimation. In tribal societies this may be drawn from an analogy with relationships between plants and animals, or parts of the body, or different roles of men and women. In the affluent world, it may appeal to credit ratings, a celebrity endorsement or viewers' votes in a television competition.

The point here is that these ideas and images construct a shared basis for claims both of social value *and* often also of access to material goods. Douglas (1987, p 51) pointed out that, in tribal societies descent from ancestors conferred identity and autonomy, but also property rights, and ancestors were discursively involved to justify inheritance claims. Ownership of economic resources was therefore conceived in terms of ideas derived from the social order, and as part of an understanding of social relations. In affluent societies, the sanctity of individuals confers social value on their choices and commodities they choose.

So cultures provide the meanings and symbols within which social value is negotiated and disputed. Because of the diversity of modern affluent societies, and the several organisational spheres within which coordination between individuals' actions is sustained, there is ample scope for competing claims to value, and several rival sources of legitimacy against which to test such claims. Archer (1996, p xvii) distinguishes between 'cultural system integration' (the logical relations between the different ideas that comprise a society's culture) and 'socio-cultural integration' (the relationships between the members of that culture). There is scope for innovation and change through both the contradictions and incoherences of the former, and the power relations of the latter. People can use ambiguities or absurdities in the cultural system to resist or overthrow the authority of individuals and groups in families, communities or organisations.

The dominance of the economic model in the political sphere has been greatly facilitated by its spreading influence in the other spheres that make up the cultural system. While the ideas, images and practices of the economic model were being imposed by neoliberal governments on the public sectors of the Anglophone societies, a set of discourses of individualism – of the rights of the self to the full realisation of personal potentials, and the claims of each to the resources for such development (Rose, 1996) – were mobilised in interpersonal relationships across society, and in all the other organisational spheres.

The logic of these rights and claims, by analogy with those of rational utility maximisers in markets, and of relationships, by analogy with those of contractual exchange, was able to subvert the cultural traditions derived from earlier family, kinship, workplace and civic relationships. For example, the innovations in intimacy in partnerships and parenting described by Giddens (1991, 1992) and Beck and Beck-Gernsheim (1995, 2002) use discursive resources from the model of the self-responsible economic agent, negotiating and choosing in markets, and contracting for services, in pursuit of a project for self-development. 'The self is seen as a reflexive project for which the individual is responsible.... We are, not what we are, but what we make of ourselves.... [W]hat the individual becomes is dependent on the reconstructive endeavours in which he or she engages' (Giddens, 1991, pp 75, 78).

These conceptions borrow fairly literally from the versions of customer identities purveyed by advertisements for cosmetics, plastic surgery, counselling and exercise regimes, as seen on television. People are told that they have a right and a duty to make their public selves into their best inner selves, 'because you're worth it'. Variations on these themes are then adopted in such spheres as education, training and memberships of associations, all seen as aspects of an overall project of self-development, in which sacred individual potentials are realised, and in whose name various claims on others are framed.

So even the intimacy of sexual experiences has, according to Bauman, been reinterpreted to fit consumption styles and projects of self-realisation.

> 'Purification' of sex allows sexual practice to adopt such advanced shopping/hiring patterns. 'Pure sex' is construed with some reliable money-back guarantee in view – and the partners in a 'purely sexual encounter' may feel secure, aware that 'no strings attached' compensates for the vexing frailty of their engagement. (Bauman, 2003, p 50)

Indeed, it seems clear that all interactions have been transformed to fit the model of serial choices among options, taken as the expression of inner desires, and summing together cumulatively as the manifestation of identities; and all relationships enduring over time as agreements to supply certain services to others engaged in projects of this kind. All other social arrangements are being adapted to suit this model in which social value is created and exchanged through market-like interactions or contract-like relationships. How can institutional transformations accommodate such shifts?

Institutions, change and value

In a complex culture, the discourses that structure the various spheres gain legitimacy by drawing on analogies and metaphors from each other, as well as from nature. A bureaucracy has its 'head' and its various 'branches', it 'reaches out' to the public and 'listens' to complaints. These terms from human or natural physiology give a kind of authenticity to what might otherwise seem an inanimate machinery for rational decisions. But conversely, people in informal interactions express their claims to regard and respect in terms of the validity of categories and classifications in science, technology and mass communications. Within organisations, managers and supervisors draw on a range of public discourses, from politics as well as industry, to justify their authority and the grounds for their decisions. They construct 'a machine for thinking and decision-making' in which 'an analogy matches a structure of authority' and 'the social pattern reinforces logical patterns' within the discourse (Douglas, 1987, p 65).

In some spheres, such as marketing and technology, innovation is built into the cultural system; but all old collective ideas are open to revision, and some are systematically rejected and forgotten (Douglas, 1987, chapters 6 and 7). Where there are strong mutual reinforcements between the categories of thought that apply to a number of organisational spheres, as in the compatibility of individualistic versions of identity and the economic model of public life, institutional thinking becomes invisible, because it is taken to reflect reality itself. For instance, the heads of organisations such as immigration control agencies and universities now un-self-consciously refer to them as 'businesses'. Douglas argued that this had begun during the period of neoliberal ascendancy.

> Since all social relations can be analysed as market transactions, the pervasiveness of the market successfully feeds us the

> convictions that we have escaped from the old non-market institutional controls into a dangerous, new liberty. When we also believe that we are the first generation uncontrolled by the idea of the sacred, and the first to come face to face with one another as real individuals, and that in consequence we are the first to achieve real self-consciousness, there is incontestably a collective representation ... [and] primitive solidarity based on a shared classification is not completely lost. (Douglas, 1987, p 99)

In other words, our claims to build lives of personal self-realisation out of reflexive choices within self-developmental projects (Giddens, 1991) are constructed out of ideas derived from the economic model, and limited by the prescriptions of its conceptual framework. It is within this collective representation of life's possibilities, and the culturally authorised ways of achieving them, that we make such naive statements as 'I have a right to do what I like', and come to believe that 'more is better'. We draw on the institutional thinking of the economic model as much for our ways of having sex, eating, drinking, raising a family and civility as for shopping or buying a house.

Indeed, what is striking about this culture and its institutions is not its capacity to sustain individual autonomy and negotiated social value – all human cultures are required to do this, or at least to provide options, such as exit to another group, which allow individuals to vote with their feet. It is the fact that it subjects all interactions to the same calculus of economic value, and the same criteria of welfare as utility maximisation (Becker, 1976, p 14). In so far as the economic model has been imposed as an ideological project of institutional transformation since the early 1980s, and has been adopted by individuals, especially in the Anglophone countries, this represents a remarkable feat of cultural imperialism.

Other cultures, even highly individualistic ones, have adopted institutions that address the hinterland between the individual and the group, between consumption and social value, between wealth and status, and between private and public. They have found ways, through institutionalised ideas and practices, of bringing the requirements of markets and private property into line with those of a sustainable social order.

For example, there are still many societies in which there are strict rules about which goods can be traded in markets. Goods with special ritual value, or which are considered to supply the basis for sharing among the group, cannot be exchanged in this way (see pp 117–18). Food, for instance, is not marketed in many societies, even though other kinds of commodities are (Sahlins, 1974, chapter 5). 'A particular social relation may constrain a given movement of goods, but a specific transaction – "by the same token" – suggests a particular social relation.…The bias is that of an economy in which food holds the commanding position' (Sahlins, 1974, pp 186–7).

But even in much more developed societies, where 'grid' differentiations (see p 40–1) still classify individuals by age, gender and occupational status, and rules govern the types of interactions allowed between these categories of members, there are prescriptions that enable trading and other commercial contacts, while still regulating much of the social order. In India, for example, a sophisticated modern economy in the cities co-exists with many grid-based prescriptions for family, kinship and community relationships.

Finally, even in 'low-group, low-grid' societies, in which individuals move easily between social units, and status is open and negotiable (Douglas, 1978, pp 193–7), there are institutions that balance the rivalry and uncertainty generated within interactions. Because social value is accumulated only through competition for contracts, and no gains in wealth and support are ever secure, social interactions are used to seal connections and try to command loyalty, however temporary. 'The large scale feast is a way of maximising the use of time in personal contacts. Ostentatious hospitality is a feature of Papuan, Kwakiutl, West African, modern industrial and any other low-grid ethnography' (Douglas, 1978, p 197).

So the question about well-being in all societies, whether their members gain social value predominantly through sharing in group activities, or through access to high-status circuits, or through individual endeavour within a competitive context, is how successfully institutions overcome potential conflicts, insecurities, exclusions and isolations, to allow the cooperative creation of intimacy, respect and the sense of belonging. Every society will experience various forms of coordination problem requiring institutional solutions. Every institution must, in turn, allow individuals to negotiate social value, within a framework that guides them towards the resolution of these problems (even though none can be completely successful in doing so).

Equally, every culture must give meanings to material objects, which allow them to enter into the creation and exchange of social value, and must incorporate production and trade into this interpretation of human interactions. What is specific to the economic model is its abstraction of such material processes from their social context, and conversely its interpretation of social processes within an economic analysis of welfare. How did it gain ascendancy, and what are the strengths and weaknesses of the model in achieving these purposes, given the wider context of affluent societies in the global economy?

In and between organisations

The institutional transformation undertaken in the name of the economic model was, as I have argued, neither a bottom-up cultural innovation (like Methodism, the Romantic Movement or Black Pride), nor a spontaneous shift in patterns of behaviour. It was a political form of collective action, but one that drew on cultural and behavioural changes in society, and enabled them to accelerate. It gained support through individual frustration with the failures of post-war institutions (welfare states) to achieve their stated purposes, including increased economic welfare for members.

What those organisational systems claimed to have accomplished was coordination between the spheres of industry, government and civil society, resolving the stalemates of the interwar period, and drawing members of all classes into the common status of citizenship (Marshall, 1950). This approach put government at the heart of the machinery for coordination, and relied on the assumption that capitalist firms could be tied into arrangements under which investment was planned, and labour organisations would reach agreements over distributional shares. It relegated voluntary organisations and families to largely subordinate, invisible, taken-for-granted roles in the social order, ensuring civil society participation and the basic socialisation of citizens respectively.

In retrospect, it is obvious that the tasks of governments within this model were too broad and difficult, given that they were territorially bounded, and unable to escape responsibility for such a diversity of functions and people. By contrast, capitalist firms, which were both much more specialised and more mobile, increasingly saw better opportunities through internationalisation of their productive operations, and fewer advantages in the arrangements under which they bound themselves to national plans. Eventually labour organisations, too, became disillusioned with agreements within which they felt more constrained than advantaged. Especially in the UK at the end of the 1970s, the institutions through which this organisational system was sustained broke down.

Meanwhile, individuals and households had been finding ways to use their mobility and fluidity to escape the restrictions of a government-led order. Using markets and property to access commercial facilities, and through strategic access to voluntary organisations (such as church schools), they gained competitive advantage, and thus such positional goods as university degrees and priority in healthcare, even within state systems (Jordan et al, 1994; Jordan, 1996).

Their strategies followed an economic logic that was well captured in the new political model, and defied the collective logic of social citizenship in welfare states. The neoliberal project aimed to dismantle the institutions of that order, by further enabling these self-interested strategies.

The questions never raised by those who inspired and led this transformation concerned the social purposes of organisations in general, or the institutions that guided individual actions in the spaces between them. Why, for example, had distinctive organisations developed for sports, cultural activities and education? What was the significance of different kinds of authority? Why were some whole areas of social life apparently not organised at all? The economic model abstracted two main types of organisation – markets and hierarchies – and addressed issues of efficiency mainly within these two categories.

Social theory, by contrast, had long been concerned with questions about the nature of organisations, and how they influenced actions. Going back to Weber (1922) they analysed how order and compliance were achieved, and predictable interactions sustained, in various kinds of organisational regimes, from religions to political parties, and distinguished between the types of authority deployed. The controlled performance of individuals, whether in bureaucracies, military forces or schools, relied on defining membership boundaries, roles and tasks, but used complex mixtures of sanctions, incentives and norms to achieve this standardisation (Etzioni, 1961; Perrow, 1986; Scott, 1987). So organisations were seen as imposing routine and 'seriality' (a patterned succession of interactions, repeated over time) on members and employers (Sartre, 1976; Giddens, 1984).

But this did less than justice to the ways in which organisations also enabled social value to be created by members, rather than simply controlling and constraining them. These other aspects have become clearer in retrospect since the economic model has been imposed across each sphere, making public services and voluntary agencies accountable to much the same logic of costs and benefits as commercial firms. For instance, the culture of academic life enabled a type of collegial cooperation and sharing that has been largely obliterated by the requirements of efficiency and productivity. In the UK, competition for position on league tables has increased research activity and published output, but at the expense of many nostalgically valued aspects of the old collective life.

The economic model promised to give individuals more sovereignty and autonomy, and to make organisations more responsive to their requirements, projects and purposes. The paradigms for this transformation became the consumer and the fee-paying affiliate, both of whom could set the standards they demanded for their money, and shift to another supplier if these were not met. Individuals were also taxpayers, and the best way they could get 'value for their money' in public services was if these were managed on commercial lines. Instead of bureaucrats and professionals seeking power and economic rents in these organisations, they were called to account by the same criteria as banks or supermarkets (Jordan with Jordan, 2000). So, instead of each kind of organisation having an ethos related to some esoteric purposes, all could respond to the same logic, and to individual members of the public.

In principle, this empowered individuals moving between organisations. Instead of being required to adapt to their cultural requirements, they could demand a more transparent version of the value they could expect to receive. In practice, it enabled a far more instrumental approach to organisational affiliation of all kinds, even membership of churches. In a more anonymous, mobile population, sorting themselves into self-selected groups, 'people shop around for places to go, even to worship' (Cox, 2002, p 338).

Indeed, the rise to prominence of social capital theory and research can be traced to a recognition that societies made up of such individuals, moving about in search of positional advantage and best value, was in danger of losing cohesion and common identity. Putnam's study of the US found that the creation of 'lifestyle enclaves', with homogeneous memberships, was damaging to associational life (Putnam, 2000, p 209). Suburbanisation in particular generated no issues to draw citizens into the public realm (Oliver, 1999, p 205). Indeed, Putnam (2000, p 214) concluded that 'sprawl has been especially toxic for bridging social capital'.

Conversely, the transformation of the collective landscape did resolve some of the problems that had beset governments. Having set themselves the task of coordinating between organisations under the post-war settlement, and made themselves responsible for the diverse vulnerabilities of their citizens, they had become unpopular and ineffective. The deals between organisations that they tried to broker had become messy compromises, which pleased no one (Ahrne, 1990, pp 99-100). State welfare agencies themselves gave rise to conflict, protest and frustration (Offe, 1984, p 148).

It proved more successful to make individuals responsible for their own risks and remedies, through an ideology of freedom, choice and self-fulfilment. This was extended and consolidated under the Third Way regimes of Clinton, Blair and Keating (Cruikshank, 1994; Rose, 1996; Jordan, 2004). The mainstream of citizens, instead of enduring the restraints of sharing in collective risk-pooling, were invited to discipline themselves, by accepting the rules of the marketplace, as a context for their projects of selfhood. In acknowledging that governments were too clumsy and flat-footed to meet the challenges of globalisation, or counter the strategies of capitalist firms, the new order gave individuals the freedom to choose their own paths through a collective landscape of opportunity and affluence, but to manage the risks themselves.

The illusion of autonomy

In the Anglophone countries since the early 1980s, the official collective representation of social life has featured individual choice as its central dynamic. But this implies that vulnerabilities, problems and failures are the consequences of such choices, for which individuals must also take responsibility. As rational maximisers of utility, under projects for personal self-development, they must make judgements about future risks and needs, as well as present ones, and negotiate over these with partners, kin and fellow members of whatever social units they care to subscribe to.

Theorists of late modernity (Giddens, 1991, 1994) or postmodernity (Harvey, 1989) see this as a new form of autonomy, transcending both the constraints of traditional social relations and the standardising logics of state-led, industrial, collective organisations. What this fails to recognise is the extent to which those same constraints also provided institutionalised meanings and practices, through which social value was created and shared, without the conscious effort of members. The very traditions and organisations that were overthrown in the name of freedom and choice were also sources of social value that were significant for well-being.

This applies across a range of issues in social life, as has been recognised in a number of recent studies. One whole group of these – saving for retirement, moderation in eating and drinking, prudence in driving, fidelity in sexual relationships – concerns the value placed on the future, as against the satisfaction of immediate desires. As Hume (1739, book iii, part 16, section vii) recognised, the tendency to prefer 'what is present to the distant and remote' is often a 'fatal error', and social institutions are designed to promote prudence, loyalty and solidarity, and control instant gratification.

The primary purpose of such institutions is to bind the individual to sacrifices of present pleasures for the sake of future security, health and quality of life. This is partly achieved through commitment in social relationships. The first element of this is a promise enforced by one's own self-discipline and mental rules (Ainslie, 1992, pp 133-5). Failure to keep these damages self-image and self-esteem. The second element is the mobilisation of others in interactions that remind one of commitments, and help keep one to them. Avner Offer (2006, p 49) calls this combination of strategies 'commitment technologies' or 'commitment devices', to avoid 'myopic choices', which are harmful to the individual in the longer term.

Here again, the emphasis of the analysis is on constraint, but Offer also recognises that social institutions are productive of well-being, because the cultures they sustain give *quality* to experience – as Ainslie (1992, p 296) put it, 'the main value of other people is to pace one's self reward', and thus help turn us from gluttons and debauchers into connoisseurs of the good life.

> Quite apart from their function, as 'enforcers' in self-control agreements, 'other people' help to pace social interaction, and also provide a source of surprise and novelty, which protects from habituation and keeps up arousal levels. That is also the function of literature and art, to amplify that variety, and generate unpredictability. In that sense, a good life might also be regarded as a creative 'work of art'. (Offer, A., 2006, p 57)

In Offer's account, the economic model's assumptions about an individual's capacities for rational choice in markets are challenged by affluence itself, the chief achievement of the model, and the goal of the Enlightenment theorists. Individuals are assumed to have a set of well-ordered preferences, knowledge of the alternatives, ability to put decisions into effect and capacity to follow a consistent strategy through the life cycle. But the unreliability of individual calculation means that they fall back on social conventions and institutions, which are 'the fabric of civilisation'. This recalls Douglas's account of social interactions and social value as efforts to bind others into one's consumption plans (see pp 113-14). Offer's emphasis is on self-control through commitment, and the interactive expertise this requires. It draws on our heritage of 'social and national cultures of institutions, law, governance and commerce'. In his interpretation of the evidence on issues like debt, obesity, drink and drug addictions, and (above all) rising rates of divorce, these processes have become fragile, and have lost much of their effectiveness.

> In competitive market societies, the flow of novelty and innovation undermines existing conventions, habits, and institutions of commitment. It reinforces a bias for the short term. To secure commitment, people accept a great deal of voluntary restraint and even compulsion. A large trend of the twentieth century has been the growth of active government and regulation. Incrementally, voters have narrowed their own freedom of choice and surrendered control of their futures to social agencies.... Government is the commitment agent of last resort, and frequently of first resort also. (Offer, A., 2006, p 358)

Offer argues that the market, through advertising and use of the physical environment of commerce (for instance, the design of supermarkets), has undermined both rationality and commitment. The practices that supported various kinds of conventional restraints, such as family meals, have been abandoned, leaving individuals to improvise their own regimes. Television and cars further eroded both family and associational patterns of interaction. Positional competition and status inequalities damaged post-war solidarities, and the labour market shifts increased working time, by women especially, at the expense of family and other relationships. Offer explains the Easterlin paradox in terms of these factors, reaching the general conclusion that 'the capacity for self-control declines with societal affluence over time, even as it rises with individual affluence at any given point in time' (Offer, A., 2006, p 364).

This emphasis on technologies for restraint as the main beneficial products of social interactions is, I would argue, only a part of the story. Offer acknowledges that he has focused on individuals

> and how their well-being is affected by choices made in the market and at home. There is another dimension which consists of the agencies and agents empowered to manage well-being. The dimension of social choice, in governance and the public domain, is part of the same

agenda, although it is largely left out of this volume. (Offer, A., 2006, p 363)

Offer's methodology is individualist, so although he is highly critical of the effects of adopting the assumptions of the economic model, he does not reject its basic premises about utility maximisation. The approach that I have adopted sees cultures and institutions as productive of something far more fundamental than 'commitment technologies' or 'laundered preferences'. It argues that individuals and their projects gain value only within socially constructed contexts, through interactions that have ritual meaning.

For example, labour markets provide the organised settings for individuals to develop their projects for contributing to society's work effort, and for identifying the distinctive value of their individual contributions. Although men tend to develop 'careers' in organisations more conventionally than women (Jordan et al, 1994, chapters 2 and 7), and hence to rely more on status-based exchanges for the value they accumulate, even the more personal developmental accounts of employment choices given by women deal in the opportunities for learning and contributing through interactions with colleagues and the public. Employment is an institution through which identities and capacities, experienced as individual and chosen, are enabled by organisational structures for the creation and distribution of social value.

This is why the fragmentation and casualisation of labour markets has important implications for well-being. If the organisational structures for the development of careers, the valuing of experience, and the appreciation of quality rather than instrumental competence, are sacrificed in the name of flexibility and adaptability, individuals are denied the contexts for meaningful employment planning (Haagh, 2007). Work becomes a means of gaining income, but its significance and satisfaction is reduced along with the security to perceive it as a site for individual and collective projects of social value.

This is an example of how institutions do more than restrain impulsive, short-term behaviour. They also shape the rewards and opportunities for people to develop their abilities, and to give a wider social significance to their aspirations. Institutions allow collective interpretations of the value of work, leisure, politics, relationships and care to be formed, and individual identities and lifecourses to be planned and revised within the frameworks supplied by cultures.

All these institutional factors help explain the Easterlin paradox, because individuals largely accept the responsibility to 'make something of themselves' within the settings that have been transformed by economic restructuring, but find it increasingly difficult to do so, as a result of fragmentation, insecurity and the conflicting demands from the different spheres of their lives (Lane, 2000; Frank, 2005). For example, Michael Pusey, in his study of *The Experience of Middle Australia: The Dark Side of Economic Reform* (2003) found that most mainstream citizens were highly critical of the transformation of the 'lucky country' from an egalitarian to a pyramid pattern (with more poor people at the base) and of its consequences for solidarity and mutual support. They saw gender equality as a gain, but thought that the negotiation of decisions about work and family required 'the necessary institutional support, directly from the state, from employers – or indirectly through a more firmly regulated market? – [which] should provide them with the legal and economic resources to do so' (Pusey, 2003, p 89).

There were clearly winners and losers from the Australian transformation; graduates and people with skills in 'symbolic analysis' were still able to realise personal projects within these structures, but others wanted to return to a 'fair do' society, and were nostalgic about a 'golden age' of greater civic engagement, and when government was more proactive in shaping social relations (Pusey, 2003, pp 100-20). As in all the Anglophone countries, working-class employment, its cultures and institutions, have been the main casualties, leaving individuals with fewer skills exposed and insecure in the face of restructuring.

So the economic model, while encouraging the individualistic pursuit of self-realisation through work and consumption, undermines the cultures and institutions through which individuals can win esteem, status, security and a set of reliable social interactions, conducive for well-being. This is the challenge for public policy that will be addressed in Part Three of this book.

Conclusions

The economic model does not deny the importance of institutions. Indeed, it argues that, 'How to design institutions that provide good incentives for economic agents has become a central question of economics' (Laffont and Martimort, 2002, p 1). However, its individualistic methodology means that this issue is reduced to an analysis of how to write contracts for those with particular responsibilities – such as central bankers (Walsh, 1995) – or arrangements for specific situations, such as asymmetric information (Stiglitz and Greenwald, 2003, pp 3-4) or incompleteness of contracts (Bolton and Dewatripont, 2005, chapter 11).

I have argued that institutions supply meanings within which the pursuit of social value becomes attractive and feasible. They provide the contexts for commitments to long-term relationships, careers, movements and causes. They give coherence and stability to the groups and associations through which cultures are reproduced and transformed. In other words, they supply the collective frameworks that allow social value to be reliably produced and distributed among members of a community.

Where a problem such as the Easterlin paradox arises, it indicates that institutions for maximising welfare are at odds with those for promoting well-being. Douglas argues that most fundamental conflicts concern institutional modes of understanding and responding to the world – in this case, those based on individual utility and social value. 'Only changing institutions can help. We should address them, not individuals, and address them continuously, not only in crises' (Douglas, 1987, p 126).

Individualism and choice as central motifs of cultures and institutions are not unique to present-day affluent societies, nor are they necessarily inconsistent with the production and exchange of the social value on which well-being seems to depend. But such societies need mechanisms and processes through which individuals can gain the intimacy, respect and sense of belonging through which their projects of self-realisation are validated and made meaningful. The economic model, which sees choice and contract as the fundamental mechanisms of social exchange, directs attention away from the features of cultures and institutions that might supply these needs in an individualistic society. It also induces rivalries and insecurities that undermine potentially socially valuable interactions, and generates stigmas, isolations and exclusions that inhibit such interactions.

The gains from individualism come from tolerance of difference, even of deviance, and the creation of enclaves for original thinking and experiment. The losses stem from uncertainty, and the requirement on individuals to create their own meanings, interpretations and identities. Innovation, through the creation of new media and new standards, is always one option, but it is open only to the most original and gifted. Rewards for success in achieving such changes are enormous, but the risks are high. In an ever-shifting cultural context, celebrity and obscurity are sometimes close neighbours, and the most ambitious are likely to experience both, often in quick succession. For most people, who are neither famous nor notorious, the predominant feeling is of marginality – of not ever being quite where the action is.

> If there were any poignant thing which individuals would
> have shared in common, it could be a sense of being fringy.
> Since in this cultural type there is no centre, each individual
> is the centre to his own world, each knows what it is to be
> peripheral to whatever else is going on. The Rosencrantz-
> and-Guildenstern feeling fosters reluctance to define norms
> sharply, even if the intellectual tools for doing so were at
> hand. (Douglas, 1978, p 195)

In this social environment, although some individuals make rash and desperate bids for recognition and fortune, many simply make minor miscalculations about how to achieve their purposes, and are then discouraged; they 'infer from early failures an unwarranted and disabling incompetence' (Lane, 2000, p 9). Above all, there are few cues from the institutions prescribed by the economic model to point people towards relationships of support, mutuality, loyalty and solidarity for the social value to sustain well-being.

All this puts an enormous strain on our closest relationships, because the individualist ethic places responsibility on everyone to realise their full potential, and gives them a right to claim the resources for that project from those chosen others mobilised to cooperate in that quest. Despite the claims of Giddens (1991, 1992) and others about the advantages of 'negotiated and democratic' intimacy between equals, the individualistic ethic raises expectations in partnerships, where the other is the main resource for personal self-development.

In a wide-ranging review of survey evidence, using responses from thousands of men and women born in the post-war UK, Ferri and Smith (2003, p 110, table 4.1) found that, among married couples in their early thirties, born in 1946, only 2% of men and 4% of women said they were dissatisfied with their spouse. Among those born in 1970, 22% of men and 26% of women were dissatisfied. Dissatisfaction among cohabiting couples increased almost as markedly. This steep rise suggests that, given the importance of close relationships for overall well-being (Myers, 1999; Helliwell, 2003), a huge strain is being placed on these relationships under the collective arrangements sponsored by the economic model.

But the institutional transformations of the 1980s to the present have equally influenced associational life, making it far less likely that those outside the mainstream of the economy participate in organisations. Whereas the middle-aged, property-owning citizen in the UK is as involved in some such activities as their parents were in the 1960s and

1970s, the same is not true of poor people and members of excluded minorities.

As part of the same comparison of survey evidence, Bynner and Parsons (2003, p 266, table 10.19) found that among male respondents in social class V (unskilled manual workers) born in 1946, 37% were members of trades unions (compared with 43% of the whole male sample from that cohort) at age 26. Among those born in 1970, and surveyed at age 30, only 6% of social class V men were members of unions, compared with 17% overall. Conversely, among social class V men born in 1958 (the 1946 figures were not available), 13% had at some time been arrested; among those born in 1970, 47% had been arrested (Bynner and Parsons, 2003, p 290, figure 10.9).

In other words, among the poorest men in young adulthood in the welfare state era, trades union membership was almost three times as prevalent as the experience of arrest, but after the economic restructuring of the final two decades of the 20th century, arrest was almost eight times as likely as trades union membership. Decline in organisational participation among poor men was at a similar rate.

All this suggests that the social sources of well-being, through close and associational interactions, were better sustained in the semi-collectivist regimes of the post-war era than after the transformations achieved in the name of the economic model. Whatever the advantages of individualism, it requires cultures and institutions that sustain social value, just as high-group and high-grid societies do. What can public policy do to influence such issues?

Part Three
Public policy

NINE

Welfare economics and public policy: 'sputtering out'

The Easterlin paradox stems from a growing gap between the economic welfare accumulated by individuals and their overall satisfaction with the quality of their lives. In liberal democracies, government policies should be responsive to the views of individual voters, so the experience that additional work effort and income for the average citizen does not produce increased well-being should lead to political debate and policy change. How does the analysis of well-being in terms of social value relate to debates about such political principles as justice, equality and liberty? How might political forces around the notion of social value express themselves, and towards what kind of programme?

There is nothing very new about the idea of a political struggle between economic and social value, and hence between welfare and well-being. In the intellectual history of modernity, some such antinomy has constantly been framed as an underlying motif of political contest, as my reference to Ruskin (1860) (p 37) indicated. Yet (apart from those periods in which totalitarian versions of socialism, fascism and religion have controlled the ruling apparatus of modern states) this has been a catchweight contest. Whereas the logic of markets and capitalism has been all-encompassing and relentless, the attempt to protect social value has been fragmented, reactive, incoherent and largely localised, drawing on many different ideas and organising principles. It has seldom been able to develop coherent principles or put together a programme of policies around which political forces could unite, or draft a set of measures capable of withstanding the progress of economic rationality.

This was the underlying story of Karl Polanyi's (1944) *The Great Transformation*, in which a set of diverse interests, from landed aristocracy and the church to crafts, guilds and corporations, resisted the 'Utopian project' of creating a global, self-regulating market economy. This largely disorganised 'movement' of historically antagonistic forces came together at various moments to protect the 'human and natural substance of society' from the assaults of the capitalist juggernaut – a process captured in its British form in the novels of Dickens, George Eliot and Mrs Gaskell. Many of the elements in this shifting alliance were backward-looking and reactionary, yet they served to delay, and sometimes to divert, the march of 'creative destruction'.

> [L]ogically enough, the first groups to oppose the unlimited play of economic rationality were the aristocracy and landowners. As Karl Polanyi has shown, there was a 'Tory socialism' well before the birth of working-class socialism. Indeed, Polanyi defines socialism as the *subordination of the economy to society* and of economic goals to the societal goals which accompany them and assign them to their subordinate place as a means to an end. Economic activity must be put to the service of ends which go beyond it and which establish its usefulness, its meaning. Thus there may be a 'Tory socialism' endeavouring to restrain economic activity so that it neither abolishes pre-capitalist social bonds in the countryside, destroys social cohesion, causes the decline of agriculture, makes towns uninhabitable, or air unbreathable, and so on, nor gives rise to a wretched proletarian mass, reduced to beggary, theft, prostitution, 'ducking and diving', and the like. (Gorz, 1989, p 130; emphasis in original)

The point about this often inarticulate, and seldom coherent, set of ideas, embracing Robert Owen, Cardinal Newman and Benjamin Disraeli, was that it recognised social value as derived from collective relationships – from cultures and traditions, which in turn relied on institutions. Whether individual autonomy was accountable to religion, patriotism or class solidarity, it was subject to moral principles and social standards derived from collective sources. So the right to maximise utility, and the programme for maximising aggregate welfare, were balanced by the power of these forces.

> While on the one hand markets spread all over the face of the globe and the amount of goods involved grew to unbelievable proportions, on the other hand a network of measures and policies was integrated into powerful institutions designed to check the market relative to labour, land and money. (Polanyi, 1944, p 72)

The problem was that the principles behind these forms of social protection were inevitably drawn from local and particular cultural traditions, which could not be stated as universal rules. This made them vulnerable to processes of economic and social change, in which well-motivated attempts to protect certain features of social relations or ways of life became ossified, and ultimately self-defeating (or worse). Polanyi gave the examples of the Stuart kings' social policies (fatally compromised with authoritarian paternalism) and the Speenhamland system of poor relief (which became a form of forced labour that tied workers to the land, when better opportunities were available in the cities).

Within these traditions, ringing denunciations of the barbarities perpetrated in the name of utility (as by Oastler, Sadler, Carlyle or Disraeli himself) have seldom given rise to clear definitions of the nature and origins of social value, or the principles by which it could best be defended and enhanced. As we have seen from the work of Ruskin, one approach has been to try to link social value to the value of life itself, in its collective form, and hence to ideas of a sustainable set of practices for quality of life. For instance, there is something almost Ruskinian about an equally outraged diatribe against global capitalism, written at the turn of the present century.

> A functioning life economy consciously selects *for* life goods, rather than against them. At the most basic, it selects for *life capital – means of life that produce more means of life*.... [A]ll life is a process, and this process always follows the pattern of life sequencing of *life > means of life* (e.g. child > food, care and housing > healthy and developing child). *Life capital*, in turn, is like any capital, wealth that can create more wealth – with the wealth in question as *life capabilities and their enjoyments in the individual, the bio-regional or the planetary form*.... *Life capital* can then be defined as the *generic and non-consumed bearer of the means of life in an economy's overall sequence of value through generations*, (McMurtry, 2002, pp 139-40; emphasis in original)

This sounds like a universalisable statement about the nature of value, but it lacks convincing contextualisation. It could be applied very differently in any number of situations of economic development around the world. What it aims to do is to link social protection with environmental conservation, which is unquestionably a response to a specific crisis of global capitalism – but its interpretation would vary widely between regions or even districts of the globe.

This illustrates the challenge facing an attempt to introduce social value, and hence well-being, into public policy decisions. Any measures that are contingent on current contexts are, like those of Stuart kings,

Speenhamland magistrates or welfare state administrators, vulnerable to processes of decay. They can suddenly become open to valid criticism in the name of the individual liberty and the possibilities of gains in economic welfare that they inhibit. As yet, no convincing replacement for welfare states has emerged – partly, according to Gorz (1989), because it was never a comprehensive challenge to liberal capitalism.

> Social-democratic policy has never, in fact, been the sort of socialism defined by Karl Polanyi: it does its utmost to create *enclaves* in the heart of economic rationality but without in any way limiting its domination over society. These enclaves, on the contrary, were themselves dependent on the good working of capitalism and intended to promote it. (Gorz, 1989, p 131; emphasis in original)

This part of the book examines how the analysis of well-being in terms of social value relates to the various challenges to welfarism introduced in Chapter One. It considers whether the attempt to make economic development accountable to social ends, understood in terms of collective cultural standards and processes, can be framed in terms of principles of justice, equality and liberty, and contested within liberal political institutions. In this chapter, I address the relationship between normative challenges to welfarism and the economic approach to public policy – welfare economics.

Welfare economics and its challengers

The main philosophical challenges to the dominance of welfarism in political thought and public policy have sought constitutional principles that are not derived from individual preferences. For instance, Nussbaum (2000, p 5) argues for normative standards 'that should be respected and implemented by governments of all nations, as a bare minimum of what respect for human dignity requires'. Her principles are not drawn from preferences, but from the 'central capabilities' that are fundamental for quality of life.

Those who defend variants of welfarism as a basis for public policy concede many points to their critics, but adopt a number of strategies to retain individual preferences and utility gains at the core of government decisions. Some allow that moral principles other than those derived from preferences should be enshrined in legal and political institutions, but still see welfare as the main criterion for substantive policies (Posner, 1995). Others seek to transform actual preferences into more moral and rational ones, in order to make them more reliable guides for governance (Brandt, 1979; Elster, 1982).

The point here is that both challengers and defenders of welfarism regard culture as part of the problem, rather than part of the solution to their theoretical endeavours. Nussbaum, Sen and Pateman, for example, seek normative principles that will command universal consensus, but also allow cultural diversity. But these principles are not drawn from cultures, any more than they are drawn from preferences; 'most cultures have exhibited considerable intolerance of diversity over the ages' (Nussbaum, 2000, p 49).

Like their critics, welfarists encounter theoretical difficulties with the 'adaptive preferences' that stem from cultures – for instance, women who accept various forms of subordination or abuse. They treat such phenomena as part of the problem of rationality and justice in social choices derived from preferences, which may be based on inadequate information or relational constraint. Modifications in welfarism have often focused on ways to improve or discount preferences that are unenlightened (Harsanyi, 1982), or require cognitive psychotherapy (Brandt, 1979), or reveal a lack of autonomy (Elster, 1982).

Neither the principled challengers to welfarism, nor the attempt to modify it in pragmatic ways, have achieved significant shifts in the application of economic analysis to public policy. The reasons for this lie in the evolution of welfare economics and its adoption by governments.

As we saw in the Introduction and Chapter One, the basis on which government was supposed to make decisions about welfare was poorly and inconsistently defined in the literature of public finance and public policy, from the start of the 20th century (pp 56-7). Welfare economics was concerned with normative questions – 'not to describe how the economy works but to assess how well it works' (Begg et al, 1997, p 240). This involved both efficiency and equity, and how they were reconciled. Equity, in turn, implied both that identical people were treated identically (horizontal equity or neutrality), and that different people were treated differently, to take account of any consequences of this variation (vertical equity).

However, looming over these questions was the all-powerful principle of optimal resource allocation – Pareto efficiency – that for a given set of consumer tastes, resources and technology, it is impossible to move to another allocation that would make some people better-off and nobody worse-off. The General Welfare Theorem, formalising Adam Smith's Invisible Hand, is the cornerstone of welfare economics. If every market in an economy is a perfectly competitive free market, the resulting equilibrium throughout the economy will be Pareto efficient because the independent actions of producers, setting marginal benefits equal to price, ensure that the marginal costs of producing a good just equals its marginal benefit to consumers.

Under the assumptions behind the use of the Pareto criterion, therefore, since different Pareto-efficient allocations correspond to different initial distributions of resources with income-earning potentials, government might concern itself only with the equitable distribution of these endowments, and leave markets to allocate the resources thus efficiently redistributed. The outcome would then be sure to be somewhere on the Pareto frontier.

But as we have seen (pp 78-9), if there are various kinds of distortions – coordination problems, including imperfect markets, externalities leading to divergence between private and social costs and benefits, and market failures through incomplete information, for example – then society's marginal cost of producing a good does not equal its marginal benefit from consuming that good. The result is that government must then seek the 'second best'. Rather than simply acting to cause a different distortion, in an attempt to compensate for these ones, it should try to use its powers, such as taxation and regulation, to spread distortions and balance across the economy as a whole.

We have also seen that interest in social capital has focused on its ability to improve efficiency in second-best situations of this kind (pp 78, 82). It was obviously attractive for market-minded economists such as Becker (1996) to have evidence that informal social interactions, rather than government interventions, could contribute to reducing the effects of such distortions. In this way, social considerations could be introduced into the theory of welfare allocations, just as psychic or social value could be incorporated into individual utility.

Yet none of this gives substance or purchase to any clear normative principles concerning policy decisions. On the contrary, it provides a rationale for such principles to be subordinated to a model in which markets are the fundamental mechanism, unless strong reasons can be given for 'distorting' them through interventions. Given the wealth of philosophical and economic exploration of the issues of justice, equality and well-being throughout the 20th century, how did these have so little influence on public policy by the end of the millennium?

'Weak welfarism'

The central moral intuition of welfarism is that individuals must have an active commitment to any standards or actions claimed to make their lives good *for them*. As Dworkin (1990, p 77) puts it, 'my life cannot be better for me in virtue of some feature or component that I think has no value'. This rules out versions of the good life derived from 'objective' sources (Finnis, 1980; Griffin, 1986; Qizilbash, 1998; Nussbaum, 2000, 2005), or universal human needs (Doyal and Gough, 1991), or even collective goods such as language, culture and morality (Sher, 1997). It installs individual moral sovereignty as paramount, and rejects as 'perfectionist' any substantive version of the good society (Van Parijs, 1995, p 28).

However, most welfarists allow that governments should adopt deontological prohibitions on actions that may increase overall welfare, but are repugnant to ordinary moral intuitions, such as executing an innocent suspect to quell a riot, or telling lies to save suffering (Kagan, 1989; Thomson, 1990; Brand-Ballard, 2004). The question is therefore whether such principles can be made consistent with a policy regime that gives priority to individual preferences, and hence deploys the basic instruments of the economic approach, such as cost-benefit analysis. Adler and Posner (2006) argue for a version of 'weak welfarism', which retains a modified Pareto standard.

The pure Pareto principle is not, in fact, a very serviceable instrument for policy decisions. It states that, if a regulation or project makes one person better-off, according to their actual preferences, and no one worse-off, then this action is socially desirable. But the Pareto standard cannot be used to justify most government interventions, or to reject them. Nearly all proposals make at least one person worse-off, and the Pareto principle's requirement to identify such people, to measure their losses of utility and to give compensations would be immensely expensive to implement (Adler and Posner, 2006, p 20). The test is too strong for real-world decisions.

The main alternative to the Pareto criterion to be generated within economics was the Kaldor-Hicks test of hypothetical compensation – whether those who gained from a government intervention could in principle compensate the losers and have something left for themselves. But this solution was rejected by many welfare economists (Graaff, 1957, pp 169-71) as generating paradoxes, intransitivities and other problems. Within economics, other solutions were also rejected (Chipman and Moore, 1978, pp 547-8; Dasgupta and Pearce, 1972). Adler and Posner (2006, p 11) go so far as to say that 'welfare economics itself has sputtered out'.

For the evaluation of specific policy measures, Adler and Posner's version of 'weak welfarism' is required to 'launder' preferences, in order to cleanse them of 'non-ideal' elements (Adler and Posner, 2006, pp 35-6) – see pp 231-2 – and also those that are drawn from general moral principles, but in no way self-interested (Broome, 1978, pp 91-5). The aim of these moves is to end up with a version in which preferences are restricted in ways that give rise to a plausible basis for welfare (or well-being, which they treat as synonymous).

This is intended to overcome problems that would otherwise be difficult for the economic model as a basis for public policy. Economists are obviously concerned about normative criteria that might seem to challenge the fundamentals of their model, for instance by failing to justify exchanges through which gains in utility are achieved. They are keen that the standards applied to government decisions should endorse the Pareto principle: 'Among serious scholars of morality it is far and away the most widely accepted moral axiom. Virtually all welfare economists and, many, probably most, moral philosophers endorse it' (Adler and Posner, 2006, p 55).

The urgency with which this is asserted indicates how important it is for the economic model to uphold the Pareto criterion; without it the whole edifice of its analysis, and of the labours of liberal materialists since the Enlightenment, come into question. Economic welfare

> exerts a moral tug on us, independent of moral rights, distributive considerations, or other moral factors. Why? The crucial point, here, is that the Pareto principle applies *even where the benefited person(s) is/are already well off, and have no moral rights against those who can improve their welfare*. (Adler and Posner, 2006, p 55; emphasis in original)

In support of this, it is argued that – without claims from individual and overall welfare – all kinds of moral and political choices would defy our deepest intuitions. Pure egalitarianism, without the balancing pull of a form of welfarism, would require us to 'level down' to Pareto inferior outcomes, in order to make the rich worse-off. Pure rights-based theory would not require us to try to rescue a person in extreme jeopardy, unless they had a specific moral claim on us (Kagan, 1989, pp 16-17). Finally, without the Pareto principle, there could be no moral reason for me to give someone an otherwise worthless object that happens to be a cure for his painful illness if he was rich and comfortable in other ways (Adler and Posner, 2006, p 55).

The problem with the Pareto principle (apart from the issues already identified) is that it justifies making rich people richer, and hence increasing inequality, so long as poor people are not made poorer. Yet advocates of 'weak welfarism', such as Adler and Posner, are unwilling to accept any version of 'prioritarianism', involving overall weighted welfare, in which a greater weight is given to those who are worse-off, or leximin versions, giving priority to the worst-off (Rawls, 1971).

This is because, so long as the group in question are worse- (or worst-)off, gains for them are more important than gains for any other group; and because this is true no matter how small this group may be, or how large any other group may be (Adler and Posner, 2006, p 57). This is why the latter choose a form of 'weak welfarism' in which the Pareto principle trumps prioritarian ones; welfare gains are more morally important than equality, at least to the extent that rich people's utility is no less morally significant than poor people's. So Adler and Posner (2006, p 36) settle for a version of 'weak welfarism' in which each person's welfare is based on their preferences, but only those that are self-interested and survive an 'idealisation test' (see p 230-1) – they are not based on a morally untenable theory of the good.

So the kind of normative principles that appeal to economists, and indeed to the commonsense moral intuitions of the public in a liberal individualist culture, focus on rules that justify increases in individual and overall economic welfare, through voluntary exchanges. They say little or nothing about the contexts in which such exchanges take place – the institutions through which the collective life of a society is conducted. In so far as governments can justifiably initiate structural changes to reduce distortions and improve coordination, this derives from a modified version of the Pareto principle, based on an individualised calculus of utility gains, in which social value of the kind discussed in Part Two of this book is largely invisible.

In this version of 'weak welfarism', social and moral standards (including those on social justice and environmental protection) are to be settled through political debate and legal determination. They should not form part of the cost-benefit analysis that informs policy choices, because they involve 'disinterested preferences', in which individuals have no self-interested stake (Adler and Posner, 2006, pp 133-7). This leaves a very problematic link between the normative principles that govern issues of justice, equality, liberty and diversity, and the domain of individual welfare (see pp 186-7). But it also separates decisions of the latter kind from considerations of social value.

The liberal-communitarian version of public policy

So far, my discussion of the normative basis for public policy seems to reflect the situation in the Anglophone countries during the ascendancy of the neoliberal governments (1980-94), and more widely of the

Washington Consensus. It does less than justice to the innovations of Third Way leaders, such as Bill Clinton, Tony Blair and Paul Keating, or to the modifications of the Washington Consensus made, partly under the influence of Amartya Sen, by leading figures in the World Bank from the mid-1990s (Stiglitz, 2002). These innovations have been referred to as liberal-communitarian approaches to public policy (Seeleib-Keiser et al, 2005), in which more attention was paid to social relations, especially to districts that generated expensive problems such as unemployment, lone parenthood, crime and drug abuse. All political parties have seemed to converge on this compromise (Huber and Stephens, 2001).

It has been under the influence of these regimes that social capital became the focus of policy, both in governments and in international organisations. This was why I devoted the whole of Part One to investigating whether social capital represented a convincing concept through which to analyse the Easterlin paradox. If it was, then some of the policy initiatives of the past 10 years might ultimately be expected to raise levels of well-being.

The challenge for Third Way governments, faced with the success of neoliberal regimes in increasing the economic welfare of the mainstream members of Anglophone countries, but the increasing demoralisation of impoverished minorities, was to find a normative justification for programmes to reconstruct the social fabric of poor communities that did not rely on discredited Keynesian economics or welfare state transfers and services. The advantage of social capital theory was that it picked up some of the themes of communitarianism (Etzioni, 1993), and translated them into a form highly compatible with the economic model.

If the integration of the world economy demanded that citizens of affluent societies became adaptable, flexible and self-responsible, ever willing to update their human capital to the requirements of a transforming 'knowledge economy' (Reich, 1993), then the counterpart to this was not the public provision by a state concerned with equality and standardisation, but the building of social capital. Just as individuals realised themselves through choices and projects of self-responsibility, so families and communities assumed similar control over their collective lives (Driver and Martell, 1997).

Social capital theory legitimated initiatives under which governments funded neighbourhood regeneration and support for non-governmental organisations and community groups, through 'partnerships', which enabled this kind of responsibility for issues such as homelessness, truancy and drug-dependency (Jordan with Jordan, 2000, chapter 2).

The terms under which these programmes were described and justified in the UK have shifted substantially over time. Initially, the primary concern was with strengthening the bonds between members of what were seen as fragmented communities (Blair, 1996; DH, 1998). After the riots in Bradford, Burnley and Oldham and in the summer of 2002, this shifted towards 'community cohesion', emphasising bridges between distinct ethnic districts (Worley, 2005), and following the logic of Putnam's (2000, pp 22-3) definitions of the two types of social capital. This was accompanied by a more general emphasis on 'civil renewal' – the strengthening of associational and political participation (Blunkett, 2004). Finally, after the suicide bombings on the London transport system in July 2005, it focused more specifically on the integration of young Muslim people.

The weakness of this type of legitimation of public spending on social programmes was that it could be justified only in terms of the costs otherwise generated by irresponsible, deviant or illegal behaviour. Social capital was supposed to reduce all these kinds of actions (Helliwell and Putnam, 2005, p 438), partly by providing the norms and networks through which poor people could achieve the same purposes more effectively by other, more orthodox means, and partly by getting government agencies and voluntary organisations to function better.

But this claimed a rather different type of logic for the reduction of costs of irresponsibility and illegality in the impoverished sector of society from the one that operated in the mainstream. There, if social capital worked to overcome coordination problems, it was within an overall structure of markets and market-like exchanges, in which choices were enabled (over group membership and collective goods provision as well as private consumption) for the sake of maximising overall welfare. It was therefore difficult to justify building social capital for its own sake, even if social capital could be welfare enhancing, since social capital was supposed to be a by-product of interactions among utility-maximising individuals.

So there was always a tension between the rationale of social cohesion and community responsibility as a basis for government programmes in the Anglophone countries, and that of enforcement through criminal justice, surveillance or other social control measures. Since the logic of social arrangements for the mainstream relied on choice under personal responsibility, underpinned by the enforcement of contracts, the idea of state-funded community responsibility in newly created 'invited spaces' (Gaventa, 2004) for partnership and participation was always artificial and tenuous.

In the UK, the fact that problems like truancy, drug dependency and alcoholism did not decline in the most impoverished districts was taken as evidence that this approach was flawed. Indeed, in an interview just before he left office, Tony Blair declared that he regretted sponsoring large-scale programmes for community cohesion and civil renewal, when it would have been more effective to focus resources on correctional programmes targeting individual deviants and criminals (Blair, 2007).

These tensions between aspects of a liberal-communitarian compromise were less evident in the continental European countries with strong Christian Democratic traditions. Those emphasised the mutual responsibilities of social classes under corporatist 'social partnership' arrangements, as the main elements in sustaining social cohesion (Van Kersbergen, 1995). As a result, there was more cultural and political resistance to the adoption of Anglophone versions of liberal individualism; but, once reforms began to accept some features of this approach, under pressure of global economic integration, there already existed both institutional and discursive resources for implementing the communitarian aspect of the compromise (Seeleib-Kaiser et al, 2005), both in the public and the voluntary sectors.

As with its role in social theory and research by the World Bank (see pp 91, 103), social capital offers no normative principles for redistribution to the poor. It merely seeks to explain, in highly generalised terms, how better cooperation among poor people might alleviate their disadvantages, and link them better into the mainstream. Its success might indeed be attributable to the fact that it is 'the rich and powerful speculating about how to improve the lot of the poor through prompting their self-help and organisation without questioning the sources of their economic disadvantages' (Fine, 2001, p 199).

Subjective well-being and public policy

By contrast, several of the researchers who have used evidence of 'stalled well-being' to provoke debate about the Easterlin paradox have been critical of the assumptions and methods of the economic model. For instance, Kahneman et al (1999, p xii), in their introduction to the major source of research data on the topic, state:

> At present, economic indicators hold the most sway in policy circles. Yet, the economic approach is limited in several ways. First, it focuses on those aspects of life that can be traded in the marketplace. Thus, desirable goods

such as love, mental challenge and stress are given little consideration.... Second, the economic view presupposes that individuals will choose the greatest amount of utility for themselves; yet a great deal of evidence now contradicts this proposition. Third, economics assesses variables that are only indirect indicators of something else – subjective fulfilment.

Similarly, Lane's critique of market democracies, which makes use of subjective well-being (SWB) data, addresses the basic assumptions of the model:

> Why, then, do the constituent individuals (of such societies) not make better use of these instruments and choose paths that will maximize their well-being? The short answer is that people are not very good judges of how, even within the private spheres of their own lives, to increase, let alone maximise, their happiness.... The problem is that people often choose of their own accord paths that do not lead to their well-being, they escalate their standards in proportion to their improved circumstances, choose short-run benefits that incur greater long-term costs, fear and avoid the means to their preferred ends, infer from early failures an unwarranted and disabling incompetence. (Lane, 2000, pp 8-9)

The problem for those who address these issues is that they demand the institution of a different maximand for individual choices and public policy, which implies a different set of organisations and programmes for this purpose. Whereas the claims made for social capital fell quite safely within the scope of a slightly adjusted economic model, those of SWB might appear authoritarian and paternalistic. Would SWB be able to yield politically persuasive measures of individual and aggregate well-being, and criteria for public policy decisions?

Layard (2005) argues that it could. Advocating a return to Bentham's utilitarianism, he proposes overall SWB as the criterion for law and policy (p 112), counting each person as an equal, and discounting Nozick's (1974, p 43) famous objection against subjective happiness as the standard, that it could be attained by a 'happiness machine' (or by drugs), overriding the other objections (such as non-ideal preferences), and building in rules and rights to 'prevent expediency and protect vulnerability' (Layard, 2005, pp 14-19). He goes on to attribute most of the Easterlin paradox to externalities, which are not actually compensated under policies derived from the Kaldor/Hicks principle (which he regards as the dominant standard in affluent market societies); and on the use of Gross National Product (GNP) as a proxy for overall well-being (Layard, 2005, pp 131-4).

Layard then contends that data on SWB, which reveal cardinal preferences, allow the work of Meade (1970), Sen (1970); Mirrlees (1971) and Atkinson and Stiglitz (1980), which postulate the diminishing marginal utility of income for the rich, and under which the gains from redistribution should just outweigh the losses in overall well-being, to be operationalised in public policy, because individual gains and losses can now be measured and compared.

In a more academic paper (Layard, 2006), he makes three clear recommendations. First, there should be a 'corrective tax' that 'will reduce work effort to a level where the fruitless incentive to raise your relative income has been fully offset: the external cost has been fully internalised' (p C27) – effectively a 'truce' to end the rat race (social comparisons leading to excessive income-aspirations). The second is a tax on 'addiction' to earning and consumption – the adaptation effect that leads to overestimation of the SWB to be derived from additional income and consumption. The third is that the government should regulate those activities that stimulate tastes not conducive to improved SWB – such as advertising directed at children and performance-related pay – and should promote those that foster a more cooperative social environment.

With the collaboration of all social scientists, this should inform a new approach to policy, in which increased happiness is the goal; the 'the progress of national happiness should be measured and analysed as closely as the growth of GNP' (Layard, 2005, p 147). This would allow better account to be taken of how others affect individuals' utility in policy makers' cost-benefit analyses.

> I conclude that economics uses exactly the right framework for thinking about public policy. Policy instruments are set to maximise the sum of (cardinal) utilities, with additional weight being given to those whose utility is low. What is wrong is the account we use of what makes people happy. (Layard, 2006, p C31)

Layard's goals for policy also include improved training and job security, reduced unemployment, better education and support for parenting, better planning of the built environment, reduced mobility (including immigration control), and increased spending on mental health services (all in the UK context) (Layard, 2005, chapters 10 and 11, and pp 23-4).

All this would represent a transformative agenda. Although Layard (2006, p C31) insists that economists should not set themselves up as moralists, he is arguing for nothing less than a 'culture shift', away from the excessively competitive environment of individualism towards the common good. But although he blames economists for inspiring the neoliberal programme, he still claims a hegemonic role for economics in public policy. His programme of reforms is confidently justified within 'the cost-benefit framework which is the strength and glory of our subject' (2006, p C24). It is highly paternalistic – for example, claiming that the moral assumptions of neo-utilitarianism should be imposed by government for the sake of improved happiness without persuading the electorate, or achieving an actual (political) truce over increased income and consumption.

His views are important, because Layard has had the ear of the UK government, and has been given a substantial budget to put some of his ideas into practice, even being described in the media as the 'Happiness Czar'. However, the extent to which the economic model adopted by New Labour's ministers is open to modification through these arguments is indicated by the priorities that Layard himself has adopted (or has been required to accept). It is his proposal for increasing spending on mental health services that has received official endorsement, along with some extra funding for 'personal education' in secondary schools, concerned with individual emotional issues. It is a bit as if, despite the bold sweep of his recommendations, Layard has settled on pursuing a no more ambitious goal than the right to one of Nozick's 'happiness machines' in every home.

One aspect of the difficulties faced by his proposals is that, despite his forceful advocacy, utilitarianism still provokes a good deal of opposition, not merely among academic philosophers. These concern the value of happiness itself, whether Socrates and the contented Fool are equally able to evaluate their lives (Griffin, 1986, pp 116-7) and whether 'myopic choices' can be corrected without excessive paternalism. Furthermore, even Kahneman himself expresses dissatisfaction with retrospective assessments of well-being, and seeks to measure 'objective' pleasure experiences, building from single moments to episodes and ultimately whole lifetimes, in order to give reliable interpersonally comparable data (Kahneman, 1999). With so much at stake in proposing overall SWB as the new criterion for policy decisions, these doubts are telling.

Second, Layard shrugs off objections to this principle that stem from other moral standards, such as equality and justice, by postulating a prior structure of rights, under a constitution, and a private set of moral rules for interaction in civil society (Layard, 2005, pp 115-23). These are claimed to provide the framework within which policies for overall SWB are pursued, but the relationship between them and the overarching principle is not explained. I shall return to this question in Chapter Eleven.

But the most important doubt about his proposal is how he derives his specific policy recommendations from the criterion of maximising overall SWB. To take two examples that are very prominent in current political debate (see pp 192-3), he makes it clear that he supports 'activation' and welfare-to-work measures, and also immigration controls. On the first, he states: 'We should eliminate high unemployment. Here tough-and-tender works best. After a time everyone should be given a chance to work, but should have to take advantage of the opportunity in order to continue receiving support' (Layard, 2005, p 233).

On immigration, he presents the case for controls in terms of the value of community – 'a high-turnover community is rarely friendly', and 'geographical mobility increases family break-up and criminality' (Layard, 2005, p 179). Stable communities have dense friendship networks, crime is lower, and people trust each other more; 'mental illness is more likely if you live in an area where your group is in the minority than if you live in an area where your group is in the majority'. Hence, geographical mobility should be discouraged, and 'many of the arguments used in favour of immigration are fallacious' (Layard, 2005, p 180).

In deriving policy goals such as support for family life and subsidisation of community activity (Layard, 2005, p 233) from his principle of maximising overall SWB, Layard, seems to go beyond the limits of liberal neutrality, and to be promoting a particular version of the good life. Even though, in average terms, conventional family structures and stable communities, along with employment, may be associated with higher levels of SWB, public policies to subsidise and strengthen them, or to make divorce, mobility or non-participation more costly, are not adequately justified by his criterion, within an overall scheme of individual liberty and market interactions.

The difficulty for Layard's proposals lies in the tension within them between two aspects of the default welfarist approach to public policy – the support for choices based on individual preferences, and the goal of overall welfare maximisation. Layard starts by rejecting GNP, and hence by implication the sum of individual utilities, as the basis for his principle, insisting that aggregate SWB should be paramount. But he never rejects market exchange, or individual choice within markets, as the main mechanisms for social interactions.

As a result, all public policies, from taxation and subsidisation to regulation and enforcement, have to be presented as corrections of distortions in such markets, which stem from externalities or information deficits, for example. In a system of social relations still driven by individual utility maximisation, an overall principle derived from aggregate SWB will often conflict with individual freedom of choice, for instance on geographical mobility. Hence, the principle of maximising SWB comes under intense scrutiny as a justification, which it cannot always bear.

Conclusions

The attempt to introduce social and moral principles into public policy in a systematic way has always been dogged by the local and particular nature of collective institutions for the protection of interpersonal and communal value. As Pareto himself recognised, despite the best attempts to derive such principles from logical processes, they inevitably represent a compromise between past beliefs and arrangements about human life and relationships, and current political interests. In his sociological writings, he distinguished between individual and social utility (Pareto, 1896, p103), and thought that government should aim to combine the pursuit of both 'logical' and 'sentimental' goals.

> If political economy as a study has progressed further than sociology, this is to a large extent due to the fact that its concern is with logical action…. [M]athematical economics … can now claim to be on the same level as the other natural sciences…. The art of government lies in finding ways to take advantage of … sentiments, not wasting one's energies in futile efforts to destroy them – the sole effect of which is simply to strengthen them…. Legislation can be made to work in practice only by influencing interests and sentiments. (Pareto, 1916, pp 196, 244)

As we have seen, however, moral and political philosophers have tried to influence public policy through the logical application of general principles of exactly the kind Pareto ridiculed. It is a slight exaggeration to claim, as Adler and Posner (2006, p 11) do, that welfare economics 'sputtered out' in the 1970s. More accurately, the high hopes pinned on normative justifications for redistribution and other government interventions, following on from the work of Rawls (1971) and the early Sen (1970), turned out to be unsustainable. Moral and political philosophers disputed each other's criteria in telling ways, and the damning evidence of 'stagflation' in welfare states, especially in the Anglophone countries, left the field open for neoliberal programmes. Welfare economics continued to operate with a kind of default approach, based on the Pareto principle and modified utilitarianism. As Adler and Posner (2006, pp 2-8) show, cost-benefit analyses, applied to public policy under the influence of neoliberal governments bent on deregulation in the 1980s, were retained by Third Way administrations in the 1990s, for the sake of improving the efficiency of programmes.

In their comprehensive review of decision procedures in public policy, Adler and Posner opt for a 'weak welfarist' approach to these analyses, in which the Pareto principle is qualified, and welfare (or 'well-being', as they interchangeably call it) is based on self-interested preferences that survive the idealisation test. Their modest aim is to apply a plausible moral theory to specific tasks and practices in government agencies, so as to enhance transparency and allow better political and legal oversight. They regard cost-benefit analysis as a way of providing full information for politicians and courts, and hence overcoming principal-agent problems in policy implementation (Adler and Posner, 2006, pp 103-23). Unlike Layard, they remain unpersuaded of the advantages of shifting to an approach based on SWB. Their position therefore has the advantage of being more clearly consistent with the economic model's assumptions about individual utility maximisation through markets.

However, neither Layard nor Adler and Posner address the institutional frameworks within which policy decisions are made. They take the structures and cultures of both markets and government agencies as given, both in their analyses of externalities and information deficits (Layard) and of costs, benefits and regulatory processes (Adler and Posner). The political transformations of the period since 1980 have targeted organisations and cultures, especially in the public sectors of the affluent Anglophone countries, to enable utility-maximising individuals to seek advantage within the collective infrastructure. Public choice theorists have justified this, on the grounds that gains in efficiency benefited all in the long term, and breached no plausible principles of equity.

In Part Two of this book I argued that those who wish to explain the Easterlin paradox must use an analysis in terms of social value to account for the gap between the utility accumulated by individuals and their evaluations of their overall satisfaction with their lives. Social value, in turn, can be understood in terms of the cultures and institutions within which it is generated and exchanged. Hence, it is to the cultural and institutional transformation, sponsored by governments since 1980, that we must now turn, to see whether public policy is susceptible to significant modification in the direction of improving well-being.

Seen from the perspective of social value, the whole purpose of this transformation was to install individual utility maximisation as the sole measure of value, in all kinds of interactions (political and personal-emotional, as well as material), and contract as the sole relationship in which to transact such exchanges. Through changes in official discourses, categories and concepts, as well as in roles, organisations and their justifications, governments sought to impose these ideas, images and institutions on populations, and to enable commercial interests to reinforce them through their communications and activities.

So the question for public policy over well-being is not, as Layard implies, whether it can offset the distortions caused by externalities and information deficits concerning the sources of well-being; nor is it, as Adler and Posner suggest, the refinement of cost-benefit analysis to achieve a better approximation to maximum overall welfare. It is whether there can be a cultural and institutional shift, consistent with economic efficiency and liberal neutrality, such that individuals can more reliably gain social value through their interactions.

As we have seen, the Enlightenment philosophers assumed that this would occur through extra-contractual activities and relationships, under the influence of instinct, and through the forces of nature. These would supply both the resources for interpersonal sympathy and benevolence, and the impulses to enjoy the aesthetic pleasures of our natural environment and the healthy exercise of our bodies. Now that these spheres for interaction and experience have been taken over by markets and contracts, it is necessary to review them, to see whether any alternative, better suited to the generation and distribution of social value, is still viable.

TEN

Social value and public policy: making citizens

Throughout this book, I have used the example of the Israeli nursery's penalty for parental lateness (Gneezy and Rustichini, 2000) as a kind of parable for the shifts in public policy that have taken place in the Anglophone countries in the past 30 years. I am not, of course, suggesting that governments in the period after the Second World War did not follow economic principles, including elements of information and contract theory, in questions of public finance. They were, for instance, well aware of issues concerning redistribution and incentives, and the optimum taxation problem (Vickrey, 1945, pp 329-30), leading to the conclusion that 'the ideal distribution of income, and hence of the proper progression of the tax system, becomes a matter of compromise between equality and incentives' (p 330). They were also aware of problems of performance and incentives in the public sector (Marschak, 1955; Hurwicz, 1960), and of inducing behaviour consistent with the goals of policy through the sharing of relevant information (Schultze, 1969; Gibbard, 1973).

However, partly because of the Cold War competition between liberal capitalism and Soviet state socialism, and the need to combat internal subversion by communist parties, they also sought the loyalty of citizens, by making explicit the normative goals, such as equality and justice, that were claimed to underpin their policies, and by including working-class (and later women's and minority) movements in the political process. At the same time, political theory aimed to provide analyses that were the ethical counterparts to these endeavours.

For example, long before Rawls (1971) elaborated his *Theory of Justice*, Harsanyi (1955) proposed expected utility as a criterion of justice in a world where an individual could select a variant of the economy he would adopt, assuming that he would then have an equal chance of landing in the shoes of each member of that economy (compare Vickrey, 1945, p 329).

Thus, the era of welfare states was marked by institutions and political discourses of citizenship, which in turn influenced the cultures of their public spheres. These regimes attempted to regulate their societies through negotiations between groups within this culture, even when (as in the Anglophone countries) they did not adopt systematically corporatist schemes for planning through representatives of the state, employers and trades unions. So it was a major transformation that has now produced an approach to policy based on contract theory, in which the issues for public policy can be largely restated in terms of the principal-agent problem, as concerned with the acquiring of information about preferences for public goods, the regulation of monopolies, insurance risks, or auctions of public resources, all of which involve incentives and asymmetric knowledge (Laffont and Martimort, 2002; Bolton and Dewatripont, 2005).

This has implied that government should set up 'independent', arm's-length boards and regulators should seek suitable contracting arrangements for every aspect of its programmes, and distribute risks and incentives in optimal ways, right down to the level of individual citizens. This applies as much to school pupils and claimants of disability benefits as to the actions of financial institutions and insurance companies.

For example, in the UK in late 2007, both the government and the Conservative opposition set out plans under which responsibility for placing claimants of Jobseeker's Allowance in employment would be contracted out to commercial firms. This would be done in such a way as to ensure that these companies had incentives to maximise successful placements, because they would be paid only after claimants remained in these jobs for a certain period. The companies, in turn, would of course seek to engage with jobseekers under terms that took account of the moral hazard associated with unobservable behaviour, and the adverse selection issues about undisclosed information. Both the government and the opposition commended the proposals as gains in efficiency, in value for taxpayers' money, and ultimately in welfare for claimants.

In this chapter, I shall analyse the consequences of this approach to public policy, and the possible alternatives, which pay attention to culture and social value, and hence to well-being. These questions can be tackled at two levels. The first is that of ideas – the concepts through which issues in public policy are constructed, and the ways in which these are deployed in defining the actions open to citizens within the structures created by government activity. Social value might be introduced into the aims and purposes of policy programmes, as a rationale for new initiatives, rather as independence, choice and utility maximisation were introduced into the reforms of the public sector by neoliberal governments in the 1980s. Just as these and subsequent Third Way regimes self-consciously aimed to change the culture within which interactions between staff and service users took place – to 'break the mould of the old passive system, and accomplish a change of culture among claimants, employers and public servants' (DSS, 1998, p 24) – so new programmes could aim to introduce ideas and images more appropriate to the creation of positive social value.

The second level is that of political economy – how policy programmes enable new forms of interaction to be introduced into a sphere of social life, so as to alter social and economic relations. In this chapter, I shall use the example of social care for people with disabilities and the frailties of old age to illustrate how the economic model of government has allowed the logic of capitalism – improving the productivity of time – to enter the sphere of social reproduction, and to become the principle guiding social interactions. I shall go on to argue that individualism itself, as a culture in which social value is exchanged, now incorporates this principle into decisions about welfare, personal and social, in every sphere of life.

This poses the greatest challenge for any attempt to introduce social value in public policy decisions. On the one hand, the ideas and interpretations of social reality derived from the economic model have entered government documents, and the wider discourses in which policy issues are debated, as the official culture of the public sphere. On the other hand, reforms have enabled firms and public–private partnerships to treat such fields as education, health and social care as opportunities for achieving greater efficiency, greater productivity of time, and hence – through opportunities for profits – greater overall welfare. This in turn has led to citizens adopting a standard for all their social interactions derived from the economic model. The culture of individualism subordinates social to economic value, even in the spheres of household, association and community.

So the question is not simply one of defining a sphere of social interaction in which social value might be adopted as the appropriate standard for evaluating policies. It is that the type of social value that is the currency of exchanges in all spheres is increasingly an individualistic one, which is derived from ideas and interpretations of the economic model. And it is also that the organisational landscape of all spheres, and the opportunities available within it, in turn reflect the logic of that model.

This chapter aims to trace the steps by which this dominance of economic interests and a culture that reflects the methodological individualism of the economic model was established. The welfare state compromise between the claims of economic and social value in public policy was forged from a fusion of idealist political philosophy and a welfare economics that left room for government and non-market action. The former was derived in the UK from neo-Hegelian concepts of interdependence in the common good (Freeden, 1978; Vincent, 1984; Harris, 1992; Boucher, 1997; Carter, 2003; Offer, J., 2006). The latter came from the recognition of a non-economic sphere by Pigou (1920), and of market failure by Keynes (1936), and their followers. This approach justified the creation of a whole sphere of social life in which the population interacted primarily in terms of the social value of *citizenship* – as equal members of a democracy in which risks were pooled, and facilities shared respectfully.

At the level of ideas, this government-led version of social value was vulnerable to many attacks derived from the liberal tradition in which it was grounded. Despite the political ascendancy of welfare state institutions in the post-war years, the fundamental moral framework of rights and distributions remained that of individual liberties and private property.

Both these and new rights to protection against racial and sexual discrimination, which were derived from discourses of human rights (Dean, 2004), concerned the equal moral sovereignty of such individuals. Once welfare economics ceased to justify state intervention to rectify large-scale market failures (see Chapters Three and Six), the rights of individuals to follow their preferences in pursuit of their welfare could be invoked to apply a thoroughgoing methodological individualism to the whole field of social interactions.

For example, these moral rules give a special status to childhood, both as a vulnerable period of life, and as one in which the individual acquires the competences for adulthood. But the infrastructures in which children grow up have been redesigned in line with the requirements of individualism. Nurseries, schools, training organisations and child protection agencies reflect the increased scope for choice and competition, and for the participation of private finance and management. The curricula and organisation of these agencies give priority to the skills for improved productivity and utility maximisation in a market economy.

More generally, the public infrastructure is now structured to the requirements of an 'information-theoretic' version of the economic model (Laffont and Martimort, 2002; Stiglitz and Greenwald, 2003; Bolton and Dewatripont, 2005). Since fluctuations in such an economy are to be understood as the consequences of responses to shocks by rational economic agents, government interventions are likely to do more harm than good, as they can be neutralised by such agents anticipating their intended impact (Fine, 2001, p 8). Market imperfections, since they are attributable to incomplete and asymmetric information between customers and suppliers, call for more published statistics about outcomes of school examinations and hospital procedures so that people eligible for education and treatment can make better choices in these as well as open market issues.

I shall examine the scope for introducing social value considerations into issues of social reproduction, and whether this can be distinguished from the productive economy. This would not entail a return either to the idealism of the neo-Hegelians or to the statism of the mid-20th century. It might involve the reassertion of certain features of social life, and of services in particular, which are not well captured in the economic model, or in its derivative approaches to public policy.

The purpose of this chapter is therefore to take the first steps towards identifying the scope for making social value a criterion for public policy decisions. It aims to analyse how earlier attempts to make some aspects of such decisions accountable to some such standard have been almost completely eclipsed by the imperatives of maximising overall welfare, according to the requirements of the economic model. This can provide important indications of how previous efforts to operationalise social value in public policy failed, and about the directions for any future attempt to improve well-being, and narrow the Easterlin gap.

Social value and the welfare state

The interpretation I have put on the Easterlin paradox is very similar to the central issues for the future of industrialised societies identified by many political and social philosophers and social theorists at the end of the 19th century, and in the years leading up to the First World War. Although the terminology and intellectual frameworks were different, they were centrally concerned with whether individualism and materialism could sustain the development of human potentials, with how various kinds of social bonds could continue to provide sources of well-being in capitalist societies, and with how collective and institutional contexts could enable cooperative and mutually beneficial social relations among citizens.

Although the groups of theorists to which I am referring were very diverse, and often disagreed about fundamentals, it is arguable that all of them sought to make economic issues accountable to the social needs of populations in questions of public policy. This intended elevation of social value to the dominant position in government decisions could, of course, be recognised also in the writings of Marx in the period leading up to this debate. The communist revolution was to make it possible for individuals to unite in contributing freely to the common interest.

> Only then will the separate individuals be liberated from the various national and local barriers, be brought into practical connexion with the material and intellectual production of the whole world and be put in a position to acquire the capacity to enjoy this all-sided production of the whole earth (the creations of man). (Marx and Engels, 1847, p 235)

Where Marx differed from the other theorists considered here was that he explicitly demanded that the whole system of production and exchange be totally subjugated to a transformed set of social relations. But the neoclassical economic orthodoxy of the time, in excluding the 'non-economic' sphere of households and civil society, allowed others, many of whom called themselves socialists, to postulate a new order in which capitalism would be modified by institutions for the common good. Without challenging the institutions of property and markets, they argued that social life represented the potential for achieving normative ideals, and that public services could supply the framework in which these ideals could best be realised – that 'private and public virtue were interdependent, that "state-conscious idealism" was the goal of citizenship, and that social-welfare policies should be ethically as well as materially constructive....' (Harris, 1992, p 133).

> An individual has no life except that which is social, and that he cannot realise his own purposes except in realising the larger purposes of society....Whatever the difficulties may be in finding the unity of the social organism, if we hold to the doctrine and make it more than a metaphor, we must recognise that society and individuals actually form such a whole, and that apart from each other they are nothing but names.... (Jones, 1883, p 9)

The notion that society was an organism was common to much social science in this post-Darwinian period – for instance in Durkheim (1893) – but the neo-Hegelians adopted it as the basis of their theory of how (in direct distinction from individualism and materialism) social relations of citizenship could raise individuals to a 'higher life' (den Otter, 1996, p 81). They called the social environment in which the state allowed its members to develop as fully as possible 'socialism'. 'Socialism teaches that man is, in his essence, united into society with his fellows, and that his inner self can only realise through a social Polity, which is himself, though it be more than himself' (Holland, 1900, p 31).

There was always a tension in this tradition between the liberal wing, which favoured voluntarism, and the Fabian one, which emphasised the role of the state. Although they disagreed about specific proposals and reforms in the period before the First World War, they were united in their opposition to the revolutionary politics of Bolshevism (although the Webbs notoriously pronounced themselves impressed by its outcomes in the 1930s). For the mainstream idealists,

> Human affairs are not governed by mechanical laws and do not move towards necessarily determined conclusions.... [I]f there is no change in the spirit among men, the class war might proceed to revolution and to the victory of the proletariat, but it would not really ameliorate the lot of men or give them liberty, it would only substitute a bureaucratic tyranny for a plutocratic. (Gore, 1922, p 10)

This idealist element in the socialism that informed welfare state proposals long outlasted its influence in academic philosophy. Tawney (1922, p 18), for instance, considered that social issues were matters 'not of quantities, but of proportions, not the amount of wealth but the moral justice of your social system'. He regarded the Fabian and Marxist theory of value as erroneous, because it mechanistically equated what workers deserved with their productivity, not their social function.

> Ideally conceived, society is an organism of different grades, and human activities form a hierarchy of functions, which differ in kind and in significance, but each of which is of value on its own plane, provided that it is governed, however remotely, by the end which is common to all. (Tawney, 1926, p 34)

This sounds more like German Christian Democracy than socialism (Van Kersbergen, 1995), with its emphasis on the mutual responsibilities of the constituent parts of the social order. Capitalism undermined the functional order, and concealed the value of relationships. The shared values and culture of a society should enable individuals to have equal access to social opportunities, despite inequalities. The principle of equality required, 'not necessarily ... an identical level of pecuniary incomes, but of equality of environment, of access to education and the means of civilisation, of security and independence and of the social consideration which equality in these matters usually comes with' (Tawney, 1926, p 17).

This aspiration was later echoed in T. H. Marshall's version of the equality achieved by the welfare state in his *Citizenship and Social Class* (1950). It also found expression in the work of G.D.H. Cole, raised in the Guild Socialist tradition of William Morris, who argued that the health and education services should shake off their 'capitalist character' and the 'spirit of greed, grab and acquisitive struggle' (Cole, 1920, pp 967). When the social services were in the process of being established, he wrote that charity, the ethos of the pre-war voluntary services, under the new regime,

> transforms itself ... into communal service, designed to widen and deepen the expression of the spirit of democratic cooperation. As long as there are rich and poor, this will tend in some degree to reflect inequalities in class and income. But under modern conditions there can and does enter into them much of a different and more equalitarian spirit. This democratic element is fostered by the growth of the salaried professions upon whose members an increasing amount of the actual work devolves. (Cole, 1945, p 29)

In retrospect, it is easy to see that these hopes were realised mainly through the common experiences of wartime adversity, and the government controls, such as rationing and the direction of labour, which prevailed during and immediately after the war. The post-war order was to be 'governed by the same principles of pooling and sharing that governed the emergency measures of the war' (Marshall, 1965, p 76).

But the culture shift that these conditions enabled did transform social relations in many ways. That these did not long survive the restoration of free markets and the relaxation of state planning was due partly to the shortcomings of idealist social thought, and partly to the poor coordination between this and the public economics of the day (see pp 56-8).

Ultimately, there was a contradiction between the liberal individualism of the Anglophone political tradition since the Enlightenment, which required free markets for the expression of diverse preferences, and perfectionism implicit in the idealist vision of society, together with reform of the rational understanding and moral character of individual British citizens. Social policy was not viewed as an end in itself, nor were the recipients of welfare ends in themselves; on the contrary, both policies and people were means to the end of attaining perfect justice and creating the ideal state. (Harris, 1992, p 126)

That there was space for any such project in the first half of the 20th century was partly due to the circumscribed claims of welfare economics – the recognition of a non-economic sphere of social interaction and possibility of divergence between total and economic welfare (Pigou, 1920, pp 11-21). This accepted that the 'satisfactions' measured by economists were limited, and that 'cognitions, emotions and desires' were also relevant for overall welfare. The latter were influenced by aesthetic and ethical considerations, such as work settings. Pigou recognised the part played by common interest, cooperation and 'the social virtues', loyalty and *esprit de corps* (Pigou, 1920, pp 15-16).

He noted that certain environments debased or elevated experiences; the 'effect upon the quality of people produced by public museums, or even by municipal baths, is very different from the ... effect of equal satisfactions in a public bar' (p 17). Finally, character and virtue, developed through education and experience, were 'an important element in the ethical value of the world'. Different cultures nurtured different contributions to non-economic and economic welfare (pp 13-14). 'In the great cooperative movement, for example, there is a non-economic side at least as important as the economic' (p 15). Changes in the *status* of working people, giving them more control over their lives, might thus improve overall welfare. The nationalisation of industries, or state-recognised national guilds, 'might increase welfare as a whole, even though they were to leave unchanged, or actually to damage, economic welfare' (p 17).

This last sentence indicates the scope for idealist-inspired policies to reconcile the increase in 'overall welfare', including 'non-economic welfare', with the perfectionist approach to social relations. Taken together with the conviction, derived from Keynesian theoretical innovations in the 1930s, that government interventions were required to correct market imperfections, especially in relation to full employment, this gave a substantial role for government in both the economy and society – far beyond that allowed by today's economic model, with its extension into all social interactions, and with total welfare defined in terms of the sum of individual utilities.

As the pioneers of the new model began to exert their influence on public policy in the Anglophone countries, this left the last defenders of idealist thought in embattled defence of their rationale for the social services. In the UK, the figure of Richard Titmuss is associated with this last stand for the welfare state in the 1970s, in terms of an egalitarian moral purpose, and as the 'general will' of the people (Titmuss, 1974, p 24). At the end of his life, he wrote about his experiences of being treated for cancer in an NHS hospital as a reflection of how social policy had helped 'to actualise the social and moral potentialities of all citizens' (1970, p 238).

> In some of the things that I have said and in some of the things that I have written in some of my books, I have talked about what I have called 'social growth'. I believe that my experience at the Westminster [hospital] provides some of the unquantifiable indicators of social growth. These are indications that cannot be measured, cannot be quantified, but relate to the texture of relationships between human beings. (Titmuss, 1974, p 150)

What I have tried to convey in this section is both the strongly ethical and perfectionist features of the idealist approach to social policy in the UK (which found its counterpart in Christian Democracy in post-war Europe), and which might be regarded as a stronger influence than the materialist socialist tradition. But I have also indicated that the welfare economics of the day made a substantial space for this version of how social value might define the standards to which economic welfare should be accountable within public policy. How else might the following have passed for a definition of social policies in a prestigious lecture on the topic?

> Social policies are concerned with the right ordering of the network of relationships between men and women who live together in societies, or with the principles which should govern the activities of individuals and groups so far as they affect the lives and interests of other people. (Macbeath, 1957, p 1)

The new economic model that emerged in the 1970s was to be far more all-embracing and dismissive of social value, as we have seen. By conceding nothing to the non-economic, by insisting on methodological individualism, and by using overall welfare as the dominant standard, the model sets a far more formidable challenge.

The scope for social value as a standard

Despite the shortcomings of the idealist approach, the political programme of the welfare state received overwhelming electoral support in 1945, and the 'post-war settlement' shaped politics in the UK for the next 30 years – in continental Europe it endured considerably longer. This implies that, in Pigou's terms, 'economic welfare' was made accountable to 'non-economic welfare' across a wide range of issues during that period. This was possible, I shall argue, because the economic model of the day allowed scope for 'non-economic' factors to govern political and social life, and for the economy to be answerable to these standards.

This scope was as much a consequence of the self-limitations of the current economic theory (and specifically of its welfare economic analysis) as of any coherence in idealist arguments for collective arrangements. The Pareto standard was assumed to apply only to the sphere of material production and consumption. In arguing that non-economic standards could trump the requirements of economic welfare for the sake of social and cultural goals, Pigou used the precedent of Adam Smith's case for agricultural protection for the sake of defence – to avoid the risk of blockade of foreign imports during war (Smith, 1776, p 333). Even during a long peace,

> the effect upon economic welfare of the policy which a State adopts toward agriculture, shipping and industries – producing war material is often a very subordinate part of its whole effect. Injury to economic welfare may need to be accepted for the sake of defensive strategy. (Pigou, 1920, p 19)

This meant that the divergence between the economic welfare and the requirements of non-economic welfare could in some spheres be very wide. Above all, Pigou quoted John Stuart Mill in support of the recognition that:

> [T]he effects upon economic welfare produced by any economic cause are likely to be modified by the non-economic conditions, which, in one form or another, are always present, but which economic science is not adapted

> to investigate.... [T]he effects of economic causes are certain
> to be partially dependent on non-economic circumstances,
> in such wise that the same cause will produce somewhat
> different effects according to the general character of, say,
> the political or religious conditions that prevail. (Pigou,
> 1920, p 21)

This enormous concession, along with the growing scope for the
state to intervene to correct market failures in employment levels,
investment rates, healthcare, secondary education and social care under
Keynesian and Beveridgian principles, explains how economics itself
accommodated welfare states. It acknowledges, in effect, that economic
welfare, defined in strictly material terms, must always be accountable
to political and social standards. This opened the door for 'pooling and
sharing' in peacetime as well as during the two World Wars, and for
the kind of moral audit required by Titmuss's idealism, for instance in
his account of *The Gift Relationship* (1970) – that universal collective
health systems enabled free donation of blood by citizens.

It was economic theory, as much as the neoliberal politics it supported,
which changed during the 1970s to block these kinds of claims. The
advance of a far stricter version of methodological individualism,
applied to the sphere of organisations and politics as well as markets
for commodities (Buchanan and Tullock, 1962), and further developed
in public choice theory (see Chapter One), as well as the extension of
economic analysis into the fields of marriage, the family, criminality
and other non-market interactions (Becker, 1976; 1981), closed down
the space for social value as a standard. The high tide of neoliberal
regimes in the 1980s and early 1990s, reflected in the Washington
Consensus as well as government programmes in the Anglophone
countries, subordinated collective and social considerations to market
ones, in driving back the role of the state.

As we saw in Part One, since the mid-1990s economic analysis
has developed further. As Fine (2001) argues, the spectacular rise of
social capital theory in economics and the other social sciences signals
both the further extension of methodological individualism, rational
choice theory and information theory into what Pigou called the
'non-economic', *and* the recognition that social norms, institutions
and movements demanded explanation. The failures of neoliberal
programmes – increased poverty and inequality, concentrations of social
problems in deprived areas, the persistent development lags of whole
continents, continued ethnic conflicts and civil wars, even after the
collapse of the Soviet bloc – required analysis of such factors. But social

capital theory subsumes all such issues into its framework, explaining them in terms of responses to market imperfections, information asymmetries and so on.

> Social capital explains what is otherwise inexplicable and is the factor that allows society to function successfully. In limited respects, parallels can be drawn with utility as used by economists. For this is also all-embracing – putatively explaining why we behave the way we do as well as providing us with our welfare. In the case of social capital, however, our sights and ambitions are raised from the level of the individual to the level of society, from market to non-market, and from narrowly defined individual motivation to customs, norms, institutions and rules. (Fine, 2001, p 189)

It might be thought that this renewed focus on the 'missing link' between the macro-level and its micro-foundations, which supplies the 'glue' holding society together, would supply an opportunity for social value to be reasserted as a standard for public policy decisions. But, as we saw in Chapters Four and Five, its incorporation within the new economic model serves a quite different purpose. Because this model now analyses the issues facing public policy in terms of a 'second-best world', of multiple equilibria, market imperfections, asymmetric information and other coordination problems, social capital explains how individuals act to deal with these distortions, either improving or worsening the overall situation (Fine, 2001; Durlauf and Fafchamps, 2004). The goal of public policy is not to attempt to apply an overall standard (such as the 'common good' in the idealist welfare state model), but to deal with a diverse set of specific problems as they arise, in terms of this complex pattern of interactions. Within the overall aim of increasing welfare, it should be concerned with improving bonds and linkages within and between communities and associations.

The point here is that the economic model still dominates public policy, as it applies to the mainstream in different Anglophone countries, and to affluent countries generally in a global context. To illustrate this, and to show how social value could represent an alternative standard, I shall consider the example of how services contribute to social reproduction in such societies.

Social reproduction is the process by which a society is reproduced and transformed over time. In the version of welfare economics set out by Pigou (1920), most of social reproduction concerned non-market interactions in households and communities, which supported but were separate from economic activity. But as Marxian political economists have long been aware, under capitalism firms are constantly competing over the whole field of social relations in search of profits. Any sphere of activity in which productivity can be increased may be a source of profit, and of competitive advantage for these enterprises.

So, for example, in the 1940s and 1950s, although the participation of married women in formal labour markets was low by historical standards in the affluent Anglophone countries, the domestic work of mainstream housewives was transformed through the sale of washing machines, vacuum cleaners, electric cookers and refrigerators, as the household sector became a target for large-scale industrial production. In the next section, I shall consider how the expansion of employment in services represented another such incursion of the commercial economy into the sphere of social reproduction, as part of the broadened scope for the version of welfare promoted by the economic model.

Services and social relations

In economic theory, the main distinction between goods and services is still the one identified by Adam Smith (1776, p 330) – that services 'perish in the very instant of their performance', and hence cannot be stored, traded on for other goods, or used to produce something else. 'Goods are physical commodities such as steel and strawberries. Services are activities such as massages and live theatre performances, consumed or enjoyed only at the instant they are produced' (Begg et al, 1997, p 2).

But this misses the other very obvious aspect of most services, that because they involve face-to-face transactions between people, they inescapably also require the production and distribution of social value of some kind. Whereas goods acquire symbolic significance through their use in various forms of social exchange, services directly concern the meanings embodied in social relations, and use cultural resources to communicate these meanings. Begg et al's examples are instructive: massages communicate very different meanings between members of tribal societies from the ones conveyed within the social relations of physiotherapy clinics, which in turn are different from those in private health spas or massage parlours.

Theatres are organisations through which cultural images and ideas are communicated to large groups of people sharing in an experience as members of an aesthetic or entertainment community. All of these, in different ways, require institutions within which such interactions are interpreted, and become part of a wider set of resources for creating and sharing social meanings.

As we have seen (pp 197-202), welfare state theorists such as Tawney, Titmuss, G. D. H. Cole and T. H. Marshall tried to define a distinctive political and moral framework within which citizens in these societies were supposed to act both in the public sphere (in a democratic and egalitarian spirit), and particularly with staff and each other in the public social services. Although it is easy now to be cynical about the earnestness (and possibly drabness) of this endeavour, what was remarkable was the extent to which these high-minded principles did actually win political support, and were respected even by the predominantly Conservative governments that ruled during the 'golden era' of welfare states. Although Macmillan, Eisenhower and Menzies may have used the cultural resources of post-war rhetoric rather differently from Attlee, Truman or Whitlam, their programmes and policies were aligned with the social relations enabled by a politics of organised labour and public services.

The restructurings, reforms and 'modernisations' of those services, which began in the early 1980s, all applied the logic of the economic model, and specifically of commercial finance and enterprise, to their organisation. I shall take the transformation of social care in the UK as a (brief) example of the rationale under which these changes were made.

One possible option for the reforms, initiated with the 1991 NHS and Community Care Act, would have been to give people with disabilities, mental illnesses or the frailties of old age cash or vouchers, creating a market in social care to replace the network of local authority, voluntary sector and commercial facilities that existed at the time. But the current orthodoxy was that these service users would have lacked the information and judgement to make good choices in the aftermath of such a radical shake-up. Instead, under the 'new managerialism' (Clarke et al, 1994; Clarke and Newman, 1997), the reform process

> gives managers the right to manage, ensures the disciplined use of resources, the pursuit of objectives aimed at reducing costs and improvement of organisational performance. It also increases the use of information technology to bring about changes. (Gibbs, 2000, p 229)

It is important to note here that this approach was framed in terms of an analysis of value in the social services, which explicitly rejected the moral goals of the idealists. It was one of 'best value for taxpayers' money'

– that health authorities and local government departments should purchase (or 'commission') services according to criteria of economy, efficiency, effectiveness and 'quality' (Fletcher, 1998; Thompson, 2002 p 101). This involved measurement and comparison, competition and consultation with service users and local residents. The 'modernisation' programme adopted by New Labour (DH, 1998) developed the themes initiated by the Conservative government.

In social care, as in health (and across the whole public sector), each item of service could be broken down into its constituent elements, which could then be measured, both in terms of its price and its outcomes for service users. For each need, and each entitled person, there was an appropriate 'care package', to be 'delivered' in the most cost-effective way, after an assessment by a care manager. The aim of the care package was to 'promote independence' and be tailored to each individual's needs (DH, 1998, para 1.8), after taking account of any risks they faced (DH, 1998, chapter 2).

This approach has since been overtaken by a more radically choice-promoting, individualised one, reflecting the rationale that was rejected in the early 1990s. Government ministers had been critical of the lack of flexibility and responsiveness of public services, even under the new regime. 'We live in a consumer age. People demand services tailor made to their individual needs.... People expect choice and demand quality' (Milburn, 2002, p 2).

The reforms of social care had already required local authorities to initiate schemes for 'direct payments', under which some service users could be given cash to purchase their own care and support (DH, 1998, paras 2.14–15). The principle was now extended to use 'individualised budgets' as the basis for a new system.

> [W]e have already seen in social care how the use of direct payments, for example, has helped improve services and transform lives. Our task now is to continue this transformation right across the field of social care for adults as people are given more choice, higher quality support and greater control over their lives. We need to ensure the services we deliver are flexible and responsive enough to meet the differing needs of individuals. (Blair, 2005, p i)

In its Green Paper on Social Care, *Independence, Well-Being and Choice* (DH, 2005), the UK government set up a dichotomy between old-style public provision (of low quality, and standardised in form) and individualised flexible services (often supplied by firms or voluntary agencies, and of higher quality). Because service 'consumption' is treated as a series of separate experiences, each of which derives from a choice among options, this model pays little attention to the overall context for well-being or interactions as a way of making sense of social relationships. These choices enable greater independence, choice and control over how needs are met. The principle of self-assessment is introduced to the process of compiling individual budgets, minimising paternalistic procedures. 'People who are currently the passive recipients of services become consumers with the ability to shape and control the services they are willing to buy and shift the culture of care planning' (DH, 2005, p 35).

The goal of allowing consumer demand to be directly expressed is in turn to transform the supply of support services. Individual purchases will 'stimulate the social care market to provide the services people actually want, and help shift resources away from services which do not meet needs and expectations' (DH, 2005, p 35).

This approach is not derived solely from the government's economic model of services and their consumption. It is also based on the campaigns of people with disabilities, and especially younger people with physical disabilities. Their associations have come together in a social movement, demanding the recognition that, with sufficient support and assistance from paid and unpaid carers, from technology, and from the government, they can live a life as full members of the workforce and society (Oliver, 1990, 1992; Oliver and Sapey, 2006). The approach promoted by the Green Paper fits well with this demand.

However, the introduction of individual budgets is still tied to eligibility criteria and means tests, which severely ration entitlement to payments of this kind. Many people who develop disabilities in middle or older age are not eligible, and have to finance their own support. These criteria often restrict government assistance to people who have become too disabled to benefit from 'choice' or 'independence' in meaningful ways, and who need home or residential care simply to sustain their physical functioning. This puts the focus back into questions about whether social care services can be adequately analysed within a framework of individual rights, independence and the purchase of utility-maximising support.

First, does the discourse of human rights, pursued by the United Nations since the Second World War, and taken up by the European Union in its Charter of Fundamental Social Rights in 1989 (further extended by the Maastricht and Amsterdam Treaties of 1993 and 1997), fully capture the value of individuals in society? The idea that each person (or 'soul') is of equal moral worth is fundamental to liberal and Christian Democratic ethics, but when linked to a market-driven programme for the transformation of the public services, it says little about the social relations in which such rights can be implemented by people with severe physical and mental frailties.

As Dean (2004, pp 13-14) points out, the discourse of human rights can be grounded either in a view of society as made up of self-interested, competitive individuals, or of vulnerable human subjects who require collectively organised systems of cooperation and support for their well-being. The former view sees these rights as maintaining order among rivalrous and potentially conflictual individuals; the latter as responses to interdependence among members of an order giving each other mutual recognition (Honneth, 1995). Dean finds echoes of the former view, even in the United Nation's *Human Development Report, 2000*, in which, following Sen (1985), human rights are linked to vulnerable groups' claims to the realisation of capabilities. He sees the United Nations' interpretation as 'more akin to that of human or social *capital*' (Dean, 2004, p 15; emphasis in original), and as adopting some of the language of the 'new managerialism'.

The alternative view, which locates social care within relations of interdependence, is (in the Anglophone literature) largely derived from a feminist perspective. People with learning disabilities, for example, are not held responsible or expected to control their own development, and are valued for their relationships with others. Unlike the mainstream, they are allowed to be primarily 'affective' or 'communicative' citizens (Smith, 2001), whose contribution lies in the responses they give to others, and evoke from them. Although the new thinking encourages them to choose friends and companions (Vernon and Qureshi, 2000, p 256), their reliance on others is not seen as 'burdensome'. It is only within an 'ethic of care' (Tronto, 1994; Sevenhuijsen, 2000; Meagher and Parton, 2004) that they can be given full worth and recognition, despite depending on others for their daily needs.

One tradition within feminism emphasises that women have represented this ethic of care, even amid the rising tide of utility-maximising individualism of the neoliberal ascendancy (Elshtain, 1981, 1998). In this view, the social value that stems from interdependence and mutual recognition can only be sustained within social relations of family, kinship and community. The individualism of the economic model is in constant tension with this ethic, and women's well-being in particular is adversely affected by the demands of Anglophone political cultures (Williams, 2001; Pusey, 2003, pp 99-105; Ellis, 2004).

Under the explicit influence of the economic model, public policy in the UK has promoted a view of social services in which the relational content is subsumed within a framework of individual utility maximisation. Care is taken out of its context of interdependence and reciprocity over the life cycle, and recast as the consumption of efficiently organised systems of support. The craft or expertise in care professions, especially in communication and relationships, is largely ignored, in favour of technocratic management of specific 'packages' (Sennett, 2008, pp 46-50). In so far as those spending their individual budgets choose social interactions in group or associations, these are treated as episodes (such as attending a football match, or taking a holiday) rather than the elements in a meaningful life, within a network of communication of social value. In the next section, I shall consider how this view of services is derived from the economic model.

Time, productivity and the consumption of services

The example of social care is a vivid illustration of how UK public policy shifted from the idealist goal of social services, as expressions of the social value of citizenship, to the perspective in which they are consumed by individuals as items of utility. However, the Easterlin paradox poses a more fundamental question about the consumption of services generally. Why did individuals and households in affluent countries substitute the consumption of commercial services for so many informal activities and interactions during the final quarter of the 20th century, if these were less conducive to well-being and quality of life? Even if government policies in the Anglophone states were aimed at promoting such substitutions, as parts of market-orientated transformations, and for the sake of economic growth, why did people persist in choices that did not increase their overall satisfaction with their lives?

The relative success of the Anglophone economies during that period (compared with Japan and the continental European countries) has been attributed to the growth of private service employment (Esping-Andersen, 1990, 1996, 1999). By sacrificing income equality to budgetary restraint and employment expansion in this sector, these countries increased their Gross National Product (GNP) faster than those that gave higher priority to protecting the living standards of the least advantaged (Iversen and Wren, 1998). But these policies required consumers in the Anglophone countries to change their patterns of spending as well as their supplies of labour power to new 'flexible' forms of employments in services.

Restaurants, theme parks, package holidays, health spas, gymnasia, fitness centres, counselling and therapy all expanded in this period. For example, expenditure by US citizens on meals out increased from 25 to 45% of spending on food between 1950 and 1995; in the UK the growth was from 10 to 18% in the same period, but from 15 to 32% if takeaway meals and snacks are included, in the same period (Offer, A., 2006, p 147, figure 7.2).

The expansion of services of this kind has defied the tendency of such products to become more expensive, relative to the prices of goods. The productivity of workers in these services is not susceptible to much improvement through new technologies; hence, some commentators predicted that 'self-provisioning' of various kinds would increase (Gershuny, 1983). In fact, despite the fact that affluent economies with large service sectors were vulnerable to the 'Baumol cost disease' (Baumol, 1967; Baumol et al, 1985), consumption went on rising as relative prices increased – even among populations whose real wages were falling, as among many manual workers in Australia and the US (Gregory, 1998) in this period.

However, faced with the apparent paradox that expenditure on these services increased as their relative price was rising, the economic model addresses the opportunity costs of informal and commercially packaged alternatives. If the constraint on individuals' *time* is taken as the one that determines such choices, the shift from self-provisioning, informal entertainment, neighbourly support and friendly advice to paid services becomes explicable. People act as if their only scarce resource is the limited amount of time available to them to achieve their ends (Becker, 1976, p 6). They choose to allocate all the other resources at their disposal as if they were priced in terms of the time required to realise their contributions to utility.

> Even without a market sector, either directly or indirectly, each commodity has a relevant marginal 'shadow' price, namely, the time required to produce a unit change in that commodity; in equilibrium, the ratio of these prices must equal the ratio of marginal utilities. Most importantly, an increase in the relative price of any commodity – i.e. an increase in the time required to produce a unit of that commodity – would tend to reduce the consumption of that commodity. (Becker, 1976, p 6)

Any such explanation of how individuals allocate scarce means to accomplish competing ends assumes that preferences are organised into a single, consistent, utility function. Such an assumption is important for the explanation of behaviour in response to changes in prices, taxes and other incentives and costs. But it does not allow for important shifts in preferences, and in the ends sought, through long-term changes in the physical and social environment. It appears that a sociocultural change was occurring in this period, making time constraints the main criterion by which individuals, and especially women, evaluated opportunity costs, in spheres where no such calculus had previously been applied.

Especially in the US and UK, women contributed many hours to paid work, even in occupations and activities in which their hourly salaries were declining relative to men's, or in absolute terms. Between 1940 and 2000 in the US, female labour market participation rose from 30 to 81% as a proportion of male participation rates, but female wages declined from 65 to 57% on average in relation to male wage rates (Offer, A., 2006, p 243, figure 11.1).

Economists have devoted very little attention to this shift, or to the changes in consumption priorities that it has produced. The reason why this is so should be obvious. It represents the extension into the household, friendship network and community of the very principles on which the commercial economy operates – treating non-market relations as if they were markets. Becker's work is an example of this approach. But what is striking is how the logic of markets, and of capitalist production, has come to be adopted by individuals as the basis for decisions in all forms of social interactions. The idea of increasing the productivity of their time, and of economies on time, is the clearest illustration of this. 'Capital is the productivity of time…. Ultimately, capital is anything that provides for an enhanced stream of utility over time…. In this respect, capital is not physical but rests in the mind or in experience and skills' (Fine, 2001, p 40).

The point here is that, in so far as people adopt this framework for their everyday decisions about social interactions, they make informal relations accountable to the rationale of income generation and consumer spending. The social value of intimacy, respect and belonging is reduced to an item in a bundle of preferences. The cultivation of relationships of all kinds is time-consuming; it requires communication, and the creation of cultural resources, through which reliable sources of such value are sustained. Within a utility function in which time is the constraint, such interactions are seen as costly, compared with the purchase of commercial services. It is more efficient to pay for several hours of counselling than to cultivate a friendship through reciprocal exchanges in an open-ended relationship, where long-term costs are uncertain.

The economic model succeeds in spreading the dominance of capitalism to what Pigou regarded as non-economic spheres by turning people into methodological individualists. In using market-like calculations over our social relationships, we unconsciously reduce them to exchanges under cost-benefit analyses. By incorporating them into utility functions alongside the commodities we purchase in shops, we subordinate intimacy, respect and the sense of belonging to consumer values. This is, after all, the aim of the huge international corporations that market services, and the governments that see trade in services as the future opportunity for affluent societies (Jordan, 2006a, part 1c).

It is very difficult, therefore, to see how the devaluation of non-market social interactions could be reversed, so long as the culture of individualism generated by the economic model continues to dominate. As we saw in Part One, all social phenomena can be absorbed into the current version of the model, as responses to market imperfections and information asymmetries. Social capital theory is the manifestation of the absorption of all social relations into the model, and all social interactions into its analysis of individual utility maximisation (Fine, 2001). People adopt friendly, associative or communal ways of doing things when distortions of this kind block market solutions.

Social reproduction and social value

I have argued that the economic analysis of services in the current model has enabled both the public social services of the post-war welfare state and the non-market interactions of the household, friendship and communal sphere to be absorbed into the commercial sector of Anglophone economies. By substituting a market logic of choice and consumption for both the political relations of citizenship and the social relations of intimacy, respect and belonging, it has allowed both to be subject to the utility functions of consumption-orientated individuals. This has meant that social reproduction – how society as a whole is reproduced and transformed from one generation to the next – has been perceived within the perspective of policies for increasing the total welfare of all such individuals, through the improved productivity of their lives, and specifically through the greater efficiency of service delivery.

This is not simply a transformation of the cultures and institutions of welfare states, and of the preferences and goals of societies' members. It is also a radical departure from the notion of social reproduction in economic theory from the time of the Enlightenment philosophers. They set themselves the task of analysing the underlying structure of 'conventions' (Hume) and 'institutions' (Smith), through which social interactions of reliable cooperation were sustained. Markets were only one such set of features in the collective landscape. The others, driven by appetites and desires (providentially including sympathy and benevolence), involved social relations of mutuality, politeness and justice. All these supplied the essential underpinnings for economic prosperity.

Even in Smith's political economy, where the work of monarchs, judges and lawyers was as much 'unproductive labour' as that of flunkeys and buffoons (Smith, 1776, pp 330-1), services were essential for social reproduction in ways that were not susceptible to market analysis. They provided the link – through the institutions of government, the armed services, the professions, the household and the local community – between the social value of interpersonal interactions, and the commercial value of production and consumption. Without these links, individuals would float in a social void. Merchants, for example, would only commit their wealth to the improvement of productivity in their societies if they became engaged with politics and communities, through ownership of land (Smith, 1776, pp 451-3).

In the current economic model, most of the interactions that make up social reproduction in the non-market sphere are more efficiently performed by commercial service firms, or public agencies acting within market principles. The residue of non-market interactions, and the social units to which they give rise, and within which they are conducted, can be understood through the catch-all category of social capital. They stem from market imperfections and information asymmetries, and so can be analysed under the economic model. Referring to the work of Coleman (1990), Fine (2001, p77) comments:

> For economists, the starting point is a perfectly working market, which is then reconstructed with a social content in economic rationality in the light of information imperfections. Sociologists, on the other hand, start from the social as defined by their disciplinary traditions and seek to reconstruct it on the basis of rational choice.

This in turn transforms the role of the state in social reproduction. The functioning of affluent societies relies on individuals' abilities to acquire and use physical, human and social capital, making rational choices in the face of such informational imperfections. The state should equip its citizens for these roles and tasks, and should correct their behaviour and improve their judgement if they show themselves to be incapable of exercising this independence.

A clear example of this in the UK has been the government's decision to enforce education, training or employment for young people between the ages of 16 and 18, announced in the Queen's speech to Parliament in October 2007. Quoting the statistic of 200,000 people in this age group in none of these categories, the government will insist, under sanction of criminal charges, that they must prepare themselves for future labour market activity in one of these three ways, to improve their skills and aptitudes.

Presumably there will be some mechanisms under which a 'gap year' can be accommodated in this programme, but it will be required to be justified in terms of acquisition of human or social capital – learning a language, or doing voluntary work at home or abroad. Adolescence, in other words, is redefined in terms of preparation for the tasks of rational choice, the independent assessment of the means to achieving the income flows necessary for utility maximisation, and for self-realisation over the life cycle.

Conversely, the UK government's response to evidence of increased mental distress among people of working age has been partly to fund increased treatment provision – under the guidance of Lord Layard (see pp 183-4) – and partly to develop programmes for reducing benefit claims for invalidity. Both policies address these conditions as individual afflictions, rather than expressions of social malaise. New treatment facilities, in which cognitive behavioural therapy is to be prominent, will aim to restore mainstream citizens to their status as fully competent, rational economic actors. The reformed regime of tests for new claimants of invalidity benefit will require them to be assessed for their abilities, not their disabilities, in order to establish what work they *can* do. As part of a package of getting them back to work, those claiming for mental illnesses (at that time, over half of the 2.7 million claimants of invalidity benefit) will also be offered cognitive behavioural therapy, to try to return them to the labour market (BBC Radio 4, 2007).

All these programmes and regulations follow logically from the assumptions of the model. Individuals require training and (in some cases) therapy to be able to make rational choices about work and consumption in a complex set of interactions, including large areas of uncertainty. They also require certain skills to be able to access the social capital through which groups and associations deal with information deficits and other distortions. Together with initiatives to regenerate deprived communities that directly address their 'negative' social capital (gang culture, drug culture, crime, truancy and so on), these form the main elements of a social policy programme driven by the model (Jordan with Jordan, 2000).

Because the culture within which social value is produced and exchanged under this regime is a low–group, low–grid, individualistic one, the isolation, stress and stigma generated within its constituent interactions is interpreted and experienced in terms of failure of personal responsibility. Since individuals are required to be in control of their projects for self-realisation, to make choices about their welfare, and to satisfy their own preferences (including those for associational membership), it is their faulty functioning that must be addressed if these do not produce the desired outcomes. So the system of social reproduction in the UK requires 80,000 people to be held in prison (a lower proportion than in the US, but higher than anywhere else in Europe). It also leaves the UK, next to the US, with the lowest rates of child well-being in the OECD 21 affluent countries, with particularly bad scores for relationships with parents and peers, and for risky behaviour (Innocenti, 2007). An individualistic version of social value, within economic relations of competition and insecurity, is not conducive to well-being.

Conclusions

Two obvious difficulties confront any attempt to introduce social value, as the basis for well-being, into public policy debates. The first is that it stems from practices and cultures that are diverse, fragmented and incoherent. Unlike the economic model, which can claim internal logical consistency and an all-embracing scope, social value is derived from many sources and traditions. Indeed, when postmodern social theory claims that the universal principles of the Enlightenment have lost their credibility in today's world, they seem to be referring to this fragmentation and diversification of cultures. But they fail to notice that the main bearer of the Enlightenment project – the economic model – has a more total stranglehold on collective life than at any previous time.

The second problem, which is linked to the first, is that social value inescapably involves those emotions and relationships that have been regarded historically as irrational and subversive of good order, because they lead to conflict and destruction. These fears are borne out when, for example, the greatest threat to liberal democracy is seen to come from a violent and totalitarian form of religious fanaticism, which threatens to propel societies back into the Dark Ages. This justifies the armed imposition of forms of individualism and 'democracy' on 'rogue states', according to the requirements of the economic model.

However, on the side of social value there are two strong counter-arguments. The first is that services – the bases for the economies of affluent societies – are directly concerned with social relations, and help to shape them. They cannot be convincingly reduced to transactions involving commodities, not because they have no enduring value, but because the value they create is (in part at least) of a different kind, and consists in what is produced through face-to-face interactions, groups and communities, but sustained by institutions in enduring systems for social reproduction.

The second is that culture is always an alternative to contract as a way of regulating relationships, and is often more conducive to well-being, if not to welfare. As examples of the shortcomings of the contract as a mode of interaction, and a means of exercising power, continue to proliferate, attention refocuses on culture. Even if it cannot be formulated in highly generalised, mathematical models, it may be worth re-examining as a way of sustaining quality of experience and standards of behaviour in many spheres of human interdependence. Even financial services are now castigated as having a culture of arrogance and complacency, in the light of the 'credit crunch', and as the failures of government and central banks to regulate them adequately illustrate the shortcomings of the contract approach.

Cultural influences are not confined to interpersonal transactions, such as those between officials or professionals and the public. They also concern the associational life of civil society, civility, public behaviour, and citizenship itself. None of this can be adequately regulated by the contract, and ideas about social capital are too vague and residual in current theory to be useful. An approach through the building of institutions that promote cultures of mutuality, respect and belonging is therefore a real alternative.

The UK government has become concerned about its role in 'making citizens'. The former Solicitor General has proposed a quasi-contractual oath-swearing ceremony for adolescents, and the Prime Minister has attempted to define British values. These efforts to capture social value for the sake of social cohesion miss the point about the distinctive qualities of a politics for sustainable social reproduction.

The same government has run against the problem of an unforeseen tension between the pursuit of welfare through economic efficiency and the maintenance of well-being through institutions for social value, over its programme for closing rural post offices. Significantly, Cabinet ministers who approved post office closure programmes have backed protest campaigns over specific post offices in their constituencies (Jenkins, 2008).

Government concerns over healthy eating will also be drawn into cultural issues. Even such apparently private, individual behaviour as eating is more effectively regulated by collective culture than by personal self-monitoring. Food culture was, after all, an important aspect of the 'civilisation process' (Elias, 1939; Mennell, 1985). The paradox of French cuisine has been that such a rich diet has still allowed healthy lifestyles and lower levels of obesity than in Anglophone countries. Dieting and individual self-regulation, by contrast, are associated with ineffective control (Offer, A., 2006, chapter 7).

This implies that public policies which seek to address well-being, and thus the Easterlin paradox, will have to foster cultures that offset (or at least balance) the individualism that is at the core of the economic model. The attempt to make economic value (welfare) accountable to social value (well-being), even in spheres of everyday social interaction, also represents a challenge to some of the fundamental principles of liberalism. This will be the topic of the next chapter.

ELEVEN

Justice, equality and social value

In this chapter, I shall deal with the potentially strongest objection to the proposal that social value should be a criterion for public policy decisions – that it is derived from a particular way (or ways) of life. In this view, any priority given to a substantive version of the good life, other than the many different lives freely chosen by individuals, is a violation of the principle of liberal neutrality. All the constitutional rights and protections, and the systems of distribution of resources, which make up the basic framework for interactions, should be drawn up with this principle in mind. In particular, our concepts of justice and equality, and the institutions through which we seek to establish them in practice, must avoid favouring a particular set of social relations (such as the heterosexual partnership, the two-parent family or the classical European musical tradition) over other possible relationships and activities.

I have argued in Part Two of the book that social value is derived from interactions between individuals and groups within cultures, which form just such ways of life. Particularly in an integrated world economy, with high rates of mobility across borders, and substantial minorities (of ethnicity, faith and culture) within almost every society, how can the social value created by such interactions influence a political authority committed to liberal equality and justice?

As we have seen (pp 46-8), the liberal approach to this set of issues seems to be in line with the methodological individualism of the economic model. Like that approach (Buchanan and Tullock, 1962, pp 4-5), it starts from the assumption that people have different preferences and life projects, and seeks to design principles and institutions in which they can conduct advantageous exchange, in pursuit of their various purposes. Justice and equality demand that social arrangements allow them opportunities for these activities and exchanges, which do not give some the chance to impose their versions of the good life on others. But the framework of rights for citizens must also restrain the government from imposing its version of the good life on them. This would rule out, for example, a socialist version of social value, as residing in a particular collective system of cooperative social relations through common ownership of productive resources. It would also rule out a fascist version, in which a particular racial or cultural tradition was imposed on all, as the only source of social value, or a theocratic one.

The liberal approach does not necessarily, of course, uncritically endorse capitalist economic and social relations. The history of political thought in this tradition since the Enlightenment has been one of the extension of rights, initially confined to men of property, to women, slaves, workers, black people, people with disabilities and so on. But this has also entailed the spread of contractual relations to more and more spheres of interaction, and the penetration of what had been seen as non-market activities (such as social care) by capitalist firms and their products. The current economic model may be taken as the latest of such expansions, in the former public sector, for the sake of individual independence and choice on issues of education, health and social support.

The liberal rejection of specific versions of the good life as the basis for political institutions is closely related to the criticisms of 'objective theories of well-being' (see pp 22-4). As we saw in relation to Nussbaum (2000, 2005), such theories root well-being in a set of qualities, or characteristics or capabilities that enable the good life. The liberal objection, also used by proponents of overall welfare as the main criterion for public policy, is that a life that contained these elements, but was not freely chosen or valued by the person living it, could not be claimed as constituting well-being for that person. Much the same criticisms could be levelled at the neo-Hegelian idealist and Christian Democratic versions of the good society as a basis for well-being – that they favoured particular social relations of interdependence and mutuality over other ways an individual might choose to live a life (see pp 197-203).

But the rejection of these versions of well-being (often referred to as 'perfectionism') has not deterred those political philosophers who work in the liberal tradition from continuing to seek more coherent and convincing versions of justice and equality, which are consistent with the requirement that each individual should be free to choose among alternative means to and ends of the good life. The energy devoted to these explorations was enhanced by the publication of John Rawls's *Theory of Justice* (1971), which spawned an accelerated output of work in the liberal tradition, and also many critical ripostes from libertarian (Nozick, 1974) and communitarian (MacIntyre, 1981; Walzer, 1983; Taylor, 1989) standpoints.

The search for moral principles for just and equal distributions of roles and resources in complex and diverse societies dealt in individual rights, generalised across whole populations. It also returned to the

Enlightenment tradition of contract theory, seeking to identify the terms on which a society's members might engage fairly with each other. It sought to abstract its rules and principles from the messy business of everyday social relations, for much the same reasons as Hobbes (1651), Locke (1690) and Rousseau (1754) had done – because these local and particular practices distracted from the central issues of law and politics. So, as communitarians and feminists pointed out, they were far more engaged with economic concepts of property and contract than with the negotiation of social value in relationships and associational life.

Just as the Enlightenment political theorists had tried to rule out the absolutisms and authoritarianisms associated with cultures of ethnicity, nationality and religion, so modern versions of contract theory, in avoiding perfectionism, attempt to sideline those aspects of social relations that give rise to irrational conflicts and abuses.

The question of this chapter is therefore whether this implies that well-being, defined in terms of social value, is an unsuitable goal of public policy.

I shall approach this question by considering one proposal for a major reform of the tax-benefit system, which is clearly rooted in the tradition of liberal individualism – basic income. Philippe Van Parijs, whose major study *Real Freedom for All: What (if Anything) Can Justify Capitalism?* (1995) has attracted worldwide attention, presents a 'real-libertarian' argument for a public policy proposal – a universal, guaranteed basic income, distributed to each individual member of society, without conditions – as the basis for justice between such members. The first reason for this choice is that his arguments are clearly rooted in the contractarian tradition of the Enlightenment and Rawls, and hence in liberal individualism. The second reason for this selection is that I have been associated with this proposal for many years (Jordan, 1973, 1987, 1996, 2006a), although my arguments for it have been rather different. The third is that this is one of the few radical ideas in social policy that has emerged in recent years, and has attracted attention from a broad range of progressive perspectives from feminism to environmentalism (Fitzpatrick, 1999, 2003). And a fourth is that many authors have, from different standpoints, argued that a post-basic income society would allow a transformation in social relations, such that many of the negative features of capitalism would be transcended. Several of these claims seem to imply that something like social value might replace economic value as the standard for individual and public policy decisions, and that something like well-being might be the goal of social interactions, rather than economic welfare.

So I shall use Van Parijs's arguments for basic income as my starting point in considering whether reforms in the distribution of rights and resources of this kind might in themselves be enough to rectify the divergence between welfare and well-being (the Easterlin phenomenon). Would 'real freedom for all' be sufficient to reorientate individuals, groups and societies from the pursuit of overall utility through individual maximisation to some other goals, which embraced social value, and thus well-being? This was implied by Van Parijs in a seminal article, written with Robert Jan Van der Veen, 'A Capitalist Road to Communism' (Van der Veen and Van Parijs, 1986) – that the social relations enabled by basic incomes for all could transcend the exploitations and abuses of that system. If this claim is justified, then it is unnecessary to look further for a way of introducing the pursuit of social value into public policy processes. Basic income would allow interactions that met social needs in conditions of justice, and well-being would be reconciled with welfare.

I shall argue that many of the claims made by other political philosophers in support of the basic income proposal are unconvincing, because they do not address issues of social value directly. Unlike Van Parijs, who acknowledges that people would simply be able to live any life they chose, however worthless, they suggest that society would be in some sense better through the freedom and equality bestowed by an unconditional income on all its members. I shall suggest that, without other ways of promoting social value, there is little reason to believe that the Easterlin paradox would be overcome by this measure alone.

Real freedom and social value

Political theory in the Rawlsian tradition takes up the device of a social contract between society's members, as a counterfactual way of imagining how the terms of such a covenant between free individuals, first posited by the Enlightenment philosophers at the birth of modernity (see pp 30-1), might be recast to extend the scope for freedom, reduce exploitation and equalise resources. Rawls argued that what was at stake in questions of distributive justice was not just income, but also wealth, power and the social bases of self-respect, and at one point advocated a guaranteed minimum income as the means of redistribution (Rawls, 1971, p 275). Van Parijs takes up Rawls's difference principle, under which the most disadvantaged get priority in this distribution, to argue for an unconditional basic income at the highest sustainable level. This would give all the freedom to choose their work, as well as to spend their earnings and accumulate and dispose of property.

Van Parijs equates power with exploitation, and defines exploitation in terms of holdings of natural endowments and material resources, which influence the performance of paid work, and hence earnings. So the rationale for basic income is to compensate individuals for natural disadvantages, and enable them to choose their version of a good life in an economic environment that is neutral between possible choices. In relation to natural talents, his criterion ('undominated diversity') is designed to ensure that only people with 'handicaps' that everyone would recognise as disadvantaging would get compensation, and for material resources each member should receive shares that are 'equally valuable in terms of the potential uses by others that have to be foregone as a result of the allocation that has been made' (Van Parijs, 1995, p 57). This implies that:

> If … all the available resources are sold at suitable competitive prices, that is, auctioned off to the highest bidder among the perfectly informed and equally endowed (members), no usable resources will be left unused and the equality of the budget-sets will be enough to guarantee that no-one could achieve more of what she wants with the resources another person has access to than with her own. (Van Parijs, 1995, p 52)

His preference for capitalism over socialism, argued in the final chapter of his book, rests on its greater efficiency in maximising the basic income, and hence real freedom. This implies that property, markets and contracts will be as fundamental in post-basic income societies as current ones. Above all, it implies that members of such societies will interact with each other in terms of contracts. Not only is the justification of basic income framed within a social contract between rational individual utility maximisers, it is also clear that the maintenance of real freedom for all will require them to continue to relate to each other as agents of this kind.

This real freedom consists of the ability to choose among the various lives one might wish to lead, including that 'to live as unconventionally as one might fancy' (Van Parijs, 1995, p 33). The examples he chooses to justify his redistribution of the assets associated with various endowments and resources illustrate the individualism of his assumptions; they are activities such as surfing, sunbathing and sitting about, taken as alternatives to formal production by spuriously female individuals with names such as Lovely and Lazy.

As one of the minority lifestyles that individuals might choose to lead, he does mention 'the preservation of interpersonal relations free of monetary considerations' (Van Parijs, 1995, p 33), but this is the closest he gets to analysing the social content of the interactions that would be enabled by the introduction of basic incomes, or how the power relations established under capitalism and liberalism might be transformed by anything other than exit options.

This, as he makes clear, is because he wishes to avoid rooting his theory of justice in a 'particular substantive conception of the good life' (p 27), which he calls 'perfectionist'. But he does accept that societies may have other goals, and make other trade-offs in pursuit of these ends.

> It does not follow that, for a real–libertarian, the extent to which a society is a good society is determined exactly by the extent to which it is a free society. Perhaps one should depart from strict or maximal justice, for example, if doing so would enable us to make social relations more fraternal. What will be attempted here, however, is to work out and define a conception of justice while abstracting from the other properties of a society that may be desirable for reasons that do not reduce to their contribution to social justice. (Van Parijs, 1995, p 27)

There seem to be two possible ways of arguing that social value should be a criterion for public policy decisions, which are potentially consistent with this statement. The first is, as Van Parijs hints, to argue that justice is not the whole of morality, and must be weighed against the objective of promoting good social relations. This implies that social value is external to justice, and there may have to be trade-offs between them, for good moral reasons. The second is that, even though justice demands that our basic structures (or 'institutional set-up', as Van Parijs calls them) are non-perfectionist, particular relationships and activities are required to realise or stabilise justice. In this view, the value of these relations lies in promoting justice and the interactions on which it relies (solidarity, respect, trust and so on), rather than on their contribution to a better way of life (Birnbaum, 2008).

In the second view, it is recognised that public policy is required to be concerned with the qualities of social relations in order to achieve and stabilise justice between members. But this does not imply that interactions giving rise to social value should be prioritised or promoted for their own sake. In this sense, well-being is not a goal of policy, but welfare still is, under the modified terms of the interactions chosen by individuals whose security and freedom is protected by their basic incomes.

This illustrates how liberal neutrality favours welfare as utility maximisation by individuals following their preferences over any version of well-being based on social value. But in spite of this, in the wake of Van Parijs's work, several other political philosophers have made claims about the consequences of basic income on social relations that go beyond the justice of this policy measure. These will be examined in the next section.

Social relations in 'basic income societies'

These claims are all, in a sense, variants on the idea that the individuals created by modern liberal capitalist societies (according to the blueprints of the Enlightenment philosophers) lacked one or more dimensions of freedom to realise their ends as social beings. In this view, the improved freedom enabled by basic incomes is transformative of the potential of individuals, and hence of societies. For example, Brian Barry (1997, pp 161, 165) writes:

> [B]asic income is not just another idea for rejigging the existing system. Rather, it would be seen as offering a genuinely new deal – a different way of relating individual and society.... I do not think it too fanciful to claim that those who learned their socialism from William Morris and R. H. Tawney may recognise the introduction of a subsistence-level basic income as a practical way of achieving some of their central aims. Indeed, if we can manage to strip away the appalling legacy of 'really existing socialism' and go back to Marx's utopian vision, it is not absurd to suggest that a subsistence-level basic income is a far more plausible institutional embodiment of it than anything Marx himself ever came up with.

Barry goes on to argue that basic income would provide a basis for funding post-school education and training, to design a rational transport system, staffed in appropriate ways, to improve urban environments, and other socially desirable goals, because it would make low-productivity, part-time jobs more attractive. 'Provided that the basic income is genuinely adequate, we can say that nobody is exploited, however low the pay. For the job is freely chosen in preference to an acceptable alternative of not having a job' (Barry, 1997, p 167).

Barry's claims highlight the issue raised at the end of the previous section. Liberal neutrality, as the basis for justice through this special kind of freedom, sanctions a set of economic and social relations in which risk and uncertainty are taken as given. Barry's labour market repopulated with railway station personnel and park-keepers seems cosy and nostalgic, but actually reflects a society in which work has been deregulated and fragmented under conditions of radical indeterminacy. From the standpoint of an individualistic view of social value, this represents the opportunity to live any life one might choose; from that of social value created within a culture of respect and belonging, constructed within institutions fostering security, stability and sustainability, this can create an environment in which freedom and justice are violated (Haagh, 2007).

Another set of claims concerns the transformation of class relations. Here again, the earlier work of Van Parijs linked basic income to 'A Revolution in Class Theory' (Van Parijs, 1987). If, as argued by Roemer (1982), capitalist exploitation stems from unequal distributions of alienable assets, then minimising exploitation could be achieved by equal distribution of such assets. Wright (2004) suggests that basic incomes for all citizens would, if sufficiently generous, alter the balance of power between classes, by providing workers an exit option from the labour market, reducing that dependence on capitalists for subsistence.

> [B]asic income increases the possibility of engaging in decommodified non-market activity, thus expanding the sphere of economic practices outside of capitalism; basic income increases the capacity of collective struggle by providing a guaranteed strike fund for workers. (Wright, 2004, p 79)

Here again, both these claims presuppose contexts of social relations in which these activities are valued by members. Wright's examples of 'socially productive' interactions (Wright, 2004, p 83) include caregiving, the arts and politics. There are some good reasons to think that certain unpaid activities would flourish in an individualistic culture, if they involved strong mechanisms for producing and distributing social value, including emotional support, respect and the sense of belonging. The examples given in Chapter Eight were music and sport, both of which are also well integrated into the commercial economy as professional activities, so that finance and esteem from that sector feed into the amateur one.

But care and politics are far more problematic, as is collective action by workers. All of these rely on ethical underpinnings to interactions that are in tension with individualism. As we saw in the previous chapter, care seems to demand an ethic of interdependence and reciprocity that is not well captured in the model of contractual exchange (see pp 208-9).

Politics requires collective mobilisations around ideas and images that conserve or transform social relations; while individualism and contractual exchange represent one such vision, the type of politics required by this (the economic model) is essentially managerial.

Low rates of political participation, and even of electoral turnout, especially in the Anglophone countries, testify to the problems of mobilisation within this model. As for trades union struggle, this too has been transformed into largely instrumental action for limited ends under the individualist ethos of the dominant model; in a fragmented, atomised labour market, in which exit options largely replaced voice ones (Hirschman, 1970), the culture of collective action would continue to be eroded.

As we saw in Chapter One (pp 26-9), Carole Pateman has been a longstanding critic of contractual versions of social relations, and the interpersonal power they enable. Her support for basic income rests on it providing the missing element in the freedom conferred on the individuals created by modernity (Pateman, 1988, p 16), by enabling real self-government or autonomy, which is central for democracy, including the government of the workplace and the household (Pateman, 2004, p 91).

> A basic income is a crucial part of any strategy for democratic social change because ... it could help to break the long-standing link between income and employment and end the mutual reinforcement of the institutions of marriage, employment and citizenship.... Individual self-government depends not only on the opportunities available but also on the form of authority structure within which individuals interact with one another in their daily lives. Self-government requires that individuals both go about their lives within democratic authority structures that enhance their autonomy and that they have the standing, and are able (have the opportunities and means) to enjoy

and safeguard their freedom. A basic income – set at the appropriate level – ... helps create the circumstances for democracy and individual self-government. (Pateman, 2004, pp 90-1)

Here Pateman makes it clear that she is arguing for a transformation in the social relations of households, employment and politics, with basic income as the first step in such a process. She does not suggest that it would, of its own accord, secure the changes she envisages, nor does she say how these opportunities are likely to change actual behaviour, other than that 'democratisation is at the forefront of discussion and that feminist arguments are taken seriously' (p 97) in institutional reforms, and that social reproduction will be one focus of such attention, addressing 'social relations and institutions, rather than atomistic individuals' (p 101).

So, while both Pateman and Wright (who talks about 'socially productive activity') make it clear that they consider that some forms of social value would be aspects of the gains from the introduction of a basic income, they do not indicate whether these should be seen as valuable in promoting or stabilising justice, or whether they think that these gains are available for some other moral ends. Pateman's criticisms of Van Parijs suggest that she regards self-government and democratic relations as essential elements in justice, whereas he sees them as contingently related to real freedom (Van Parijs, 1995, pp 8-9, 15-17). In so far as Pateman appears to include particular forms of social relations (reciprocal and democratic) in her view of justice, this would violate neutrality, and constitute a form of perfectionism, in Van Parijs's view.

Van Parijs, by contrast, would see various solidaristic and communitarian arrangements as consistent with his view of justice, and of the justifications for basic income, so long as none of these are legitimated in terms of a particular conception of the good life. They should be seen as enabling the highest sustainable basic income (Van Parijs, 1995, pp 231, 297), which itself, of course, is justified on non-perfectionist grounds. In other words, they are ultimately legitimated in terms of welfarist criteria (modified by the Rawlsian 'difference principle'), not by any appeal to well-being.

So we are back to the same issues defined at the end of the previous section. If it becomes clear, as I would argue, that there is nothing about the basic income principle that would make it more likely that the 'socially desirable' or 'socially productive' activities discussed by these authors would increase after its introduction, how might social relations be transformed (as Pateman demands), or at least stabilised (as Van Parijs's own expectations might require) for such a society to be sustainable?

This raises exactly the issues of social value, not captured in Van Parijs's arguments about surfers and sunbathers, about the cultures and contexts for social participation that I have been discussing in Parts Two and Three of this book.

Liberalism and perfectionism

If we accept that the individualistic version of social value, from which the methodological individualism of the economic model is derived, is simply one kind of culture, and one definition of value among many, then there is nothing sacrosanct about the lives individuals might choose. Or, to put it more accurately in terms of my analysis of social value in Chapters Seven and Eight, the value attached to individual preferences and choices in the economic mode is sacred through exactly the same cultural processes as the value that attaches to the group totems and rituals of tribespeople from the Amazonian jungle or the smallest islands of the Pacific. Symbolic value is given to people, their exchanges and the commodities through which they communicate, through interpretations derived from shared cultural resources.

From this standpoint, liberal neutrality is an idealist, not to say romanticised, view of individual freedom, which gives priority to the version of social value espoused by individualistic culture. It uncritically endorses the sacred value of the self, at the expense of all the contextual features of the social environment in which this self is embedded. It is therefore prone to devaluing those sources of social value that are derived from interactions that are intrinsic to ways of life in which interdependence and belonging are aspects of solidarity and mutual support. It prizes 'pure relationships' of intimacy, unencumbered by obligations (Giddens, 1992) over the enduring bonds of love and loyalty (Bauman, 2003). This does not imply a conflict between liberalism and social value, well-being or the good life; it simply says that liberalism tends to support a form of social value favoured by welfarism.

However, as I argued in Part Two of this book, the version of social value that is derived from the economic model has never been as dominant in social relations as it has become in government policy. Even though commerce and the transforming logic of public sector reform have deeply influenced the cultures through which people interact and interpret their social worlds, there remain many other ideas and practices through which members of social units of all kinds create and communicate value to each other, and experience their lives. For instance, although the spheres of art, music and literature have been deeply influenced by atomistic versions of individualism, the oldest themes of human society – love, conflict, power, community, continuity and change – continue to define their appeal, and supply their meaning to members. People continue to interact, and to interpret their interactions within traditions derived from other collective representations of the value of human existence.

Indeed, the hallmark of present-day societies is the diversity of their cultures. Individualism – a very uniform, reductionist and ultimately banal version of the value of life – has failed to subvert a multitude of other collective ways of experiencing social value, and sustaining it through relationships, groups, associations and communities. This is what is both challenging and stimulating about the outcomes of globalisation – that economic integration under the aegis of a homogenising, abstract model of utility maximisation has given rise to new networks, groupings, movements and ideologies, which co-exist in the same social spaces. While these include Islamic fundamentalists and drug-fuelled gangsters, as well as more traditional bigots and racists, they represent as much of a protest, and a resistance against individualism and narrow economism, as an expression of it.

So the really interesting and important questions for public policy concern the relationships between a core of moral principles, designed to enable this *collective* as well as individual diversity, and the more specific set of laws, regulations and interventions through which the economy and society are steered. Provided that the core rules and institutions reflect the values of justice and equality, and are neutral between all these different interpretations of the good life, I do not see why those other aspects of social policy should not be orientated towards well-being, as the maximisation of social value through exchanges in many kinds of cultures, rather than welfare, as the maximisation of individual utility. For example, this is what Nussbaum (2000) claims for her approach to constitutional principles and quality of life – that it is designed to enable diversity and framed within liberal political principles; it is also what Pateman (2004) is seeking through the democratisation of all kinds of social relations.

One reason why such a project – to define a set of standards for policy programmes in terms of social value – seems worth pursuing is that the attempt to frame welfarist criteria has failed. As we saw in Chapter Nine, welfare economics, even if it did not 'sputter out', certainly lost coherence in the 1970s, about the time that Easterlin (1974) stated his paradox. The challenge to it posed by that paradox, which inspired this book, has not dealt a fatal blow to the welfarist project. Indeed, as we saw in Chapter Ten, economists like Van Praag and Ferrer-i-Carbonell (2004) and Layard (2005, 2006) see subjective well-being (SWB) as the instrument for reviving a utilitarian version of the principle of maximising overall welfare.

Economists will undoubtedly continue to seek ways to absorb SWB into their analysis, just as theorists like Becker (1996) have done in relation to social capital. But I doubt whether welfarism can be convincingly modified to produce a coherent set of principles that deals with the Easterlin paradox, under any plausible interpretation of well-being. For example, as we saw in Chapter Nine, one of the most thorough and wide-ranging attempts to revive welfare economics – Adler and Posner's (2006) *New Foundations of Cost-Benefit Analysis* – seeks to modify the criterion of overall welfare, in order to avoid the pitfalls of utilitarianism, the Kaldor-Hicks criterion and objective theories of well-being. They argue that interpersonal comparisons are possible, through the use of an 'impartial spectator' mechanism, and without recourse to the data on SWB compiled by Kahneman and his colleagues (1997, 1999). But, despite their impeccable adherence to methodological individualism and a preference-based model, they are still forced, at several points in their detailed analysis, to rely on 'social' factors that are not derived from the preferences on which the cost-benefit analysis for public policy decisions are to be based.

The first of these is in their 'laundering' of the preferences to be used in the cost-benefit analyses for public policy decisions, to exclude those involving harm to others (Adler and Posner 2006, pp 35-6) (see pp 177-8). There is no way to identify these 'non-ideal' preferences, except in terms of some version of social value. If some people wish to abuse, dominate or exclude others, they may be able to find willing victims, or at least others willing to accept the consequences of their action for those dominated or excluded. Unless there are some social or moral principles in the core of the collective arrangements that proscribe such actions (by protecting those vulnerable to harm, and sanctioning forms of domination or exclusion), then the preferences of individuals for (legal) behaviour of this kind can only be 'laundered' by reference to a notion of the social value of interactions, or from an objective version of the good life.

Second, Adler and Posner concede that, because of the costs of information-gathering in cost-benefit analysis, it may often be better to use 'intuitive balancing' as a decision procedure, employing something like Nussbaum's (2000, pp 78-80) or Griffin's (1986) lists of 'dimensions of well-being' (Adler and Posner, 2006, pp 75-81). Although they say that this 'intuitive balancing' 'will not be perfectly accurate in tracking overall welfare', 'it could still be more accurate than CBA [cost-benefit analysis]' (Adler and Posner, 2006, p 98).

If even the most scrupulous analysis of overall welfare maximisation as a decision procedure is unable to hold consistently to preference-based principles, as the economic model would require, this suggests that there is an important potential role for collective action and political debate in the policy process, as well as at the constitutional and legal level. The Easterlin paradox demands that public policy pays attention to the divergence between preferences and satisfactions, and addresses issues that are not captured through the aggregation of 'compensation variations', as Adler and Posner's method requires.

Social reproduction and sustainability

One very obvious way in which the significance of this distinction manifests itself in policy is in the desire which people feel for a better society, and particularly for a better life for their children's generation than the one that they have lived. This is something quite different from the fulfilment of their own life projects, or the realisation of their personal potentials, as these are captured by the individualist model of welfare maximisation. What is at stake in such desires and motivations concerns the nature of social relations – that they should, for instance, be free from damaging conflicts, insecurities, stigmas and exclusions, and that the context of social life should promote rewarding and supportive relationships.

The economic model can deal with these issues only in the most general terms, as 'values' and 'commitments', expressed in 'mission statements' and logos, but not entering directly into decision-making processes. In the politics of the liberal-communitarian model (see pp 179-82) it is generally referred to in the phrase 'the Vision Thing', as an inspirational framework, but not a criterion for policy development. The communitarian element in Third Way programmes reflects this tendency; Tony Blair was a leader whose ability to personify vision and values obscured the fact that his major policy initiatives were derived from the economic model. As Sennett (2008, p 50) comments on the NHS reforms, quality in practice requires learning from ambiguity through experience, not a 'set of abstractions about good-quality work'.

Indeed, even those welfarists who readily concede that social and moral principles should be enshrined in law and constitutions through the political process, such as Adler and Posner (2006, pp 133-6), are anxious to exclude the opinions of activists in fields like social justice and environmental protection from the cost–benefit analyses that inform substantive policy decisions. They call the views expressed by members of such movements 'group loyalties' or 'socially influenced ideals' (Sobel, 1998), and use survey evidence (Rosenthal and Nelson, 1992, p 116) to show that even respondents themselves distinguish between these moral and political values and the money valuations (compensation variations) used for cost–benefit analysis.

But if we understand all value as socially constructed, then a great deal falls into the gap between these two categories. Opinions on issues such as the survival of species, biodiversity and ecological sustainability itself are largely generated by discussions and debates, whether in informal groups, on the internet or in associations. They are all likely to be shaped by 'group loyalties' and 'social influences' of one kind or another; we learn to value such things, and to struggle to conserve them, through social processes. Like those processes themselves, the value we come to attach to the existence of natural resources is social in origin.

The economic model, as represented by Adler and Posner, seeks to insulate strictly moral considerations about welfare from self-interested ones; but the price paid by this separation is that a huge swathe of social issues, concerned with social reproduction and sustainability, become largely invisible, and outside the scope of policy development. If issues that are 'moral' must be determined by parliamentary and legal processes, the vast majority of everyday decisions are then made in line with the economic model of welfare, according to cost–benefit analyses, which attempt to exclude issues of this kind. Because of the way representative democracy works, decades may go by before 'moral' issues are clarified, and the need for decisive action recognised. Meanwhile, both the collective social environment and the natural environment will have been transformed (often despoiled) in line with the economic criterion of overall welfare.

This is not, of course, surprising, given that the economic model subordinates social value to economic, making it a residual form of interaction, to deal with market distortions. It would hardly make sense, if social groups, associations and communities are seen as second-best responses to market imperfections, to give them priority in any attempt to increase welfare, defined as the utility maximised by rational individuals. Since it is built into economic analysis as a primary assumption that perfectly functioning markets would yield the greatest overall welfare to members of a society, the second-best world of government interventions must seek the nearest approximation to this first-best outcome. Collective action of all kinds is likely to push society further away from the most efficient and welfare-maximising available outcomes – a maxim spelt out by Mancur Olson (1982) in his *The Rise and Decline of Nations* (1982). On this account, policy should forestall the kinds of collective action that respond to imperfections such as information asymmetries, so as to distort outcomes still further.

Even on the more positive view of social arrangements enabled by social capital theory, any and every such set of interactions may produce collective goods that can be 'misused' for 'antisocial' purposes. This is why Third Way and World Bank programmes give priority to liberalisation, flexibility and privatisation in their reforms, with social capital building as a supplementary element, focused on the most deprived and excluded groups and communities, as a way of getting them to access markets and core programmes (education and healthcare). In the next section, I shall consider how a programme that recognised social value as fundamental for well-being might vary from this one.

Social reproduction and the social services

However, to make this assumption is, of course, absurd in terms of the notion of social value developed in this book. For example, the campaign for a basic income represents a political proposal that has emerged in a particular social and economic context, arising from the relations between members of liberal capitalist societies. Its advocates have traced its origins to, among others, Tom Paine (1796), Charles Fourier (1836), Jean-Baptiste Godin (1871), Edward Bellamy (1897), Josef Popper-Lynkeus (1912), Dennis Milner (1920), C. H. Douglas (1920), G. D. H. Cole (1929) and James Meade (1938) – a diverse list of radicals, Christians, socialists and outsiders, but all of whose thinking was shaped by a liberal capitalist social environment.

In its modern form, it has been carried forward by the student and claimant social movements of the UK and the US in the late 1960s and early 1970s (Jordan, 1973, 1974, 1976), before being taken up by the political philosophers quoted earlier in this chapter. If it is ever implemented, it will owe this to the cultural interactions and collective mobilisations that carried it forward in the 1920s and 1930s (Drakeford, 1988) as well as that later period, and have since then led to it being presented sporadically as an element in the election programmes of political parties all over the world.

The point here is that ideas about a better future society are developed and refined through many kinds of interactions, including experiments in living, producing and giving social support. Social forms in collective life evolve through interactions within productive and administrative organisations. The political process within which moral and social principles are debated, and public institutions reformed, is not an intellectual talking-shop; it reflects these movements and struggles. Like the basic income movement, methodological individualism and information-theoretic economics came to supply the rationale for public policy through such a process, gradually displacing idealism, welfare economics and Keynesian public economics during the 20th century.

What is sinister about the current economic model is that it has claimed to replace this battle of social forces and their ideas with a rational, scientific approach to governance – a business model fit for 'the End of History', when the competent management of the organisational and administrative branches of public policy can be conducted by technocrats, in accordance with principles derived from market dynamics, and under the oversight of a set of 'independent' boards (on the model of central banks), which apply criteria and enforce standards. This approach aims to minimise the influence of social forces that arise from interactions within wider society, either by suppressing them, or by channelling them into harmless projects that are made accountable to the principles of economic analysis.

Of course, this attempt to tame and channel social forces does not succeed, because social issues force themselves to the attention of government, and people continue to mobilise around both old and new causes. They also react spontaneously to new conditions, and their interactions transform the collective landscape. What is different about the political framework imposed under the economic model is that it systematically diverts the expression of claims and demands about collective life into ones about ways of increasing individual utility. Since the purpose of government is to maximise overall welfare, all such claims are only meaningful in those terms.

As a result of this framework for policy analysis, the social movements of the 1960s and 1970s – feminism, anti-racism, the gay movement, the movement of people with disabilities, the environmental movement and so on – have achieved important modifications in the basic structure of rights and regulations at the core of governance. But the form of political contest largely excludes new movements and ideas from achieving such transformations, and even from influencing more detailed policy development. The Easterlin paradox illustrates this phenomenon; by what processes, and through what kinds of movements, might deep concerns about well-being (for instance, about the evidence of very low levels of well-being among children and young people in the UK and US) find a voice, and lead to transformative actions and campaigns?

Because issues of social reproduction and sustainability are made invisible within the economic model, and ideas about how to build a better society can find so little expression within the political process derived from that model, it is only by challenging its definition of value, and of the goals of public policy, that this can be changed. The case of social capital theory illustrates how anything short of this cannot shift the process from its limitations, because of its methodological individualism and its exclusive concern with utility maximisation, which reduce all social interactions to exchanges in an imperfectly informed world. As a result, even with the addition of this concept, it cannot take account of the social value stemming from group and community exchanges, or the issues of power and conflict between social units (Fine, 2001, pp 143-4).

The problem for critics of the economic model, like myself, is that it is impossible to substitute for it an alternative with the spurious precision and rigour that can be gained from its highly abstract models, whose simplified assumptions make outcomes predetermined. Social value deals in units of culture (Douglas, 1978, p 189), not hard currency, so it cannot be measured statistically. Data on SWB are a broad indication of how the factors that constitute social value are affecting well-being, but they cannot be used as a simple substitute for GNP, as utilitarians such as Layard propose.

Indeed, programmes for a set of policies based on social value cannot be stipulated in advance of an opportunity for issues of social reproduction, sustainability and the creation of a better society to be redefined, and for social activity and social movements to be formed around these new definitions. This change can only come from recognition of the failures of the economic model, and an acknowledgement that well-being relies on factors that are not susceptible to analysis within its methodology. It depends, in other words, on reversing the shift whereby, in the 1980s, policy reorientated itself 'from what was vaguely right to what is precisely wrong' (Sen, 1987b, p 34).

So the political process, and policy development within it, requires something like what was achieved by idealists, socialists and Keynesians in the first half of the 20th century, when they argued that political forces should carve out a space within capitalism and markets for the expression of social relations that were not concerned with individual utility maximisation, but with qualitative aspects of interdependence. This did not rely on a consensus about the common good, or a state-led version of the good life for citizens, but it did give attention to issues of how the collective life of a society could best realise well-being for members. It encouraged participation and collective action of many kinds, and understood the benefits of this in terms that were not reduced to individual gains in utility.

There are certain very obvious ways in which policy could enable such processes. It could, for instance, look for ways of making professional practice in the social services accountable to service users, rather than managers and accountants, concerned with narrow cost-efficiency. It could provide more generous and less narrowly defined funding for community groups and associations to pursue collective purposes, concerned with the improvement of the quality of collective life. It could encourage the identification of new social and environmental issues, and mobilisation around these, in order to give new content to the political and policy processes.

I would argue that all these shifts would complement the introduction of a basic income scheme as the cornerstone of social policy, and that they would be necessary conditions for the kinds of changes in social relations that are on the wish-lists of the political philosophers who now argue for basic income. Without shifts of this kind, and within a culture of individualism and a politics derived from the economic model, neither a sustainable version of justice and democracy, nor a reliable basis for well-being, would be feasible.

Contract or culture?

The irony of the contract approach to public policy is that it has come to be associated with far more detailed interventions in aspects of social life – the economy and the public services – than its more collectivist predecessor – the welfare state. For instance, in the UK, the current rate of legislation and regulation is roughly double that of the 1960s and 1970s. This is because the attempt to devise incentives and penalties for every type of relationship in contractual terms, as the current economic model demands (Macho-Stadler and Pérez-Castrillo, 2001; Laffont and Martimort, 2002; Stiglitz and Greenwald, 2003; Bolton and Dewatripont, 2005), implies a constant frenzy of activity, to assemble huge databases of information about citizens and immigrants, to reconstruct the organisations within which exchange of all kinds take place, and to stipulate targets and quality control standards. This undermines, usually intentionally, the institutions and cultures through which things had previously been done.

At the time of writing, fundamental doubts about this whole enterprise are dawning. On the one hand, the empires of credit on which the US, the UK and Australian economies have been expanded in the recent past have been revealed as precarious. The financial services industry had devised new instruments to 'slice and dice' debt, and distribute it worldwide. But for all their risk assessments and ruling limits, commercial finance and its regulation have proved monumentally fallible. On the other hand, government initiatives, to introduce biometric identity cards, to reduce immigration, to raise schooling standards, to improve hygiene in hospitals or to cut carbon emissions, involve huge expenditures and expose the authorities to additional risks, around security and crime.

What is new in the present situation is that the economic model is in trouble in practice as well as in theory. Part of the problem is that governments can do little to explain and justify themselves to electorates, because the theory behind their actions is so rarefied, abstract and formal – they operate in what is, for most people, a virtual world of finance and contract – one in which such concepts as 'contingent ownership allocation' determine optimum control and debt financing, where venture capital contracts involve contingent–control allocations (Kaplan and Stromberg, 2003), and where, in 'a *willingness-to-repay problem*, lending for investment is feasible only if the lender can brandish the threat of cutting off the borrower from further loans in the event of a default' (Bolton and Dewatripont, 2005, p 557).

Faced with such global issues as the 'credit crunch', climate change or religious extremism, or even local issues of gun control or drug abuse, governments committed to the contract model can therefore do little to involve the public directly in their programmes. The attempt to engineer solutions to problems of well-being by modifications of the economic model, incorporating SWB as the maximand, share many of the same problems, as my discussion of Layard's (2005, 2006) proposals indicated (see pp 183-7).

Although changes in the principles under which resources are allocated through public policy would make a difference, a more important shift would involve the gradual replacement of a contractual approach to relations in the public sector, and with the public, and eventually in the whole sphere of social reproduction. Even the detailed practice of human service work, in non-governmental organisations and commercial agencies as well as public services, has come to be analysed in terms of contracts, as in 'parenting contracts', or 'behavioural contracts', or 'acceptable behaviour contracts' or 'learning contracts', in child protection, education and youth justice.

At the same time, culture (in the form of shared ideas and patterns of behaviour, regulated through communications among members of a group) has been interpreted as something to be overcome, transformed or minimised, as in 'dependency culture', or 'gang culture', or 'gun culture', or even 'public sector culture'. Indeed, contract has been perceived as a way of overcoming culture, as when practitioners use contracts to get parents, or young people, or addicts, or offenders, to make pledges to change their behaviour, and break with patterns of attitudes and behaviours through which others previously influenced their actions. Along with management, contract (as in contracting out or partnership contracts) has been an instrument used by central government for transforming the cultures of local government and health services. It involved the rejection of a collective group-think, and becoming autonomous, enterprising, business-minded and cost-conscious.

Doubts about this have begun to surface in the UK over a series of scandals, in which the contractual approach to the provision of services had led to abuses of various kinds. These scandals have been extremely diverse, covering a wide range of official and semi-official activities, in which commercial priorities took precedence over standards such as honesty, humanity or propriety. For instance, the Parliamentary Committee on Human Rights found that 20% of residential and nursing homes for older people manifested neglect, malnourishment or abuse of residents, despite 15 years of a contract and inspection regime (BBC Radio 4, *News,* 18 August 2007). The out-of-hours arrangements for general practitioner consultations were found to have inadequate continuity, consistent and reliability of care, as a result of contracting-out processes. In policing, the emphasis on measurable outcomes and the achievement of targets was leading to the arrest of victims of assaults as well as their assailants (two arrests for the price of one). Broadcasters (most scandalously the BBC children's programme *Blue Peter*) were falsifying the results of competitions, or not counting audience votes properly, for the sake of revenue or ratings (BBC Radio 4, *News*, 20 July, 2007).

The official response to all these scandals has been to call for a 'change of culture' in the organisations in question, to recognise the requirements of the standards that have been overlooked or abandoned. But it is unclear how, within a contract culture, this is to be achieved. If the aim of the reforms of services has been to make contract the basis of exchanges between individuals, the call for a new culture seems to imply that contracts are an inappropriate way to achieve good standards in these kinds of work.

After all, contract and culture are two different ways of trying to regulate how people interact with each other, to achieve coordination and minimise conflict, for the sake of gainful exchanges. Anything that can be done by contract can also be done by culture (Buchanan and Tullock, 1962, p 42). The contract approach defines private resources and assigns the rights and obligations of the agreeing parties. The cultural approach accuses the contractual one of turning people into isolated atoms, who pass up opportunities for communication and sharing, leading to the devaluation of interaction itself, of shared facilities, of public behaviour and social life.

The reason why the claims of culture are now being reasserted is the growing awareness that problems like the neglect of the urban environment, casual violence, public drunkenness and ordinary rudeness cannot be adequately regulated by a contract approach. There could be an almost infinite increase in Anti-Social Behaviour Orders or police cautions without real improvement in the quality of life of many places in which interactions occur in cities, so long as the culture of encounters between citizens puts no positive value on politeness, decency and respect, and no shame on their absence.

It also seems to be dawning on some politicians, academics and commentators that the individualism of the economic approach is destructive of social value, as created among certain key groups and occupations. For example, the loyalty and commitment that is required by carers for people with disabilities, parents, members of the armed and emergency services may be undermined by an ethos in which individual utility is the sole measure of value. There was considerable public outrage when two police community support officers stood by while members of the public attempted to rescue a boy who subsequently drowned, having jumped into a lake to try to save his sister. Their explanation – that it was not part of their terms of employment to attempt such an intervention – seemed to take the contractual approach too far (BBC Radio 4, *News*, 30 November, 2007). But even the loyalty and commitment required to be the owner of a cat or dog are undermined when there is a firm called 'Flexpetz', where you can hire one by the week or month. Because contracts deal in specific actions and the utility for eligible private consumers that stems from the defined performance of services, they are ill-suited to the tasks that may confront either auxiliary police personnel or pet owners, which require a culture of commitment to be adequately realised.

Those working in human services must, it seems obvious, deal in social value in most of their encounters with the public, whether they choose to or not. They have to try to understand the attachments and loyalties that exist between people, and the symbolic significance of places, objects, animals and so on. They must try to empathise with and minimise the hurt that comes from losses, separations, rejections, abuses and violence between people – the pain, shame and resentment that stem from losing affection, security or the sense of belonging. Social relationships create identity, self-esteem and support, and we all rely on members of groups and societies for our well-being. They are sustained within cultures, through ways of valuing people, rituals and standards of behaviour.

The contract approach often seems to put a higher priority on doing checklists, ticking boxes and counting things than on these aspects of the human services. It appears to treat the content of interactions with service users a bit like smiling and saying 'have a nice day' if one is a worker at Macdonalds. The central core of the job is defined in terms of delivering a costed package of services to achieve certain outcomes, or satisfy certain needs. It is even regarded as intrusive or patronising to pry too deeply into the private worlds of the emotions or attachments; if they go wrong, professionals can prescribe treatments, training or punishment (often in the form of contracts).

The shift from contractual approaches to ones that take account of social value cannot rely on any one reform or reorganisation. It involves the creation of many opportunities, at many levels, for issues about quality of life and relationships. This is a political process, which recognises deliberation and debate about improving well-being, and progressing towards a better society, as the only ways to address the Easterlin paradox. Instead of focus groups to inform policy proposals, it requires that official agencies and the commercial sector open themselves up to far more radical challenges about the nature of their work, and the direction of change.

Conclusions

The economic approach to public policy was a reaction to the 1960s and 1970s, which began in the Anglophone countries, in large part to reduce the influence of social movements and protest politics. Its analysis of all social interactions, and specially collective action in the political sphere, in terms of gains in individual utility, was intended to expose the rent-seeking at the heart of groups and organisational behaviour (Olson, 1965, 1982; Buchanan and Tullock, 1980). It conveyed this form of politics, enabled by the structures of welfare states, as a set of coordinated efforts to advantage members of various collectives over individuals not affiliated to such units. Government based on contract was supposed to minimise the inefficiencies, injustices and (above all) the wasteful conflicts engendered by that dynamic among organised groupings.

In a way, this made the economic approach similar to the Enlightenment project, which tried to substitute government for the sake of peace and prosperity, based on the pursuit of the 'milder vices' of avarice and greed, for the politics of faith, honour and blood, which had plunged Europe into more than a century of violent wars (Hirschman, 1977). The economic approach tried to substitute the market-orientated quest for efficiency in gaining the greatest overall welfare for a struggle around the value of political and social principles, which it presented as a disguised struggle for control over utility-generating assets. It pointed out, with some justification, that the beneficiaries of the more successful social movements were not the most disadvantaged, but leaders of their organisations.

In this book, I have argued that the subordination of social to economic value in the economic model of public policy is at the heart of the Easterlin paradox of 'stalled well-being'. Because of its methodological individualism, economic analysis cannot encompass the processes by which interactions generate and distribute symbolic social value, and regulate such processes through cultures and institutions. The rapid emergence of social capital theory in the social sciences marks the recognition that interactions do create collective goods that are of value to individuals and communities; but this insight is then absorbed into the model's analysis, as an explanation of how people deal with market imperfections, and especially information asymmetries. This leaves all collective phenomena as accountable to the first-best standard of the model – perfectly functioning markets – as aspects of a second-best world, to be dealt with as parts of a pragmatic programme for achieving better coordination within the whole economic system.

Van Parijs's (1995) argument for the highest sustainable basic income illustrates the advantages and limitations of the economic approach. As an institution, basic income aims to guarantee individual liberty, but relies on social relations of affection, loyalty and solidarity for its underpinnings. This points to a mutual accountability between economic and social value, and between welfare and well-being. A market economy is the best means to realise a basic income at an adequate level, but the social relations to enable such a scheme require bonds between members that are sustained by systems of social value.

Furthermore, the improvements in well-being claimed for a future basic income society by Barry, Pateman, Wright and many others could not be accomplished through economic mechanisms (information, incentives, contracts) but through cultural transformations. A new politics of social reproduction would redefine issues such as children's upbringing and the care of older citizens in terms of the value of emotional support, respect and participation in the public sphere, rather than efficiency in service delivery and economic growth. The conflicts between the priorities of maximising the basic income and sustaining the practices and cultures conducive for well-being would be the new stuff of democratic politics.

There are parallels here with ecological sustainability. In the face of climate change, the economic model is forced to recognise the value of what it previously treated as free goods, such as wildernesses, rain forests and endangered species. Conversely, environmentalists are required to frame their claims with reference to overall welfare, and to justice between rich and poor countries. In much the same ways, arguments for well-being through improved social relations must be framed so as to take account of income distribution and physical health, while those for greater efficiency and production must take account of the interdependence of populations.

Above all, the well-being perspective demands that issues of policy should no longer be reduced to ones of individual utility, as if society was made up of a set of contracts between rational maximisers. It argues that the quality of people's lives depends on how they relate to each other, and that this can only be understood within an analysis of cultures and institutions. Like the ecology of the natural environment, these are built up through millions of interactions, and can be enabled and steered, but not precisely planned or prescribed.

Under the aegis of the economic model, governments, especially in the Anglophone countries, have been willing to trust the rational choices of bankers, producers and consumers, in ways that would have been regarded as reckless during the era of welfare states. They have been far less trusting in the value of social interactions among citizens as a source of improved relationships and constructive innovations. This book has argued that the study of how quality of life is influenced by these interactions should become far more central to public policy.

The recent failures of organisations of all kinds – government agencies, public–private partnerships, firms – to deliver what they promise, to honour trust, and even to supply a reliable economic context, has directed attention to cultures. It has reminded more thoughtful observers that, in the absence of any coherent collective systems of meaning, purpose and integrity, people will create their own cultures of social value, and act on them, sometimes in highly destructive ways.

It is well recognised, for instance, that militant Islamic extremism is a reaction to the decline in significance and status of a whole region, and of specific groups within affluent societies – a collective response to the empty promises of a soulless commercialised individualism that is arrogant and exclusive. Similarly, knife and gun cultures among the youth of very disadvantaged districts represent systems of esteem and honour, based on prowess in violent conflict. Even internet suicide sites lay claim to prestige and fame. Cultures of social value, however perverse, occupy a vacuum created by anonymous, individualistic consumerism, and cannot be effectively countered by policies of control and punishment derived from contract theories.

The search for forms of social value that can encompass the divisions, rivalries and hostilities of affluent, mobile, ethnically diverse societies will be a long-term project, requiring detailed commitment. But it cannot even start until the shortcomings of the economic model as a basis for public policy are fully acknowledged.

Conclusion

This book has been both a critique of the economic model adopted by governments in the Anglophone countries, and an attempt to explain the Easterlin paradox of stalled well-being. It has argued that many of the social problems that afflict affluent societies would be better addressed in terms of social value – through building cultures of mutuality, respect and belonging.

This might be taken to imply that the current economic orthodoxy is sustainable, if not desirable (subject, of course, to suitable modifications for ecological survival). Yet even this seems doubtful, in view of developments that were been unfolding during the period in which the book was being written. These events appear to reveal a deeper level at which the paths of welfare (as defined by the model) and well-being diverge, in which 'welfare' corresponds to the units of virtual value accumulated in a world of electronically stored information, and 'well-being' to what occurs in the parallel universe of actual human interactions.

This double image, in which the two elements become less and less similar, is symbolised in the hapless figures of political leaders and central bankers of the US and UK. On the one hand, they cast themselves as the master manipulators of national and global economies, from whose decisions flow the streams of resources for the world's productive activities. On the other, they appear increasingly helpless in the face of banking collapses, home repossessions and debt mountains, along with a rising tide of anxiety, obesity and delinquency.

Throughout this book, I have traced the gap between welfare and well-being to a divergence between the regulation of social interactions through contract (based on the principal-agent model of relationships), and that which relies on culture (standards governing positive and negative social value within collective units). As the affluent Anglophone economies have specialised more and more as the bankers, insurers and brokers of the global system, monetary theory and macroeconomics have increasingly adopted axioms from the economics of information and incentives. The roles of governments and central banks are defined by a model in which

> the key to understanding monetary economics is the demand and supply of loanable funds, which in turn is contingent on understanding the importance, and consequences, of imperfections of information and the role

> of banks.... [A] central function of banks is to determine
> who is likely to default, and in doing so, banks determine
> the supply of loans.... [F]inancial institutions ... are critical
> in determining the behaviour of the economy, and ...
> the central features of banks and bank behaviour can be
> understood in terms of (or derived from) an analysis of
> information imperfections. (Stiglitz and Greenwald, 2003,
> pp 3-4)

This implies that governments and central banks, in regulating financial
markets, are acting as insurers for the whole economy, writing contracts
to try to regulate the behaviour, first of banks, and through them of all
other agents. '[T]he regulator (the principal) tries to *control* or *affect* the
behaviour of the bank (the agent), to make the bank act *more* in accord
with social objectives' (Stiglitz and Greenwald, 2003, p 204; emphasis
in original). The omnipotent attempt to control through incentives and
prices spreads out to the rest of the economy and society.

> Households are often not perfectly rational. Households and
> firms ... certainly don't have perfect information. There are
> often important differences in the information that they
> have access to (information asymmetries). Models based
> on more realistic assumptions ... provide an additional
> rationale for government to intervene in the economy and
> additional tools for government and central banks to stabilise
> the economy. (Stiglitz et al, 2006, p 47)

The regulatory and stabilising functions of government in the latest
variant of the economic model require it to accumulate vast databases
about every aspect of economy and society – information about all
individuals and their activities. This in turn puts government at risk
of bumbling incompetence, when computer systems prove unfit for
purpose, or crash under pressure, or when confidential details are lost.
The disparity between grandiose purposes and disastrous performance
was what made the UK's acting Liberal Democrat leader, Vince
Cable's question about Gordon Brown's transformation 'from Stalin
to Mr Bean' so appropriate. The theory behind the model is, in its
way, as totalitarian in its compass as state socialism, not because the
government actually controls anything, but because it imagines it can
fix the incentives through which firms, organisations and individuals
are induced to behave in desirable ways.

The reality is that most people have now become reconciled with a systematic disparity between glossy image and grubby reality in our daily transactions. We read between the lines of mission statements, logos and brochures, whether of government agencies or firms, and devise strategies for tricking, shaming or outflanking formal systems, and using unofficial ones. We do not imagine that anyone within an organisation will tell us what is really happening, rather than what embellishes their company's sales, or improves their position in a government league table. In other words, we do not think that there is any plausible correspondence between welfare, as measured in the statistics published by governments and firms, and the way we experience the quality of our lives.

In all this we are, after all, doing no more than fulfilling the expectations of the model. Since every individual is seeking to get the most possible utility for themselves for the least possible cost, each will act instrumentally within the terms of the set of contracts through which they relate to others. Each of us knows that the other is merely following a set of procedures that define minimum performance, and by which their returns from the activity in question are defined. As a general rule, organisations are better at claiming results and achievements than they are at actually doing things, and their members are experts in going through the motions, unless there is some other kind of pay-off at stake.

If it seems that these intrinsic features of the model, which drain meaning and commitment out of experience, are self-perpetuating and inescapable, then this is contradicted only by the moments in which we recognise something qualitatively different in our interactions with the material world or with others. These alternative sources of value can provide clues to ways of breaking the cycle of frustration that is built into the economic model. Because its hold on the collective life of affluent Anglophone societies is so totalitarian, such resistance tends to be very local, small-scale and temporary – difficult to translate into a movement, to organise and expand.

The economic model – its concepts, methods and assumptions – has penetrated the discourses of government, and defined the dominant managerial politics of the age. If the language of the model shifts from 'flexibility' and 'deregulation' to 'stability with growth' (Stiglitz et al, 2006), we can be sure that political leaders will follow. Sure enough, Alistair Darling, the UK Chancellor, in his first Budget speech, used the term 'stability' six times in the first minute, and 23 times in all, (*Guardian*, 13 March, 2008). Within a few days of her appointment, the Minister for Housing, Carline Flint, proposed a new 'commitment contract' for all new local authority housing tenants, in which they would have to promise to seek employment, in order to 'change the culture of no-one works around here' (*Guardian*, 5 February, 2008). And a report on behalf of UK police authorities has recommended a national database of primary school children seen as showing signs of serious criminal tendencies (BBC Radio 4, *News*, 16 March, 2008).

It is difficult, from a position within this culture, to conceive of a new politics of well-being, in which social value might become the focus of policy debates, and through which the cultures that sustain it might be rebuilt. It seems unlikely that this will occur by addressing subjective well-being (SWB) itself – by targeting increased happiness, as recommended by Layard (2005) and the neo-utilitarians. This would probably soon be reduced to the pursuit of shallow gratification – those forms of personal self-realisation (in the manner of a weekend colour supplement or a health spa prospectus) that are most easily accommodated within the culture of individualism. David Cameron's foray into the field of well-being represents a study in ambivalence in this regard. On the one hand, he sought to transcend narrow materialism and self-interest to 'repair a broken society'; but on the other, he seemed unwilling to commit to the kinds of collective action that might generate new sources of self-esteem and social action among members of the most disadvantaged communities.

A new politics of well-being could not return to the idealism of the neo-Hegelians or the Tory socialists, but it would require some other inspirational images and ideas about the collective identities, values and purposes of liberal, multicultural societies. In this respect, the phenomenon of Barack Obama's presidential campaign has been remarkable. He has mobilised young people, as well as African American citizens, around a vision of change and progress that owes little to the economic model. It remains to be seen whether this relies solely on oratory and charisma, or whether it can give rise to a social movement for the construction of new institutions for mutuality, solidarity and citizenship.

Another route to the creation of cultures for an improved collective version of quality of life experience, work and relationships lies through spontaneous formation of networks, including internet interactions, such as the Wikipedia phenomenon. Sennett (2008, pp 24-7) quotes the Linux code, a software kernel that (unlike Microsoft's carefully conserved intellectual property) is open to all users (Moody, 2002). Linux creates an 'electronic bazaar' (Raymond, 1999) in which an open community of software craftspeople maintain quality through information interactions, solving problems as they arise, through experiment and dialogue.

Sennett (2008) and Leadbeater (2008) suggest that these spontaneous networks are more generally significant examples of how to overcome demotivation and sterility, and particularly the prevailing disrespectful and abusive cultures of many internet chatrooms (Bunting, 2008).

Above all, well-being will not become a political priority through further expansions of the regulatory activities of government, in line with contract theory. The collapse of the Anglophone version of welfarism – in which greedy bankers made fortunes out of risky loans to insecure, low-paid workers – has been finally demonstrated by the 'credit crunch'.

The fantasy that banks and insurance companies could be relied on to sustain the common good, making the politics of well-being redundant, is now exposed as a latterday South Sea Bubble (Elliot, 2008). What are needed are political forces, mobilised around interests, and creating new ideals and purposes, to offset the power of finance capital. No government or central bank can write a contract that will bring such forces into existence.

A new version of collective life, made up of networks, movements and relationships of these kinds, would necessarily combine elements of liberalism and socialism, with both economic and social priorities being accountable to each other. Globalisation should allow this to encompass a heady mixture of ideas, images and traditions, all contributing to an excitingly diverse environment. The economic approach tends to flatten the collective landscape, and synthesise the variety of experience into abstract generalisations.

The illusory nature of economic growth based on credit, house price inflation and commercial service expansion has discredited managerial politics. While the institutions of private property, markets and democracy can easily be justified in terms of individual liberty, their claim to maximise welfare is – especially in the affluent countries – increasingly nebulous. At very least, they require to be offset by institutions through which people collectively deliberate and interpret their experiences, and try to improve the quality of their lives, outside the pressure to produce, deliver and consume.

The problem, of course, is that it has proved fairly easy to destroy the sense of commitment to common causes, to solidarities, moralities, religions and ways of life, for the sake of increased individual welfare supplied by the economic model; but it is far harder to build a new version of these forms of collective meaning. Many people remain loyal to non-welfarist communal activities, such as crafts, sports, musical styles or outdoor pursuits, but they are induced to see these as 'lifestyle choices', rather than essential aspects of well-being.

So the current crises over climate change, credit and debt, and long-term fears over security, crime, health, nutrition and general well-being provide an opportunity. This book has argued that this is the moment for the reconstruction of social value and collective culture to start.

References

Adler, M. D. and Posner, E. A. (2006), *New Foundations of Cost-Benefit Analysis*, Cambridge, MA: Harvard University Press.

Ahrne, G. (1990), *Agency and Organisation: Towards an Organisational Theory of Society*, London: Sage Publications.

Ainslie, G. (1992), *Picoeconomics: The Interaction of Successive Motivational States within the Person*, Cambridge: Cambridge University Press.

Ainslie, G. (2001), *Breakdown of Will*, Cambridge: Cambridge University Press.

Anand, P. and van Hees, M. (2006), 'Capabilities and Achievements: An Empirical Study', *Journal of Socio-Economics*, 35, pp 268-84.

Anand, P., Hunter, G. and Smith, R. (2005), 'Capabilities and Well-Being: Evidence Based on the Sen-Nussbaum Approach', *Social Indicators Research*, 74, pp 9-55.

Archer, M. S. (1996), *Culture and Agency: The Place of Culture in Social Theory*, Cambridge: Cambridge University Press.

Argyle, M. (1999), 'Causes and Correlates of Happiness', in D. Kahneman, E. Diener and N. Schwarz (eds) *Well-Being: The Foundations of Hedonic Psychology*, New York: Russell Sage Foundation, pp 353-72.

Arrow, K.J. (1951), *Social Choice and Individual Values*, New York: Wiley.

Arrow, K.J. (1971), 'Political and Economic Evaluation of Social Effects and Externalities', in M. D. Intriligator (ed), *Frontiers in Quantitative Economics*, Amsterdam: North Holland, pp 3-23.

Atkinson, A. B. and Stiglitz, J. (1980), *Lectures in Public Economics*, London: McGraw Hill.

Baldock, J. (2007), 'Social Policy, Social Welfare and the Welfare State', in J. Baldock, N. Manning and S. Vickerstaff (eds) *Social Policy* (3rd edition), Oxford, Oxford University Press, pp 5-30.

Barry, B. (1997), 'The Attractions of Basic Income', in J. Franklin (ed), *Equality*, London: Institute for Public Policy Research, pp 157-71.

Bass, B. M. (1990), 'From Transactional to Transformational Leadership', *Organisational Dynamics*, 18, pp 15-31.

Baudrillard, A. (1983), *Simulations*, New York: Semiotext(e).

Bauman, Z. (1987), *Legislators and Interpreters: On Modernity, Post-Modernity and Intellectuals*, Cambridge: Polity Press.

Bauman, Z. (2003), *Liquid Love: On the Frailty of Human Bonds*, Cambridge: Polity Press.

Baumol, W. (1967), 'The Macroeconomics of Unbalanced Growth', *American Economic Review*, 57, pp 415-26.

Baumol, W., Batey-Blackman, S. and Wolf, E. (1985), 'Unbalanced Growth Revisited: Asymptotic Stagnancy and New Evidence', *American Economic Review*, pp 806-17.

BBC Radio 4 (2007), *News*, 27 July.

BBC2 TV (2007), *Tribe*, October.

Beck, U. (1992), *Risk Society: Towards a New Modernity*, London: Sage Publications.

Beck, U. (1994), *The Re-Invention of Politics: Rethinking Modernity in the Global Social Order*, Cambridge: Polity Press.

Beck, U. and Beck-Gernsheim, E. (1995), *The Normal Chaos of Love*, Cambridge: Polity Press.

Beck, U. and Beck-Gernsheim, E. (2002), *Individualization*, London: Sage Publications.

Becker, G. S. (1976), *The Economic Approach to Human Behaviour*, Chicago: Chicago University Press.

Becker, G. S. (1981), *A Treatise on the Family*, Cambridge, MA: Harvard University Press.

Becker, G. S. (1996), *Accounting for Tastes*, Cambridge, MA: Harvard University Press.

Begg, D., Fischer, S. and Dornbusch, R. (1997), *Economics*, 5th Edition, London: McGraw Hill.

Bellamy, E. (1897), *Equality*, New York: Appleton and Co.

Bennis, W. G. and Nanus, B. (1985), *Leaders: The Strategies for Taking Charge*, New York: Harper and Row.

Bernheim, R. D. and Stark, O. (1988), 'Altruism within the Family Reconsidered: Do Nice Guys Finish Last?', *American Economic Review*, 78, pp 1034-45.

Bernstein, B. (1964), 'Social Class and Psycho-Therapy', *British Journal of Sociology*, 15, pp 54-64.

Beveridge, W. (1942), *Social Insurance and Allied Services*, Cm 6404, London: HMSO.

Beveridge, W. (1944), *Full Employment in a Free Society*, London: Allen and Unwin.

Binmore, K. and Dasgupta, P. (1986), 'Game Theory: A Survey', in K. Binmore and P. Dasgupta (eds) *Economic Organisations as Games*, Oxford: Blackwell.

Birnbaum, S. (2008), 'Just Distribution: Rawlsian Liberalism and the Politics of Basic Income', *Stockholm Studies in Politics*, 122.

Bjørnskov, C. (2006), 'The Multiple Facets of Social Capital', *European Journal of Political Economy*, 22, pp 22-40.

Blair, T. (1996), Speech to Labour Party Conference, October.

Blair, T. (2005), Preface to Department of Health, *Independence, Well-Being and Choice*, Cm 6499, London: The Stationery Office.

Blair, T. (2006), Speech on Respect Action Plan, 10 January.

Blair, T. (2007), 'I've Been Tough on Crime: Now We Have to Nip it in the Bud', *Sunday Telegraph*, 28 April.

Blunkett, D. (2003), 'Active Citizens, Strong Communities: Progressing Civil Renewal', Scarman Lecture to the Citizens Convention, 11 December.

Blunkett, D. (2004), 'New Challenges for Race Equality and Community Cohesion in the Twenty-First Century', Speech to IPPR, 20 June.

Boehm, C. (1982), 'The Evolutionary Development of Morality as an Effect of Dominance Behaviour and Conflict Interference', *Journal of Social and Biological Structure*, 5, pp 413-21.

Boehm, C. (1993), 'Egalitarian and Reverse Dominance Hierarchy', *Current Anthropology*, 34(3), pp 227-54.

Bolton, P. and Dewatripont, M. (2005), *Contract Theory*, Cambridge, MA: MIT Press.

Boucher, D. (ed) (1997), *The British Idealists*, Cambridge: Cambridge University Press.

Bowles, S. and Gintis, H. (2002), 'Social Capital and Community Governance', *Economic Journal*, 112(483), pp F419-36.

Bowles, S., Choi, J.-K. and Hopfensitz, A. (2003), 'The Co-evolution of Individual Behaviours and Social Institutions', *Journal of Theoretical Biology*, 223, pp 135-47.

Boyd, R. and Richerson, P. J. (1985), *Culture and the Evolutionary Process*, Chicago: Chicago University Press.

Boyd, R. and Richerson, P. J. (2002), 'Group-Beneficial Norms Can Spread Rapidly in a Structured Population', *Journal of Theoretical Biology*, (3) pp287-96.

Brand-Ballard, J. (2004), 'Contractualism and Deontic Restrictions', *Ethics*, 114, pp 269-300.

Brandt, R. B. (1979), *A Theory of the Good and the Right*, Oxford: Clarendon Press.

Brickman, P. and Campbell, D. T. (1971), 'Hedonic Relativism and Planning the Good Society', in M. H. Apley (ed) *Adaptation-Level Theory: A Symposium*, New York: Academic Press, pp 287-302.

Broome, J. (1978), 'Trying to Value a Life', *Journal of Public Economics*, 9, pp 90-106.

Brueckner, J. K. (2000), 'Welfare Reform and the Race to the Bottom', *Southern Economic Journal*, 66 (3), pp 505-25.

Bruni, L. and Porta, P. L. (eds) (2005), *Economics and Happiness: Framing the Analysis*, Oxford: Oxford University Press.

Bryman, A. (1992), *Charisma and Leadership in Organisations*, London: Sage Publications.

Buchanan, J. M. (1965), 'An Economic Theory of Clubs', *Economica*, 32, pp 1-14.

Buchanan, J. M. (1967), *Public Finance in a Democratic Process*, Chapel Hill: University of North Carolina Press.

Buchanan, J. M. (1968), *The Demand and Supply of Public Goods*, Chicago, IL: Rand McNally.

Buchanan, J. M. (1978), *The Economics of Politics*, London: Institute for Economic Affairs.

Buchanan, J. M. (1994), *Ethics and Economic Progress*, Norman, OK: University of Oklahoma Press.

Buchanan, J. M. and Tullock, G. (1962), *The Calculus of Consent: Logical Foundations of Constitutional Democracy*, Ann Arbor, MI: University of Michigan Press.

Buchanan, J. M. and Tullock, G. (1980), *Towards a Theory of a Rent-Seeking Society*, College Station, TX: Texas A&M University Press.

Bunting, M. (2008), 'From Buses to Blogs, A Pathological Individualism is Poisoning Public Life', *The Guardian*, 28 January.

Bynner, J. and Parsons, S. (2003), 'Social Participation, Values and Crime', in E. Ferri, J. Bynner and M. Wadsworth (eds), *Changing Britain, Changing Lives: Three Generations at the Turn of the Century*, London: Institute of Education, pp 261-94.

Cameron, D. (2006), Speech in Hertfordshire, 22 May.

Carter, M. (2003), *T. H. Green and the Development of Ethical Socialism*, Exeter: Imprint Academic.

Channel 4, TV (2007), *Meet the Natives*, 19 October.

Chipman, J. S. and Moore, J. C. (1978), 'The New Welfare Economics, 1939-1974', *International Economic Review*, 19, pp 547-8.

Clarke, J. and Newman, J. (1997), *The Managerial State: Power, Politics and Ideology in the Remaking of Social Welfare*, London: Sage.

Clarke, J., Cochrane, A. and McLaughlin, E. (1994), *Managing Social Policy*, London: Sage.

Club of Rome (1972), *The Limits to Growth*, London: Earth Island.

Cole, G. D. H. (1920), *Social Theory*, London: Methuen.

Cole, G. D. H. (1929), *The Next Ten Years in British Social and Economic Policy*, London: Macmillan.

Cole, G. D. H. (1945), 'A Retrospect of the History of Voluntary Social Service', in A. F. C. Bourdillon (ed) *Voluntary Social Services*, London: Methuen, pp 11-30.

Coleman, J. S. (1966), *Report on Equality of Educational Opportunity*, Washington, DC: US Government Printing Office.

Coleman, J. S. (1973), *The Mathematics of Collective Action*, Chicago: Alder.

Coleman, J. S. (1986), 'Micro Foundations and Macro Social Theory', in S. Lindeberg, N. E. Enkvist and K. Wikberg (eds) *Approaches to Social Theory*, New York: Russell Sage Foundation.

Coleman, J. S. (1987), 'Norms as Social Capital', in G. Radnitzky and P. Bernholz (eds) *Economic Imperialism: The Economic Method Applied Outside the Field of Economics*, New York: Paragon.

Coleman, J. S. (1988), 'Social Capital and the Creation of Human Capital', *American Journal of Sociology*, 94, pp S95-S120.

Coleman, J. S. (1990), *The Foundations of Social Theory*, Cambridge: Cambridge University Press.

Coleman, J. S. (1992), 'The Rational Reconstruction of Society', *American Sociological Review*, 58(6), pp 898-912.

Collier, P. (1998), 'Social Capital and Poverty', World Bank Social Capital Initiative, Working Paper No. 4.

Cornes, R. and Sandler, T. (1986), *The Theory of Externalities, Public Goods and Club Goods*, Cambridge, Cambridge University Press.

Cox, E. (2002), 'Australia: The Lucky Country', in R. D. Putnam (ed) *Democracies in Flux: The Evolution of Social Capital in Contemporary Society*, Oxford: Oxford University Press.

Cruikshank, B. (1994), 'The Will to Empower: Technologies of Citizenship and the War on Poverty', *Socialist Review*, 23(4), pp 29-55.

Cruikshank, B. (1996), 'Revolutions Within: Self-Government and Self-Esteem', in A. Barry, T. Osborne and N. Rose (eds) *Foucault and Reason: Neo-Liberal and Rationalities of Government*, London: UCL Press, pp 301-50.

Danilova, N. (2007), *Veterans' Policy in Russia: A Puzzle of Creation*, Bristol: Department of Social Policy, University of Bristol.

Dasgupta, P. (2000), 'Social Capital and Economic Performance', in P. Dasgupta and I. Serageldin (eds) *Social Capital: A Multifaceted Perspective*, Washington, DC: World Bank, pp 325-424.

Dasgupta, P. (2002), *Social Capital and Economic Performance: Analytics*, Cambridge: Faculty of Economics, University of Cambridge.

Dasgupta, A. K. and Pearce, D. W. (1972), *Cost-Benefit Analysis: Theory and Practice*, London: Macmillan.

Dasgupta, P. and Serageldin, I. (eds) (2000), *Social Capital: A Multi-faceted Perspective*, Washington DC: World Bank.

Dasgupta, P., Hammond, P. and Maskin, E. (1979), 'The Implementation of Social Choice Rules: Some General Results on Incentive Compatibility', *Review of Economic Studies*, 46, pp 185-216.

de Tocqueville, A. (1835-40), *Democracy in America* (edited by J. P. Meyer and M. Lerner), London: Collins (1968).

Dean, H. (2004), 'Human Rights and Welfare Rights: Contextualising Dependency and Responsibility', in H. Dean (ed) *The Ethics of Welfare: Human Rights, Dependency and Responsibility*, Bristol: The Policy Press, pp 7-28.

den Otter, S. (1996), *British Idealism and Social Explanation*, Oxford: Clarendon Press.

DH (Department of Health) (1998), *Modernising Social Services: Promoting Independence, Improving Protection, Raising Standards*, Cm 4169, London: The Stationery Office.

DH (2005), *Independence, Well-Being and Choice: Our Vision of the Future of Social Care for Adults in England*, Cm 6499, London: The Stationery Office.

Di Tella, R. and MacCulloch, R. (2007), 'Cross-National Happiness as an Answer to the Easterlin Paradox?', Paper given to the Fourteenth International FISS Research Seminar, Sigtuna, Sweden, 15-17 June.

Di Tella, R., MacCulloch, R. and Oswald, A. (2003), 'The Macroeconomics of Happiness', *Review of Economics and Statistics*, 85(4), pp 807-27.

Dobson, A. (1998), *Justice and the Environment*, Oxford: Oxford University Press.

Dorling, D. and Thomas, B. (2003), *People and Places: A 2001 Census Atlas of the UK*, Bristol: The Policy Press.

Douglas, C. H. (1920), *Economic Democracy*, Sudbury: Bloomfield (1974).

Douglas, M. (1962), 'Lele Economy Compared with the Bushong', in *In the Active Voice*, London: Routledge and Kegan Paul, pp 48-73.

Douglas, M. (1970), *Natural Symbols: Explorations in Cosmology*, London: Barrie and Rockliff.

Douglas, M. (1973), 'The Exclusion of Economics', in *In the Active Voice*, London: Routledge and Kegan Paul (1982), pp 174-82.

Douglas, M. (1976), 'Goods as a System of Communication', in *In the Active Voice*, London: Routledge and Kegan Paul (1982), pp 16-33.

Douglas, M. (1978), 'Cultural Bias', in *In the Active Voice*, London: Routledge and Kegan Paul (1982), pp 183-254.

Douglas, M. (1983), 'Identity: Personal and Socio-Cultural', *Uppsala Studies in Cultural Anthropology*, 5, pp 35-46.

Douglas, M. (1987), *How Institutions Think*, London: Routledge and Kegan Paul.

Douthwaite, R. (1992), *The Growth Illusion: How Economic Growth has Enriched the Few, Impoverished the Many, and Endangered the Planet*, Dublin: Resurgence/Lilliput.

Doyal, L. and Gough, I. (1991), *A Theory of Human Need*, Basingstoke: Macmillan.

Drakeford, M. (1988), *Social Movements and Their Followers*, London: Macmillan.

Driver, S. and Martel, L. (1997), 'New Labour's Communitarianisms', *Critical Social Policy*, 17 (52) pp 27-56.

DSS (Department of Social Security) (1998), *A New Contract for Welfare,* Cm 3805, London: The Stationery Office.

Duesenberry, J. S. (1949), *Income, Saving and the Theory of Consumer Behaviour,* Cambridge: MA: Harvard University Press.

Durkheim, E. (1893), *The Division of Labour in Society,* New York: Free Press (1968).

Durkheim, E. (1898), 'Individualism and the Intellectuals', *Revue Bleu,* 4(10), pp 7-11.

Durkheim, E. (1912), *Les Formes Elémentaires de la Vie Religieuse: Le Systéme Totemique in Australie,* Paris, Alcan.

Durlauf, S. N. (2002), 'On the Empirics of Social Capital', *Economic Journal,* 112(483), pp F459-79.

Durlauf, S. N. and Fafchamps, M. (2004), 'Social Capital', Working Paper 10485, www.nber.org/papers/W10485

Dworkin, R. (1981), 'What is Equality? Part II: Equality of Resources', *Philosophy and Public Affairs,* 10, pp 283-345.

Dworkin, R. (1990), *Foundations of Liberal Equality,* Salt Lake City, UT: University of Utah Press.

Easterlin, R. (1974), 'Does Economic Growth Improve the Human Lot? Some Empirical Evidence', in P. David and M. Reder (eds) *Nations and Households in Economic Growth: Essays in Honor of Moses Ambramovitz,* New York: Academic Press.

Easterlin, R. (2005), 'Building a Better Theory of Well-Being', in L. Bruni and P. L. Porta (eds) *Economics and Happiness,* Oxford: Oxford University Press, pp 29-64.

Edwards, B. and Foley, F. (1997), 'Social Capital and the Political Economy of Our Discontent', *American Behavioural Scientist,* 40(5), pp 669-78.

Edwards, B. and Foley, F. (1999), 'Is It Time to Disinvest in Social Capital?', *Journal of Public Policy,* 19(2), pp 141-73.

Elias, N. (1939), *The Civilising Process,* Oxford: Blackwell (1978).

Elliot, L. (2008), 'America Was Conned – Who Will Pay?', *The Guardian,* 17 March, p 30.

Ellis, K. (2004), 'Dependency, Justice and the Ethic of Care', in H. Dean (ed) *The Ethics of Welfare: Human Rights, Dependency and Responsibility,* Bristol: The Policy Press, pp 29-48.

Elshtain, J. B. (1981), *Public Man, Private Woman: Women in Social and Political Thought,* Oxford: Martin Robertson.

Elshtain, J. B. (1998), 'Antigone's Daughters', in A. Phillips (ed) *Feminism and Politics,* Oxford: Oxford University Press, pp 369-81.

Elster, J. (1979), *Ulysses and the Sirens: Studies in Rationality and Irrationality,* Cambridge: Cambridge University Press.

Elster, J. (1982), 'Sour Grapes', in A. Sen and B. Williams (eds) *Utilitarianism and Beyond*, Cambridge: Cambridge University Press, pp 219-38.

Elster, J. (1985), *Making Sense of Marx*, Cambridge: Cambridge University Press.

Eriksen, E. and Weigård, J. (2000), 'The End of Citizenship? New Roles Challenging the Political Order', in C. McKinnon and I. Hampsher-Monk (eds) *The Demands of Citizenship*, London: Continuum, pp 13-34.

Esping-Andersen, G. (1990), *The Three Worlds of Welfare Capitalism*, Cambridge: Polity Press.

Esping-Andersen, G. (ed) (1996), *Welfare States in Transition: National Adaptations in Global Economies*, London: Sage Publications.

Esping-Andersen, G. (1999), *Social Foundations of Post-Industrial Economies*, Oxford: Oxford University Press.

Etzioni, A. (1961), *A Comparative Analysis of Complex Organisations: On Power, Involvement and their Correlates*, New York: Free Press.

Etzioni, A. (1993), *The Spirit of Community: The Reinvention of American Society*, New York: Touchstone.

Etzioni, A. (1999), *The New Golden Rule*, New York: Fontana.

Fafchamps, M. (2002), 'Spontaneous Market Emergence', *Topics in Theoretical Economics*, 2 (1), Article 2, Berkeley Electronic Press, www.impress.com

Fehr, E. and Schmidt, K. (1999), 'A Theory of Fairness, Competition and Cooperation', *Quarterly Journal of Economics*, 114, pp 817-68.

Feinstein, C. H. (1976), *Statistical Tables of National Income, Expenditure and Output of the UK, 1855-1965*, Cambridge: Cambridge University Press.

Ferri, E. and Smith, K. (2003), 'Partnership and Parenthood', in E. Ferri, J. Bynner and M. Wadsworth (eds) *Changing Britain, Changing Lives: Three Generations at the Turn of the Century*, London: Institute of Education, pp 105-32.

Fine, B. (2001), *Social Capital versus Social Theory: Political Economy and Social Science at the Turn of the Millennium*, London: Routledge.

Finnis, J. (1980), *Natural Law and Natural Rights*, Oxford: Oxford University Press.

Firth, R. (1950), *We, the Tikopia*, London: Allen and Unwin.

Firth, R. (1967), *Tikopia Ritual and Belief*, London: Allen and Unwin.

Fitzpatrick, T. (1999), *Freedom and Security: An Introduction to the Basic Income Debate*, London: Macmillan.

Fitzpatrick, T. (2003), *After the New Social Democracy: Social Welfare in the Twenty-First Century*, Manchester: Manchester University Press.

Fletcher, K. (1998), *Best Value Social Services*, Caerphilly: SSSP Publications.

Foldvary, F. (1994), *Public Goods and Private Communities: The Market Provision of Social Services*, Aldershot: Edward Elgar.

Foucault, M. (1976), *Discipline and Punish: The Birth of the Prison*, New York: Vintage.

Foucault, M. (1984), 'The Order of Discourse', in M. Shapiro (ed) *Language and Politics*, New York: New York University Press.

Fourier, C. (1836), *La Fausse Industrie, morceleé, répugnante, mensongére, et l'antidote, l'industrie naturelle, combinée, attrrayante, véridique, donnant quadruple produit et perfection extrême en toutes qualités*, Paris: Anthropos (1967).

Fox, J. and Gershman, J. (2000), 'The World Bank and Social Capital: Lessons from Ten Rural Development Projects in the Philippines and Mexico', *Policy Sciences*, 33, pp 399-419.

Frank, R. H. (2005), 'Does Money Buy Happiness?', in F. A. Huppert, N. Bayliss and B. Keverne (eds) *The Science of Well-Being*, Oxford: Oxford University Press, pp 461-74.

Frank, S. A. (1995), 'Mutual Policing and Repression of Competition in the Evolution of Cooperative Groups', *Nature*, 377, pp 520-22.

Freeden, M. (1978), *The New Liberalism*, Oxford: Clarendon Press.

Freedland, M. (2001), 'The Marketization of Public Services', in C. Crouch, K. Eder and D. Tambini (eds), *Citizenship, Markets and the State*, Oxford: Oxford University Press.

Frey, B. and Stutzer, A. (2002), *Happiness and Economics: How the Economy and Institutions Affect Well-being*, Princeton, NJ: Princeton University Press.

Gambetta, D. (1988), 'Can We Trust Trust?', in D. Gambetta (ed) *Trust: Making and Breaking Cooperative Relations*, Oxford: Blackwell, pp 213-38.

Garfinkel, A. (1967), *Studies in Ethnomethodology*, Englewood Cliffs, NJ: Prentice Hall.

Garland, D. (2001), *The Culture of Control*, Oxford: Oxford University Press.

Gaventa, J. (2004), 'Towards Participatory Governance: Assessing the Transformation Possibilities', in S. Hickey and G. Mohan (eds) *Participation: From Tyranny to Transformation*, London: Zed Publications.

Gershuny, J. I. (1983), *Social Innovation and the Division of Labour*, Oxford: Oxford University Press.

Gibbard, A. (1973), 'Manipulation of Voting Schemes: A General Result', *Econometrica*, 41, pp 587-601.

Gibbs, A. (2000), 'The New Managerialism', in M. Davies (ed) *The Blackwell Encyclopaedia of Social Work*, Oxford: Blackwell.

Giddens, A. (1976), *New Rules of Sociological Method*, London: Hutchinson.

Giddens, A. (1984), *The Constitution of Society*, Cambridge: Polity Press.

Giddens, A. (1991), *Modernity and Self-Identity: Self and Society in the Late Modern Age*, Cambridge: Polity Press.

Giddens, A. (1992), *The Transformation of Intimacy: Sexuality, Love and Eroticism in Modern Societies*, Cambridge: Polity Press.

Giddens, A. (1994), *Beyond Left and Right: The Future of Radical Politics*, Cambridge: Polity Press.

Giddens, A. (1998), *The Third Way: The Renewal of Social Democracy*, Cambridge: Polity Press.

Glaeser, E., Laibson, D. and Sacerdote, B. (2002), 'An Economic Approach to Social Capital', *Economic Journal*, 112(483), pp F437-58.

Glaeser, E., Laibson, D., Scheikman, J. and Soutter, C. (2000), 'Measuring Trust', *Quarterly Journal of Economics*, 65(3), pp 811-46.

Gneezy, U. and Rustichini, A. (2000), 'A Fine is a Price', *Journal of Legal Studies*, 29, pp 1-17.

Godin, J. B. (1871), *Solutions Socials*, Quimperlé: La Digitale (1979).

Goffman, E. (1967a), 'On Face Work: An Analysis of Ritual Elements in Interaction', in *Interaction Ritual: Essays in Face-to-Face Behaviour*, New York: Doubleday Anchor, pp 1-46.

Goffman, E. (1967b), 'The Nature of Deference and Demeanor', in *Interaction Ritual*, New York: Doubleday Anchor, pp 47-96.

Gore, C. (1922), 'Introduction', in *Group of Churchmen, The Return to Christendom*, London: CSM.

Gorz, A. (1989), *Critique of Economic Reason*, London: Verso.

Graaff, J. de V. (1957), *Theoretical Welfare Economics*, Cambridge: Cambridge University Press.

Granovetter, M. (1975), *Getting a Job: A Study of Contracts and Careers*, Chicago, IL: Chicago University Press.

Gregory, R. (1998), 'Competing with Dad: Changes in Intergenerational Income of Male Manual Labour Market Income', Paper presented at the conference 'Income Support, Labour Market and Behaviour', Australian National University, Canberra, 24-5 November.

Griffin, J. (1986), *Well-Being: Its Meaning, Measurement and Moral Importance*, Oxford: Oxford University Press.

Guardian (2006), 'Pensioner Groups Call for Urgent Action on Reform', 16 November, p.14.

Gusinde, M. (1961), *The Yamana*, New Haven: Human Relations Area Files.

Haagh, L. (2007), 'Developmental Freedom, Unemployment, and Poverty: Restating the Importance of Regulation to Agency', in O. Neumeier, G. Schweiger and C. Sednak (eds) *Perspectives on Work: Problems, Insights, Challenges*, Munster: LIT Publishing.

Habermas, J. (1981), 'Modernity versus Post-modernity', *New German Critiques*, 22, pp 3-14.

Harris, J. (1992), 'Political Thought and the Welfare State, 1870-1940: An Intellectual Framework for British Social Policy', *Past and Present*, 135, pp 116-41.

Harriss, J. (2001), *Depoliticising Development: The World Bank and Social Capital*, New Delhi: LeftWord.

Harsanyi, J.C. (1955), 'Cardinal Welfare, Individualistic Ethics and Interpersonal Comparisons of Utility', *Journal of Political Economy*, 63, pp 309-21.

Harsanyi, J. C. (1982), 'Morality and the Theory of Rational Behaviour', in A. Sen and B. Williams (eds) *Utilitarianism and Beyond*, Cambridge: Cambridge University Press, pp 39-62.

Harvey, D. (1989), *The Condition of Post-Modernity*, Oxford: Blackwell.

Hayek, F. A. (1960), *The Constitution of Liberty*, London: Routledge and Kegan Paul.

Hayek, F. A. (1976), *The Mirage of Social Justice*, London: Routledge and Kegan Paul.

Hayek, F. A. (1982), *Law, Legislation and Liberty*, London: Routledge and Kegan Paul.

Helliwell, J. F. (2003) 'How's Life? Combining Individual and National Variables to Explain Subjective Well-Being', *Economic Modelling*, 20, pp 331-60.

Helliwell, J. F. (2006), 'Well-Being, Social Capital and Public Policy: What's New?', *Economic Journal*, 116(510), pp C34-45.

Helliwell, J. F. and Huang, H. (2005), 'How's the Job? Well-Being and Social Capital in the Workplace', Paper presented at the Annual Meeting of the Canadian Economics Association, McMaster University, May.

Helliwell, J. F. and Putnam, R. D. (2005), 'The Social Context of Well-Being', in F. A. Huppert, N. Bayliss and B. Keverne (eds) *The Science of Well-Being*, Oxford: Oxford University Press.

Hicks, U. K. (1947), *Public Finance*, Cambridge: Cambridge University Press.

Hirschman, A. O. (1970), *Exit, Voice and Loyalty: Responses to Decline in Firms, Organisations and States*, Cambridge, MA: Harvard University Press.

Hirschman, A. O. (1977), *The Passions and the Interests: Arguments for Capitalism before its Triumph*, Princeton, NJ: Princeton University Press.

Hobbes, T. (1651), *Leviathan* (edited by M. Oakeshott), Oxford: Blackwell.

Holland, H. S. (1900), 'Sacerdotalism and Socialism', *Commonwealth*, V(2), pp 21-40.

Honneth, A. (1995), *The Struggle for Recognition: The Moral Grammar of Social Conflict*, Cambridge: Polity Press.

Huber, E. and Stephens, J. (2001), *Development and the Crisis of the Welfare State*, Chicago, IL: University of Chicago Press.

Hudson, B. A. (1993), *Penal Policy and Social Justice*, Basingstoke: Macmillan.

Hume, D. (1739), *A Treatise of Human Nature* (edited by L. Selby-Bigge), Oxford: Clarendon Press (1978).

Huppert, F. A., Bayliss, N. and Keverne, B. (eds) (2005), *The Science of Well-Being*, Oxford: Oxford University Press.

Hurwicz, L. (1960), 'Optimality and Information Efficiency in Resource Allocation Processes', in K. Arrow, S. Karlin and P. Suppes (eds) *Mathematical Methods in the Social Sciences*, Stanford, CA: Stanford University Press.

Inman, R. P. and Rubinfeld, P. H. (1997), 'The Political Economy of Federalism', in D. C. Mueller (ed) *Perspective in Public Choice: A Handbook*, Cambridge: Cambridge University Press, pp 73-105.

Innocenti Report Card 7 (2007), *Child Poverty in Perspective: An Overview of Child Well-being in Rich Countries*, Florence: UNICEF.

Iversen, F. and Wren, A. (1998), 'Equality, Employment and Budgetary Restraint: The Trilemma of the Service Economy', *World Politics*, 50(4), pp 507-46.

Jackson, M. (2007), *Soldier*, London: Transworld.

Jenkins, S. (2008), 'Closure Mania Ignores the Real Cost of Axing Post Offices', *The Guardian*, 19 March, p 39.

Jones, H. (1883), 'The Social Organism', in D. Boucher (ed) *The British Idealists*, Cambridge: Cambridge University Press, pp 3-29.

Jordan, B. (1973), *Paupers: The Making of the New Claiming Class*, London: Routledge and Kegan Paul.

Jordan, B. (1974), *Poor Parents: Social Policy and the Cycle of Deprivation*, London: Routledge and Kegan Paul.

Jordan, B. (1976), *Freedom and the Welfare State*, London: Routledge and Kegan Paul.

Jordan, B. (1987), *Rethinking Welfare*, Oxford: Blackwell.

Jordan, B. (1996), *A Theory of Poverty and Social Exclusion*, Cambridge: Polity Press.

Jordan, B. (1998), *The New Politics of Welfare: Social Justice in a Global Context*, London: Sage Publications.

Jordan, B. (2003), 'Criminal Justice, Social Exclusion and the Social Contract', *Probation Journal*, 50(3), pp 198-214.

Jordan, B. (2004), *Sex, Money and Power: The Transformation of Collective Life*, Cambridge: Polity Press.

Jordan, B. (2006a), *Social Policy for the Twenty-First Century: New Perspectives, Big Issues*, Cambridge: Polity Press.

Jordan, B. (2006b), *Rewarding Company, Enriching Life: The Economics of Relationships and Feelings*, www.billjordan.co.uk

Jordan, B. (2007), *Social Work and Well-Being*, Lyme Regis: Russell House.

Jordan, B. with Jordan, C. (2000), *Social Work and the Third Way: Tough Love as Social Policy*, London: Sage Publications.

Jordan, B., Redley, M. and James, S. (1994), *Putting the Family First: Identities, Decisions, Citizenship*, London: UCL Press.

Kagan, S. (1989), *The Limits of Morality*, Oxford: Oxford University Press.

Kahneman, D. (1999), 'Objective Well-being', in D. Kahneman, E. Diener and N. Schwarz, (eds), *Well-being: The Foundations of Hedonic Psychology*, New York: Russell Sage Foundation, pp 3-14.

Kahneman, D., Diener, E. and Schwarz, N. (eds) (1999), *Well-Being: The Foundations of Hedonic Psychology*, New York: Russell Sage Foundation.

Kahneman, D., Wakker, P. P. and Sarin, R. (1997), 'Back to Bentham? Explorations of Experienced Utility', *Quarterly Journal of Economics*, 112(2), pp 375-405.

Kandori, M. (1992), 'Social Norms and Community Enforcement', *Review of Economic Studies*, 59, pp 63-80.

Kaplan, S. and Stromberg, P. (2003), 'Financial Contracting Theory Meets the Real World: An Empirical Analysis of Venture Capital Contracts', *Review of Economic Studies*, 70, pp 281-315.

Kelsey, J. (1995), *Economic Fundamentalism: The New Zealand Experiment – A World Model of Structural Adjustment*, London: Pluto.

Keynes, J. M. (1936), *A General Theory of Employment, Interest and Money*, London: Macmillan.

Kymlicka, W. and Norman, W. (1994), 'Return of the Citizen: A Survey of Recent Work on Citizenship Theory', *Ethics*, 102(4), pp 353-81.

Laffont, J. J. and Martimort, D. (2002), *The Theory of Incentives: The Principal-Agent Model*, Princeton, NJ: Princeton University Press.

Lane, R. E. (1991), *The Market Experience*, Cambridge: Cambridge University Press.

Lane, R. E. (2000), *The Loss in Happiness in Market Democracies*, New Haven, CT: Yale University Press.

Layard, R. (2005), *Happiness: Lessons from a New Science*, London: Allen Lane.

Layard, R. (2006), 'Happiness and Public Policy: A Challenge to the Profession', *Economic Journal*, 116(510), pp C24-33.

Leadbeater, C. (2008), *We-Think*, London: Profile.

Leonard, M. (1994), *Informal Economic Activity in Belfast*, Aldershot: Avebury.

Leonard, M. (1999), 'Informal Economic Activity Strategies of Households and Communities', Paper presented at the 4th ESA conference, 'Will Europe Work?, Amsterdam, 18–21 August.

Leonard, M. (2004), 'Bonding and Bridging Social Capital: Reflections from Belfast', *Sociology*, 38(5), pp 927–44.

Levitt, S. D. and Dubner, S. J. (2006), *Freakonomics*, London: Penguin.

Lin, N. (2001), *Social Capital*, Cambridge: Cambridge University Press.

Locke, J. (1690), 'Second Treatise', in *Two Treatises of Government* (edited by P. Laslett), Cambridge: Cambridge University Press (1976).

Loury, G. (1977), 'A Dynamic Theory of Racial Income Differences', in P. Wallace and A. LeMund (eds) *Women, Minorities, and Employment Discrimination*, Boston, MA: Lexington Books.

Lyotard, J. F. (1984), *The Post-Modern Condition: A Report on Knowledge*, Manchester: Manchester University Press.

Macbeath, A. (1957), *Can Social Policies be Rationally Tested?*, Hobhouse Memorial Trust Lecture, Oxford: Oxford University Press.

MacFarlane, A. (1978), *The Origins of English Individualism: The Family, Property and Social Transition*, Oxford: Blackwell.

Macho-Stadler, I. and Pérez-Castrillo, J. D. (2001), *An Introduction to the Economics of Information: Incentives and Contracts* (2nd edition), Oxford: Oxford University Press.

MacIntyre, A. (1981), *After Virtue: A Study in Moral Theory*, London: Duckworth.

March, F. and Olsen, J. (1989), *Rediscovering Institutions: The Organisational Basis of Politics*, New York: Free Press.

Marschak, J. (1955), 'Elements in the Theory of Teams', *Management Science*, 1, pp 127–37.

Marshall, T. H. (1950), *Citizenship and Social Class*, Cambridge: Cambridge University Press.

Marshall, T. H. (1965), *Social Policy*, London: Hutchinson.

Marx, K. and Engels, F. (1847), 'The German Ideology', in R. Freedman (ed) *Marx on Economics*, Harmondsworth: Penguin (1961), p 235.

Mayo, E. (1949), *The Social Problems of Industrial Civilization*, London: Routledge and Kegan Paul.

McMurtry, J. (2002), *Value Wars: The Global Market versus the Life Economy*, London: Pluto.

Meade, J. E. (1938), *Consumers' Credits and Unemployment*, Oxford: Oxford University Press.

Meade, J. E. (1970), *The Theory of Indicative Planning*, Manchester: Manchester University Press.

Meagher, G. and Parton, N. (2004), 'Modernising Social Services and the Ethics of Care', *Social Work and Society*, 2(1), pp 10-27.

Mennell, S. (1985), *All Manners of Food: Eating and Taste in England and France from the Middle Ages to the Present*, Oxford: Blackwell.

Merton, R. (1949), 'The Self-Fulfilling Prophecy', in *Social Theory and Social Structure*, New York: Free Press, pp 475-90.

Milburn, A. (2002), 'Reforming Social Services', Speech to the Annual Social Services Conference, Cardiff.

Milner, D. (1920), *Higher Productivity by a Bonus on National Output: A Proposal for a Minimum Income for All Varying with National Productivity*, London: Allen and Unwin.

Mirrlees, J. (1971), 'An Exploration in the Theory of Optimum Taxation', *Review of Economic Studies*, 38, pp 175-208.

Moody, G. (2002), *Rebel Code: Linux and the Open-Source Revolution*, New York: Perseus.

Mueller, D. C. (1979), *Public Choice*, Cambridge: Cambridge University Press.

Mueller, D. C. (1989), *Public Choice II*, Cambridge: Cambridge University Press.

Myers, D. G. (1999), 'Close Relationships and Quality of Life', in D. Kahneman, N. Diener and N. Schwarz (eds), *Well-Being*, New York: Russell Sage Foundation, pp 374-91.

Myerson, R. (1979), 'Incentive Compatibility and the Bargaining Problem', *Econometrica*, 47, pp 61-73.

Nash, K. (1998), *Universal Difference: Feminism and the Liberal Undecidability of Women*, Basingstoke: Macmillan.

Newman, A. L. (2002), 'When Opportunity Knocks: Economic Liberalisation and Stealth Welfare in the United States', *Journal of Social Policy*, 32 (2), pp 179-98.

Niskanen, W. A. (1975), 'Bureaucrats and Politicians', *Journal of Law and Economics*, 18, pp 617-43.

Nordhaus, W. and Boyer, J. (2000), *Warming the World*, Cambridge, MA: MIT Press.

Nordhaus, W. and Tobin, J. (1972), *Is Growth Obsolete?*, New York: NBER/Columbus University Press.

North, D. C. (1990), *Institutions, Institutional Change and Economic Performance*, Cambridge: Cambridge University Press.

Northouse, P. G. (1997), *Leadership: Theory and Practice*, London: Sage Publications.

Nozick, R. (1974), *Anarchy, State and Utopia*, Oxford: Blackwell.

Nussbaum, M. (2000) *Women and Human Development: The Capabilities Approach*, Cambridge: Cambridge University Press.

Nussbaum, M. (2005), 'Mill between Aristotle and Bentham', in L. Bruni and P. L. Porta (eds) *Economics and Happiness: Framing the Analysis*, Oxford: Oxford University Press, pp 170-83.

Oates, W. E. (1972), *Fiscal Federalism*, New York: Harcourt Brace Jovanovich.

Oates, W. E. (1999), 'An Essay on Fiscal Federalism', *Journal of Economic Literature*, 27, pp 1120-49.

Offe, C. (1984), *Disorganized Capitalism: Contemporary Transformations of Work and Politics*, Cambridge: Polity Press.

Offer, A. (ed) (1996), *In Pursuit of Quality of Life*, Oxford: Oxford University Press.

Offer, A. (2006), *The Challenge of Affluence: Self-Control and Well-Being in the United States and Britain since 1950*, Oxford: Oxford University Press.

Offer, J. (2006), *An Intellectual History of British Social Policy: Idealism versus Non-Idealism*, Bristol: The Policy Press.

Oliver, J. E. (1999), 'The Effects of Metropolitan Economic Segregation on Civil Participation', *American Journal of Political Science*, 43, pp 186-212.

Oliver, M. (1990), *The Politics of Disability*, London: Macmillan.

Oliver, M. (1992), 'A Case of Disabling Welfare', in T. Harding (ed) *Who Owns Welfare?*, London: NISW.

Oliver, M. and Sapey, B. (2006), *Social Work and Disabled People*, London: BASW.

Olson, M. (1965), *The Logic of Collective Action: Public Goods and the Economics of Groups*, Cambridge, MA: Harvard University Press.

Olson, M. (1982), *The Rise and Decline of Nations: Economic Growth, Stagflation and Social Rigidities*, New Haven, CT: Yale University Press.

Ormerod, P. (2007), 'Against Happiness', *Prospect Magazine*, 133, pp 1-6.

Ostrom, E. (2000), 'Social Capital: A Fad or Fundamental Concept?', in P. Dasgupta and I. Serageldin (eds) *Social Capital: A Multifaceted Perspective*, Washington, DC: World Bank.

Paine, T. (1796), 'Agrarian Justice', in P. F. Fouer (ed) *The Life and Major Writings of Thomas Paine*, Secaucus, NJ: Citadel Press (1974), pp 605-23.

Pareto, V. (1896), 'Cours d'économie politique', in S. E. Finer (ed) *Vilfredo Pareto: Sociological Writings*, London: Pall Mall Press (1966), pp 97-122.

Pareto, V. (1909), *Manuel d'économie politique*, Paris: Giard.

Pareto, V. (1916), 'Treatise on General Sociology', in S. E. Finer (ed) *Vilfredo Pareto: Sociological Writings*, London: Pall Mall Press, pp 167-331.

Pateman, C. (1988), *The Sexual Contract*, Cambridge: Polity Press.

Pateman, C. (1989), *The Disorder of Women: Democracy, Feminism and Political Theory*, Cambridge: Polity Press.

Pateman, C. (2004), 'Democratizing Citizenship: Some Advantages of a Basic Income', *Politics and Society*, 32(1), pp 89-106.

Perrow, C. (1986) *Complex Organisations: A Critical Essay*, New York: Random House.

Phillips, A. (1993), *Democracy and Difference*, Cambridge: Polity.

Pigou, A. C. (1920), *The Economics of Welfare*, London: Macmillan.

Piore, M. and Sabel, C. (1984), *The Second Industrial Divide*, New York: Basic Books.

Platteau, J. P. (1994a), 'Behind the Market Stage, Where Real Societies Exist: Part I: The Role of Public and Private Order Institutions', *Journal of Development Studies*, 30 (3), pp 533-77.

Platteau, J. P. (1994b), 'Behind the Market Stage, Where Real Societies Exist: Part II: The Role of Moral Norms', *Journal of Development Studies*, 30 (4), pp 577-601.

Polanyi, K. (1944), *The Great Transformation: The Political and Economic Origins of Our Time*, Boston, MA: Beacon Press.

Popper-Lynkeus, J. (1912), *Die allgemeine Nährpflicht als Lösung der Sozialen Frage*, Dresden: Reissner.

Posner, R. A. (1995), *Overcoming Law*, Cambridge, MA: Harvard University Press.

Posner, R. A. (2004), *Catastrophe, Risk and Response*, Oxford: Oxford University Press.

Powdermaker, H. (1933), *Life in Lesu*, New York: Norton.

Pusey, M. (2003), *The Experience of Middle Australia: The Dark Side of Economic Reform*, Cambridge: Cambridge University Press.

Putnam, R. D. (1993), *Making Democracy Work: Civic Traditions in Modern Italy*, Princeton, NJ: Princeton University Press.

Putnam, R. D. (2000), *Bowling Alone: The Decline and Revival of America Community*, New York: Simon and Schuster.

Qizilbash, M. (1998), 'The Concept of Well-Being', *Economics and Philosophy*, 4, p 57.

Radcliffe-Brown, A. R. (1952), *Structure and Function in Primitive Society*, London: Cohen and West.

Rasell, M. (2007), 'Social Security Reform and Well-Being in Russia', Paper presented at the FISS International Research Seminar on Issues in Social Security, Sigtuna, Sweden, 15-17 June.

Rawls, J. (1971), *A Theory of Justice*, Oxford: Blackwell.

Raymond, E. S. (1999), *The Cathedral and the Bazaar: Musings on Linux and Open Access by an Accidental Revolutionary*, Cambridge, MA: O'Reilly Linux.

Reich, R. (1993), *The Work of Nations: Preparing Ourselves for Twenty-First Century Capitalism*, New York: Knopf.

Robbins, L. (1932), *The Nature and Significance of Economic Science*, London: Allen and Unwin.

Roemer, J. (1982), *A General Theory of Exploitation and Class*, Cambridge, MA: Harvard University Press.

Rose, N. (1996), *Inventing Ourselves: Psychology, Power and Personhood*, Cambridge: Cambridge University Press.

Rose, N. (1999), 'Inventiveness and Politics', *Economy and Society*, 28(3), pp 69-84.

Rosenthal, D. H. and Nelson, R. H. (1992), 'Why Existence Values Should Not be Used in CBA', *Journal of Policy Analysis and Management*, 11, pp 116-22.

Rothstein, B. and Stolle, D. (2001), 'Social Capital and Street-Level Bureaucracy: An Institutional Theory of Generalised Trust', Paper presented at the conference 'Social Capital', Exeter University, 15-20 September.

Rousseau, J.-J. (1754), 'A Discourse on the Origin of Inequality among Mankind', in *The Social Contract and Discourses* (edited by G. D. H. Cole), London: Dent (1913).

Routledge, B. and von Amsberg, G. (2003) 'Social Capital and Growth', *Journal of Monetary Economics*, 50(1), pp 167-94.

Rubin, M. (1993), 'Incorporating Fairness into Game Theory and Economics', *American Economic Review*, 83, pp 1281-302.

Ruskin, J. (1860), 'Ad Valorem', in *Unto This Last, and Other Writings* (edited by C. Wilmer), Harmondsworth, Penguin (1985), pp 204-28.

Sahlins, M. (1974), *Stone Age Economics*, London: Tavistock Publications.

Samuelson, P. (1954), *Foundations of Economic Analysis*, Cambridge, MA: Harvard University Press.

Sandel, M. (1982), *Liberalism and the Limits of Justice*, Cambridge: Cambridge University Press.

Sartre, J. P. (1976), *Critique of Dialectical Reason I: The Theory of Practical Ensembles*, London: New Left Books.

Schokkaert, E. (2007), 'Capabilities and Satisfaction with Life', Paper presented at the 14th International Research Seminar on Issues in Social Security, Sigtuna, Sweden, 15-17 June.

Schotter, A. (1981), *The Economic Theory of Social Institutions*, Cambridge: Cambridge University Press.

Schram, S. (2006), *Welfare Discipline: Discourse, Governance, and Globalisation*, Philadelphia: Temple University Press.

Schultze, C. (1969), 'The Role of Incentives, Penalties and Rewards in Attaining Effective Policy', in *The Analysis and Evaluation of Public Expenditures: The PPB System*, vol 1, Washington, DC: Joint Economic Committee Compendium, 91st Congress, 1st Session.

Schumpeter, J. (1911), *The Theory of Economic Development*, Cambridge, MA: Harvard University Press (1936).

Scott, R. (1987), *Organisations: Rational, Natural and Open Systems*, Englewood Cliffs, NJ: Prentice Hall.

Seeleib-Kaiser, M., Van Dyk, S. and Roggenkamp, M. (2005), *What do Parties Want? An Analysis of Programmatic Social Policy Aims in Austria, Germany and the Netherlands*, Working Paper 01/2005, Bremen; Centre for Social Policy Research.

Sen, A. (1970), *Collective Choice and Social Welfare*, San Francisco, CA: Holden-Day.

Sen, A. (1977), 'Social Choice Theory: A Re-Examination', *Econometrica*, 45, pp 58-89.

Sen, A. (1984), *Resources, Values and Development*, Oxford: Blackwell.

Sen, A. (1985), *Commodities and Capabilities*, Oxford: Elsevier Science.

Sen, A. (1987a), 'Lecture 1: Concepts and Critiques', in *The Standard of Living*, Cambridge: Cambridge University Press, pp 1-19.

Sen, A. (1987b), 'Lecture II: Lives and Capabilities', in *The Standard of Living*, Cambridge: Cambridge University Press, pp 20-39.

Sen, A. (1999), *Development as Freedom*, Oxford: Oxford University Press.

Sennett, R. (1998), *The Corrosion of Character: The Personal Consequences of Work in the New Capitalism*, New York: W. W. Norton.

Sennett, R. (2003), *Respect: Character in a World of Inequality*, London: Allen and Unwin.

Sennett, R. (2006), *The Culture of the New Capitalism*, New Haven, CT: Yale University Press.

Sennett, R. (2008), *The Craftsman*, London: Allen Lane.

Sevenhuijsen, S. (2000), 'Caring in the Third Way: The Relation between Obligation, Responsibility and Care in Third Way Discourse', *Critical Social Policy*, 20(1), pp 5-37.

Sher, G. (1997), *Beyond Neutrality: Perfectionism and Politics*, Cambridge: Cambridge University Press.

Silverman, D. (2005), *Doing Qualitative Research*, London; Sage Publications.

Simon, H. (1955), 'A Behavioural Model of Rational Choice', in *Models of Thought*, New Haven, CT: Yale University Press.

Skinner, Q. (1998), *Liberty before Liberalism*, Cambridge: Cambridge University Press.

Smith, A. (1759), 'The Theory of Moral Sentiments', in H. W. Schneider (ed) *Adam Smith's Moral and Political Philosophy*, New York: Harper and Row (1948), pp 7-280.

Smith, A. (1776), *An Inquiry Concerning the Nature and Causes of the Wealth of Nations* (edited by R. H. Campbell and A. S. Skinner), Oxford: Clarendon Press (1976).

Smith, J. M. and Szathmary, E. (1995), *The Major Transitions of Evolution*, Oxford: Oxford University Press.

Smith, S. R. (2001), 'Fraternal Learning and Interdependency: Celebrating Differences within Reciprocal Commitments', *Policy & Politics*, 30(1), pp 47-59.

Sobel, D. (1998), 'Well-Being as the Object of Moral Consideration', *Economics and Philosophy*, 14, p 249.

Somers, A. (2001), 'Romancing the Market, Reviling the State; Historicizing Liberalism, Privatisation and the Competing Claims to Civil Society', in C. Crouch, K. Eder and D. Tambini (eds) *Citizenship, Markets and the State*, Oxford: Oxford University Press, pp 23-48.

Starrett, D. A. (1988), *Foundations of Public Economics*, Cambridge: Cambridge University Press.

Stiglitz, J. E. (1994), *Whither Socialism?* Cambridge, MA: MIT Press.

Stiglitz, J. E. (1998), 'More Instruments and Broader Goals: Moving Towards a Post-Washington Consensus', WIDER Annual Lecture, Helsinki, 7 January.

Stiglitz, J. E. (2002), *Globalization and Its Discontents*, London: Allen Lane.

Stiglitz, J. E. and Greenwald, B. (2003), *Towards a New Paradigm in Monetary Economics*, Cambridge: Cambridge University Press.

Stiglitz, J. E., Ocampo, J. A., Spiegel, S., Ffrench-Davis, R. and Nayyar, D. (2006), *Stability with Growth: Macroeconomics, Liberalisation and Development*, Oxford: Oxford University Press.

Sugden, R. (2005), 'Correspondence of Sentiments: An Explanation of Pleasure in Social Interaction', in L. Bruni and P. L. Porta (eds), *Economics and Happiness*, Oxford: Oxford University Press, pp 91-115.

Sunstein, C. (2005), 'Cost-Benefit Analysis and the Environment', *Ethics*, 115(2), pp 351-85.

Tawney, R. H. (1922), *The Acquisitive Society*, London: Bell.

Tawney, R. H. (1926), *Religion and the Rise of Capitalism*, London: Bell.

Taylor, C. (1989), *Sources of Self: The Making of Modern Identity*, Cambridge: Cambridge University Press.

Taylor, C. (2000), 'The Old-Boy Network and the Young-Gun Effect', *International Economic Review*, 41(4), pp 871-91.

Taylor, M. (1987) *Community, Anarchy and Liberty*, Cambridge: Cambridge University Press.

Thomson, J. J. (1990), *The Realm of Rights*, Cambridge, MA: Harvard University Press.

Thompson, N. (2002), *Building the Future: Social Work with Children, Young People and their Families*, Lyme Regis: Russell House.

Tiebout, C. (1956), 'A Pure Theory of Local Expenditures', *Journal of Political Economy*, 42, pp 416-24.

Titmuss, R. M. (1970), *The Gift Relationship*, London: Allen and Unwin.

Titmuss, R. M. (1974), *Social Policy*, London: Allen and Unwin.

Tronto, J. (1994), *Moral Boundaries: A Political Argument for an Ethic of Care*, London: Routledge.

Tully, J. (2000), 'Multicultural and Multinational Citizenship', in C. McKinnon and I. Hampsher-Monk (eds) *The Demands of Citizenship*, London: Continuum, pp 212-34.

Turnbull, C. (1962), *The Forest People*, New York: Doubleday.

Turnbull, C. (1965), *Wayward Servants*, Garden City, NY: Natural History Press.

Van der Veen, R. J. and Van Parijs, P. (1986), 'A Communist Road to Capitalism?', *Theory and Society*, 15, pp 635-55.

Van Kersbergen, K. (1995), *Social Capitalism: A Study of Christian Democracy and the Welfare State*, London: Routledge.

Van Parijs, P. (1987), 'A Revolution in Class Theory?', *Politics and Society*, 15, pp 453-82.

Van Parijs, P. (1995), *Real Freedom for All: What (If Anything) Can Justify Capitalism?*, Oxford: Clarendon Press.

Van Praag, B. and Ferrer-i-Carbonell, A. (2004), *Happiness Quantified: A Satisfaction Calculus Approach*, Oxford: Oxford University Press.

Van Praag, B. and Frijters, P. (1999), 'The Measurement of Welfare and Well-Being: The Leyden School Approach', in D. Kahneman, E. Diener and N. Schwarz (eds) *Well-Being: The Foundations of Hedonic Psychology*, New York: Russell Sage Foundation.

Van Staveren, I. (2003), 'Beyond Social Capital in Poverty Research', *Journal of Economic Issues*, 37(2), pp 415-29.

Veenhoven, R. (1989), *Conditions of Happiness*, Dordrecht: Kluwer Academic Press.

Veenhoven, R. (1999), 'Quality of Life in Individualistic Society: A Comparison of Forty-Three Nations in the Early 1990s', *Social Indicators Research*, 48, pp 157-86.

Vernon, A. and Qureshi, H. (2000), 'Community Care and Independence: Self-Sufficiency or Employment?', *Critical Social Policy*, 20, pp 255-76.

Vickrey, W. (1945), 'Measuring Marginal Utility by Reactions to Risk', *Econometrica*, 13, pp 319-33.

Vincent, A. W. (1984), 'The Poor Law Report of 1909 and the Social Theory of the Charity Organisation Society', *Victorian Studies*, 27, pp 343-63.

von Mises, L. (1966), *Human Action*, Chicago, IL: Contemporary Books.

Wacquant, L. (1998), 'From Welfare State to Prison State: Imprisoning the America Poor', *Le Monde Diplomatique*, July, pp 1-35.

Waddan, A. (1997), *The Politics of Social Welfare: The Collapse of the Centre and the Rise of the Right*, Cheltenham: Edward Elgar.

Walsh, C. (1995), 'Optimal Contracts for Central Bankers', *American Economic Review*, 85, pp 150-67.

Walzer, M. (1983) *Spheres of Justice*, Oxford: Blackwell.

Warner, W. L. (1964), *A Black Civilization*, New York: Harper and Row.

Weber, M. (1905), *The Protestant Ethic and the Spirit of Capitalism*, New York: Scribners (1930).

Weber, M. (1922), *Economy and Society* (edited by G. Roth and C. Wittich), New York: Bedminster Press (1968).

Wicksell, K. (1896), 'A New Principle of Just Taxation', in R. A. Musgrave and A. T. Peacock (eds) *Classics in the Theory of Public Finance*, London: Macmillan (1958), pp 72-116.

Williams, F. (2001) 'In and Beyond New Labour: Towards a New Political Ethics of Care', *Critical Social Policy*, 21(4), pp 467-93.

Williamson, O. E. (1975), *Markets and Hierarchies: Analysis and Anti-Trust Implications – A Study in the Economics of Internal Organisation*, New York: Free Press.

Woolcock, M. (1998), 'Social Capital and Economic Development: Towards a Synthesis and Policy Framework', *Theory of Society*, 27(2), pp 151-208.

Worley, C. (2005), '"It's not About Race, It's About the Community": New Labour and "Community Cohesion"', *Critical Social Policy*, 25(4), pp 483-96.

World Bank (1997), *Expanding the Measure of Wealth: Indicators of Environmentally Sustainable Development*, Washington DC: World Bank.

World Bank (1998), *The Initiative on Defining, Monitoring, and Measuring Social Capital: Overview and Program Description*, Washington, DC: World Bank (Social Development Family).

World Bank (2001), *World Development Report 2000/2001: Attacking Poverty*, Washington, DC: World Bank.

Wright, E. O. (2004), 'Basic Income, Stakeholder Grants and Class Analysis', *Politics and Society*, 32(1), pp 79-88.

Zalenik, A. (1997), 'Managers and Leaders: Are They Different?', *Harvard Business Review*, 55, pp 67-78.

Index